The Power Model System™
The Natural Path to Human Wisdom

HumanWisdom, LLC

www.human-wisdom.com

Licensing

With the retail purchase of this book, a single non-exclusive license is granted to the individual purchaser for personal use. Institutions, private practitioner, and groups should inquire about licensing The Power Model System™ before using in any other way except personal-private use. The Power Model System™ is copyrighted and trademarked and is the sole property of HumanWisdom, LLC.

Copyright 2008
All Rights Reserved

ISBN: 978-1-4251-4825-6 (sc)

ISBN: 978-1-4251-4826-3 (e-book)

Note for Librarians: A cataloguing record for this book is available from Library and Archives Canada at www.collectionscanada.ca/amicus/index-e.html

Printed in Victoria, BC, Canada.

We at Trafford believe that it is the responsibility of us all, as both individuals and corporations, to make choices that are environmentally and socially sound. You, in turn, are supporting this responsible conduct each time you purchase a Trafford book, or make use of our publishing services. To find out how you are helping, please visit www.trafford.com/responsiblepublishing.html

Our mission is to efficiently provide the world's finest, most comprehensive book publishing service, enabling every author to experience success. To find out how to publish your book, your way, and have it available worldwide, visit us online at www.trafford.com

 www.trafford.com

North America & international

toll-free: 1 888 232 4444 (USA & Canada)

phone: 250 383 6864 ♦ fax: 250 383 6804 ♦ email: info@trafford.com

Dedication

I dedicate this book to my daughters, Debbie and April Freitas. You two have taught me what unconditional love is and at the same time, that love is not enough. You have taught me to "let go and let God," knowing that most relationship issues are not love issues but life lessons. I have learned that both of you are only on loan from God, and God has the final say. Having you two is an experience I would not have missed *for anything*. Our love can live through anything, knowing we have our personal journeys with our Higher Power. To my grandchildren, Amanda Freitas, Caleb Rodriquez, and Carlin Freitas, thank you for keeping me young, alive, and spirited. The joy of watching you learn, grow, and challenge life is a true gift.

This book has been a lifetime in the making. The Power Model System™ has been evolving for the last twenty-five years and will continue to do so after it is published. This is a living system which forever surprises me, as does life.

I also dedicate this book to all future souls, those in their mothers' wombs, because that's where our fight or flight system is initiated.

To those who have already arrived, along with all those who have walked through my life, I've learned something from each and every one of you. Sometimes I may not have liked the lesson, but I can honestly say that, "being in reality," they were all worth it in the long haul.

I've saved the best for last. I dedicate this book to my Higher Power, which I call God. Without you, God, I would not exist, and I would not have had this opportunity to accomplish my life purpose. Thank you for life, and thank you for The Power Model System™. I can reflect back on my experiences in life and say that I have resolved them and learned my lessons. Each lesson brought me to where I am today.

Acknowledgments

Raymond and Kartika Castonguay, Linda Peace, Debbie Freitas and April Freitas (my two daughters), who continued to have faith throughout this project. MaryJo Reeves who continues to believe and apply *The Five Steps to Centeredness* to all that she does. Tracy Craft for her dedication and work on the first workbook for HumanWisdom. My friend, Kartika, thanks for your support and computer lessons. Thank you Linda Peace and Nancy Anderson for those long phone calls of support and your faith in me. Thanks to Bill and Barbara Brown, and Rick Baney for believing in this system and acknowledging the miracles it brings to individuals. When times got tough, all these people never failed to support me with hope, faith and encouragement to keep going.

I would like to offer special thanks to Linda Peace, who worked relentlessly with me on workshops, with this book, and in many other ways that made a big difference in the completion of this book. I also give deep thanks to Raymond Castonguay, who suggested four years ago that I get this book done and out to the public. He worked relentlessly with me from day one on the book and made it print ready. We can have all the good ideas and systems, but only when we team up with others can it be materialized. Thank you, Linda and Raymond, for the years of work you have put behind this book and believing in The Power Model System™. I truly appreciate all your hours of reviewing, reviewing, and reviewing one more time. And through all this, thanks to my three grandchildren, Mandy Freitas, Caleb Rodriquez, and Carlin Freitas, who continued to keep me young throughout this process.

Last but not least, I give acknowledgment to my Higher Power who I call God, because without my connection to God, The Power Model System™ would not have been created and made available to others.

Editors:
Raymond Castonguay, Ellen Beck, Renni Browne

Cover:
John Bennett: Design

Graphics:
Marcy Smith

Disclaimer

This book is not intended for readers who have deep or debilitating problems and/or a need for psychotherapy or prescribed medications. Do not, under any circumstance abandon or withdraw from the medical or psychiatric treatment you are currently receiving. This book does not claim to be considered a substitute for professional medical or psychiatric care.

For people with everyday relationship problems with themselves or others, the activities in this book should be helpful. In order to be effective you should perform only one activity at a time; that is; start the desired activity and follow it through to completion before starting a second activity. Never pursue multiple activities simultaneously. It is my hope and expectation that the activities in this book will be used appropriately with good judgment and common sense to help the reader achieve a higher degree of self-discovery.

Kay Bennett
March 5, 2008

Table of Contents

The Power Model System™ Activities

Preface

The Power Model System™ is a revolutionary system in the field of self-growth. There is nothing like it in the field to assist human beings in getting in touch with who we really are by creating a bridge between our past, present, and future.

Our past serves as a foundation for building our future. If our past is 100% full of wonderful, life-rewarding experiences and great wise teachers, our future is virtually assured. However, most of us have a past that was very difficult at one time or another and often gave conflicting messages, lessons, and experiences that resulted in chaos, confusion, and often painful consequences.

Like many people, I've found it difficult to overcome my past. Growing up, I had a lot of fear and low self-esteem. I sabotaged my success over and over again by simply "reacting" to everything. Finally, I grew tired of being a victim of circumstance, and my search for personal solutions led me to develop The Power Model System™, which has helped me and countless people since 1986.

As I applied the elements of this system to my life, I learned what was buried in my subconscious mind and that my self-sabotage came from emotions, thoughts, beliefs, and reactions formed when I was very young. Of course, I thought I had dealt with all my baggage from the past, but in reality I had only scratched the surface. Surprise! At first I didn't understand this, since I had always been a self-growth oriented person. I noticed that the changes I had worked so hard on did not last for very long. With some deep soul searching, I realized that parts of me were often in conflict with each other, causing successes to unravel a short time later, no matter what self-help program I used. I learned that this conflict came from an imbalance of my physical, emotional, mental, and spiritual human components. With this awareness, I was able to take action and balance these components and thus make more permanent changes in my life. In order to do this, I developed the self-discovery tools that I share with you.

The cornerstone of The Power Model System™ is that "you are the expert on you" and that you have been all along. By using The Power Model System™ through personal self-discovery, anyone can be at peace with themselves and become self-empowered and balanced internally. This internal balance cannot be permanently achieved unless you work on all human levels—emotional, mental, spiritual, and physical. The simple activities in Power Model System™ allow self-discovery to occur simultaneously in all these areas, while helping you to see what has been holding you back. You'll be spiritually connected to your Higher Power whatever the situation, and you'll have the ability to spiritually connect with others, no matter what their spiritual belief, age, sex, or culture. You'll find yourself feeling, thinking, and behaving differently. You'll feel younger with more abilities at your disposal, and you'll find your walk in life more harmonious than it has ever been. No one need convince you of this; you'll discover this on your own faster than you ever thought possible!

Human growth is very personal, so I use the word "you" a lot in this book to help you dig deep inside yourself in a personal journey of self-discovery. If you feel that something doesn't fit you personally, then simply go on to the next paragraph or section. This book is about self-discovery and it is not my intention to tell you what you should be doing.

May The Power Model System™ bring into your life what it has brought into mine: success in all your four human components—physical, emotional, mental, and spiritual.

Chapter 1

THE POWER MODEL SYSTEM™

You are never given a wish without also being given the power to make it true. You may have to work for it, however.
Book of Illusions

PART 1:   A FASTER AND STRAIGHTER PATH, BIRTH OF THE POWER MODEL SYSTEM™

Years ago, I thought I needed to hear what other people thought of me and then follow their suggestions. In fact, some of that reasoning still rings true for me today. But often those external observations simply didn't fit, and I didn't have the self-esteem or wisdom to recognize the difference between a rebellion of someone's advice verses knowing who I am. Meaning I did not know myself enough to determine if someone's critique of me was correct or not. I didn't have a system that would allow me to discover my feelings, my thoughts, my actions, and my spiritual beliefs—a model I could plug my information into and decide what I wanted to change or leave alone. I also didn't have a system or tools that would allow me to bring forth all the information I had learned and recreate a new *internal system* that was cohesive and worked for me. (Each of us has an *internal system* that defines how our four human components (physical, emotional, mental, and spiritual) connect and interact with each other.)

The methods I explored in the past included affirmations, grief work, twelve-step, and recovery programs. I made progress going into recovery for co-dependency and work addiction, and that progress eventually led me to teach college-level classes to people recovering from major difficulties in life. This experience gave me insight into these four human components that are part of all of us, and assisted me on this phase of my journey. At one point, I can remember saying with finality, "Now I am okay."

But still, I knew something was missing; Growing up seemed just too difficult for me and others. I knew there had to be a faster, straighter path to maturity. I wanted something visual, a step-by-step guide, so I would know if I was making progress and could keep track of my own growth throughout the years. I wanted a system I could practice and take wherever I went. I wanted it to work for me time after time.

I wanted a system that had a sense of internal balance so that with continuous use I could re-pattern how I thought, felt, and perceived the world and the people in it. While experiencing my soul's journey, I wanted to know my purpose and fulfill it. Ultimately, that meant I would have to stop *reacting* when life offered me challenges and, instead, act according to my purpose—to become all that I could be. I spent years compiling information, working with myself and my clients to develop The Power Model System™. Once I applied it to myself, I became aware of issues that hindered my growth. I was able to make my own adjustments and listen to feedback from others without my insides going crazy. The system brought rapid results, in terms of increasing internal motivation and making permanent changes in behavior. I could re-pattern my brain and change my future. As I matured (don't confuse age with maturity!), so did The Power Model System™.

Invisible Force

"Invisible force" is a phrase that many of the people I've worked with have used. They say to me, "Kay, I want to change, but there's something holding me back and I don't know what it is." I understand what they're saying. They're not the only ones who experience this force. I also see and hear speakers, educators, counselors, and others trying to work around, under, and through that same force with people they're trying to educate and help. Unfortunately, however, it doesn't yield the desired results. Because of this invisible force, people are not able to hold on to the new behaviors, knowledge, and feelings they've been taught. This invisible force continues to bring them back to their "old" selves.

So the question is, why do people pay money, spend the time, and want to learn but leave with information they can't keep applying in their lives? I see four answers to that question:

1) Every one of us has an internal system we developed in childhood that only we can uncover;
2) Each of us created this internal system in our conscious mind, and by our teen years it has become part of our subconscious mind;
3) This system affects every aspect of our lives;
4) This internal system involves your four components (emotional, mental, spiritual, and physical). Until you can understand how this all affects you, it is virtually impossible to develop true maturity on a permanent basis.

So, what is this invisible force? First, let me tell you what it is *not*.

It's *not* that you lack the desire to change.
It's *not* that you've neglected to spend time and money learning how to change.

It's *not* that you lack intelligence.

It's *not* that you're reaching for something you can't achieve.

It's *not* that you're destined to be the same way the rest of your life.

It's *not* that you've failed to apply new information you're continually learning.

Now that we've established what it's *not*, let's talk about what it *is*.

The invisible force reflects how you work internally—how you operate through your emotional, mental, physical, and spiritual components, which I call your *internal blueprint* or profile. With a few activities, you will actually be able to go within yourself and determine your unique blueprint. We will discuss more about this later in the book.

Know Thy Self

Sense of: s*ense is to become aware of; perceive. To grasp; understand.*
Self: *one's consciousness of one's own being or identity.*

The Merriam-Webster Dictionary

Deep down subconsciously, you know all the right behaviors and actions to take in order to experience the perfect relationship, the perfect career, and the perfect life. But that inner knowledge seems to be out of reach. What if you could actually learn how you and your Higher Power (as you believe him/her to be) created your internal blueprint? Would you like to understand how your emotional, mental, physical, and spiritual components work together? What if I told you that you'll be able to identify the natural defense system (fight-or-flight) that you set up long ago? Would you like to become aware of your strengths and weaknesses, accept them, take action on the elements you want to change, and then change them? That's right—actually do it yourself! After all, you're the expert on *you*. You have been all along.

Chances are, you're still letting that powerful invisible force—your subconscious mind—take over. Many decisions, reactions, and beliefs about the world originate in your subconscious mind. To change or re-pattern any of these beliefs or reactions, you'll need to become fully aware of the information in your subconscious mind and transfer it into your conscious mind. In other words, you'll have to get to know yourself intimately.

Can you truly know yourself at the most intimate level? Absolutely! But to do this, you'll need to know how to move the information from your subconscious mind to your conscious mind. Only then will you be able to recreate your system of automatic responses, decisions, reactions, and beliefs. Up until now, you've been hindered by a lack of awareness of what you created in the first place. Learning to access that awareness becomes your goal. This is simple but not easy.

A few basic Power Model System™ principles will assist you in knowing yourself:

1. Acknowledge that *you* are the expert on you;
2. Affirm that we all possess the same physical, emotional, mental, and spiritual components, but they've been put together differently and interact differently in each of us;
3. Follow a visual system in which you can see and record your information and progress;
4. Utilize tools that allow self-discovery so you don't have to rely on an "outside expert" telling you who you are;
5. Ask the right questions. Where your answers take you will deliver relevant information from your subconscious mind;
6. Honor the uniqueness that you and your Higher Power created. Doing so will help you recreate a new system so that you can experience control and self-empowerment, and take responsibility for your life.

If you were going to reconstruct a home, you would first need a blueprint of the house showing how it was built and what materials were used, i.e., concrete, wood, drywall, plumbing, electrical components, etc. If you wanted to change the structure, you'd refer to the old blueprints, draw up new ones, and then start making the changes. If you skipped ahead, you'd have a mess of mistakes to clean up. Similarly, if your car quit running and you didn't know how each part worked, you couldn't fix it until you understood its internal blueprint.

The same goes for each of us. We need to refer to our internal blueprint before we can begin making intelligent choices and changes.

> *You are who you are, wherever you go, whatever you do, and whomever you're with.*

> *Your individual internal blueprint defines how your mental, physical, emotional, and spiritual components operate and how they interact with each other.*

Your Personal Higher Power

One powerful belief that I interweave throughout this book is that my Higher Power (as I know it to be) has been at my side since the day I was born, assisting in my development as best it could while honoring my free will. This means that my Higher Power is fully aware of how my internal blueprint operates and how it came to be. Once I realized that my Higher Power and I had together created my internal blueprint in my childhood, I knew that my Higher Power and I could *recreate* a new internal blueprint. First, I needed to figure out what I wanted to change and what I wanted to keep. From there, my choices expanded, offering me more opportunities than I had ever imagined. It is my hope that you come to realize the same is true for you.

I define Higher Power as "a source of power inside and outside of us." However, the definition of that Higher Power is completely your own choosing. It might be associated with a religion, a great prophet or teacher, or the universe itself. Some well known religions and teachers are listed below. Feel free to add to the list.

This is a good time to reflect what "Higher Power" means to you personally. (If you don't have one, that's okay!)

Amish	Hinduism (Hare Krishna and others)	Shinto
Baptist	Islam (Mohammed)	Sikhism
Baha'I Faith	Jainism	Taoism
Buddhism	Judaism	
Codas	Macumba	
Confucianism	New Age	Add Yours Below
Catholic	Native-American-Spirituality	Example: Nature
Latter-Day-Saints	Osho	
Christianity (Jesus)	Scientology	_____
Unitarian	Eckankar	

What if I Don't Believe in a Higher Power?

This book stresses the importance of a Higher Power, not to advocate a particular belief system but to assist you in tapping into a source of power that is not likely known to you. At some point in our lives, we all experience events or challenges that seem overwhelming and impossible to overcome, yet we miraculously get through these times without ever knowing how or why. I believe we do this by unconsciously tapping into a power or ability that we don't know we have. For many, this power is associated with a religion. Even if we don't believe in a religion or God, we dig deep into ourselves and tap into an innate power, energy, ability, or sense of peace.

Those of you who don't believe in an "official" Higher Power may, for the purposes of this book, define Higher Power as something deep within you that allows you to momentarily detach from the outside world and get back in touch with yourself at a deeper level. An activity later in the book will assist you in discovering these deeper levels of your being, which you may refer to as a Higher Power.

The "Presents" for Staying Present

Do you knock on doors that don't open? Are you unable to see not only the doors that are open but *all* doors? Do you know you have day-to-day gifts? What if I told you that every day is Christmas? It's all in your perception. You might fail to recognize when an opportunity comes your way because you're not focused on the present. Instead, you're living in the past while looking toward the future. Consequently, all sense of "present time" disappears from your reality. That's what I refer to as "living in illusion," meaning that *you see what you see and nothing more.*

If you perform the various activities throughout this book focusing only on the results you want at the end, you won't give yourself credit for the self-discoveries you make along the way. Stop to appreciate what you learn during each activity, even if you don't like everything you discover. Take time to stay with your process. Read, perform an activity, think about it, and apply the information to your situation. Be completely "with" the page of the book that's in front of you. Think about similar information you've received in different ways. Most of all, resist the temptation to skip over something because you think you already know it or say to yourself, "Oh, this does not apply to me."

Many of us don't know how to learn, or if we do learn something, we forget it very quickly. So let's examine how humans learn.

Staying In the Present by Changing the Way You Learn

Repetition breeds knowledge. You might have difficulty digesting information the first time you're exposed to it. We all benefit from hearing the same information repeated in different contexts. You've probably noticed already that I often say the same things in different ways. This is how we learn. Each time you read the same thing, you arrive at a new awareness on a deeper level.

Having visual pictures assists you in remembering information as well. Pictures work eight times more effectively on the human brain than the spoken or written word. For example, posting a calendar filled with positive sayings (preferably pictures) in your workspace will help you keep a positive attitude because you "see" those words (or images) every time you sit at your desk. In effect, you're re-patterning positive messages into your brain.

Learning Statistics

Consider these statistics about learning[3]. One month after learning, we retain the following:

- 14% of what we hear (80% of this is distorted)
- 22% of what we see
- 30% of what we watch others do
- 42% of what we hear, see, and watch others do
- 72% when learning is connected to real or imagined life experiences
- 83% when learning is converted into a challenging activity
- 91% when we teach others

Let's apply these statistics to learning with The Power Model System™ so you will get an idea of the valuable integration that's taking place inside you as you're working this system and self-discovering who you are.

What We Hear

Often what we hear is not what was said or meant to be said. There are many reasons for this. Here are a few:

- We all interpret or perceive words in subtle different ways;
- We may hear the information, but since it is not really used in our life it is quickly forgotten;
- Because of our past, we simply don't believe what people say anymore.

What We See

You may have heard the phrase "seeing is believing." Have you ever wondered why two people can see the same movie or event and each have completely different interpretations? Here is the reason:

- Often what we see is quickly interpreted, tainted, or influenced by our past experiences. For example, a mountain cliff may be exhilarating for some and bring fear of death for others. Often these perceptions prevent us from learning.

Watching Others

Watching others in action increases learning because we get to see not only what others do but the consequences of these actions. One thing that often inhibits this learning (especially for children) is that we do not "practice what we preach."

Real and Imagined Experiences

It has been said that "experience is the best teacher." This is because consequences often follow our actions. This is why retained learning significantly increases when we are involved in the lesson. It is also true that if we visually imagine certain activities in our minds, we can learn from them. Why? Because the mind doesn't differentiate between an imagined experience and a real experience. We often don't learn from these experiences because we are on *autopilot*. While in autopilot, we aren't very aware of the cause or effect of our reactions. This will be discussed in more detail later on in the book

Challenging Activities

Challenging activities have a predetermined purpose, so you become more aware of your actions. You perform the activity with the intention of learning something. Thus, you are more "in the present" and better able to pick up the details of the experience and the thoughts and feelings that accompany it.

Teaching Others

Teaching is the pinnacle of learning. While teaching, you are mindful of what you are saying; you know you are being observed by the student. This forces you to look in the mirror and see if you are practicing what you are preaching. Often teachers will tell you that they learn much through the teaching process itself. This is because the lesson often has to be proven or improved to accommodate the individual student. Teaching others is a humbling experience, which elicits a deep awareness that we are all learning together in this classroom called Earth.

Now let's look at how The Power Model System™ utilizes these learning statistics.

As you go through this system, you'll be given activities that engage your *sight* (by visually presenting your internal system on paper) and *hearing* (by being asked the right questions, you're able to hear yourself come up with the answers).

The "Story Times" in this book allow you to hear what others have done and learn the consequences of their actions. These stories encourage you to be aware in the present by seeing the actions of others (and their consequences) in the real world. This will bring your learning retention to 42%.

Some of the activities will require you to visualize past experiences (both childhood and recent). This will increase your learning retention to 72%. Other more challenging activities might involve doing something you do not ordinarily do. These activities take personal effort and force you to stay in the present. When you stay in the present, your learning retention jumps to 83%! The Power Model System™

encourages you to share what you have learned with others. This makes you a teacher and skyrockets your learning retention to an amazing 91%!

Self-challenge, self-discovery, and sharing the experience with others are crucial factors of the Power Model System™.

Again, I encourage you to show these activities to others and share the information. The more you share this system with others, the more it will become integrated within you. I've discovered that performing the activities in groups is highly beneficial. In this way, you can assist each other. As I've said before, teaching is a powerful tool. We learn something from every person with whom we interact, but more so when we're teaching.

Expect Miracles

Miracle: an e*xtraordinary event manifesting divine intervention in human affairs.*
The Merriam-Webster Dictionary

I believe in miracles. Furthermore, I believe humans can experience as many miracles as they want by "living in the present" (connecting with their Higher Power) and fully knowing that all their worrying, wanting, demanding, and desires are already taken care of.

What does a miracle look like? How do you know if you've had one? You've paid for the books, gathered the information, and gone to the workshops. Still, something is lacking. Your mind tells you what you should be doing, but an invisible force holds you back. So you go into counseling, delve into your childhood, examine your relationships, and talk about how you want to make changes. After a while, you find yourself working on the same problems over and over—and getting few results. Your counselor, teacher, or instructor continues to tell you that you can change, but you must have a desire to change.

Of course you have the desire or you wouldn't be reading this book! But the invisible force I described earlier is holding you back and may have dampened your expectations for any kind of real miracle in your life. I guarantee that you'll understand this invisible force and bring real miracles into your life—not just one miracle, but many—if you continue to self-discover your true inner-self and make changes from within.

PART 2: THE POWER MODEL SYSTEM™ PROCESS

Figure 1.1 illustrates the formula of The Power Model System:

Emotional + Mental + Spiritual = Physical right action

Most self-help programs take you to spiritual results. The Power Model System™ will take you to a spiritual life, but the end results are the *right physical actions in life*. To connect with the right physical actions in our lives, we need to have our emotional, mental, and spiritual components working together.

We are in a physical body with a sensory system that is experienced through *emotions* (which need to be identified and processed) and *thoughts* (which need to be identified and understood). This processing and understanding will continue throughout our entire lives. We are "practicing" and evolving human beings, which means we will have moments of greatness and moments where we stumble. In other words, we will go in and out of balance our entire lives. But through the Power Model System™ we will maintain awareness of what is really happening in our lives and, thus, have the ability to constantly correct our course towards inner strength and happiness. To do this, we must see how our emotional, mental, spiritual, and physical components interact with each other.   Again, this interaction is uniquely different for each individual. As you go through life, any course corrections that need to be made will depend on you.

The Right Action Is Determined by You

A cornerstone of The Power Model System ™ is that *you choose what is right and wrong for you.* You choose what you want to change and what you want to keep in your life. The Power Model System ™ simply assists you to see what your choices are.

Right: *conforming with or conformable to justice, law, or morality, in accordance with fact, reason, or truth; correct.*
Action: *1) the state or process of acting or doing. 2) something done or accomplished; a deed. 3) organized activity to accomplish an objective. 4) behavior or conduct.*
                                                                The Merriam-Webster Dictionary

Most of us struggle throughout our lives not knowing if we're making right or wrong decisions. Wouldn't it be nice if you could know what actions are right for you? This is where The Power Model System™ comes in. You take the right action *for you* using your own spiritual belief foundation. If we all did this, we would realize that every moment offers us another choice and, thus, another opportunity to grow together!

Below is a quote from Vonny Vaughn, a woman from South Carolina who attended a three-day HumanWisdom Workshop:

"Before signing up for the workshop I thought, *should I be going to a workshop or just pray all my problems away?* Then I realized that the workshop was an answer to my prayers. God puts people in our lives to help us along in our journey…he's just thoughtful like that."

How the Power Model System ™ Works

Figure 1.1 explains The Power Model System™. This chart shows the inner workings of the system and how it can paint a picture of our inner blueprint. By performing a series of activities, your personal blueprint will come together, allowing you to effectively make decisions that will result in permanent changes from within.

The chart is made up of three main sections: *Reality, Personal Blueprint, and Illusion.* Through activities, you will discover how your Personal Blueprint can either keep you in reality and joy or illusion and despair. This is done by discovering how each of your four human components benefit in reality or suffer in illusion. It will be shown that joy in reality is always experienced through awareness, acceptance, and action, while control in illusion always leads to resistance, resentment, revenge, and ultimately to despair or death of self.

On the chart between Personal Blueprint and Reality are activities and Power Model System™ components that will assist you in your self-discovery. On the chart between Personal Blueprint and Illusion are activities and Power Model System components that will assist you in realizing what keeps you in Illusion and out of control.

At the bottom of the chart you'll see the words "Illusion" and "Control." You can choose to become aware of your desire to control people, places, or things, or you can remain *resistant* to change. If you choose to maintain your resistance, you become resentful of yourself and others because you didn't get what you wanted when and how you wanted it. This can lead to the deadly *revenge* stage where you take destructive physical action to hurt yourself or others.

The Power Model System™ is based on the theory that we are all born with a *dependent* system. That is, we are dependent on our parents and emotions to decide what we think and how we act. As we get older, we presume we are mature and think we are in control of our emotions—we don't go around crying or raging. For many of us, this is a false presumption. All we are really doing is getting better at hiding and suppressing our feelings from ourselves and others—to the point where we no longer recognize them but display negative behavior in reaction to them.

Our goal is to move through this reactive behavior or dependency to the *interdependent* stage. We can develop interdependency between our emotions, thoughts, and spirituality. When we are able to function in an interdependent manner internally, we become *independent* in our actions. By having independent actions, we can decide on the right actions for us. We are able to be independent in our actions because of the connection to our personal Higher Power. *Deep down we know when a certain action is right.* Achievement of the independent stage is the ultimate goal and a wonderful place to be.

To begin the discovery process, we will need to start at the *dependent* stage. We will then go through the stages of self-discovery of our four components. We'll look at each human component and what we will achieve within each activity, within that stage.

Dependant

When you are *dependent*, you react to your environment from your emotions. These reactions stem from illusions you have about yourself and your environment. Self-discovering your illusions will affect all four of your human components, which will then affect your whole decision-making process concerning important life events.

These eight Power Model System™ activities will help you self discover your dependence:

- The Present You
- Environment Activities
- Three Faces of Illusion
- Automatic Pilot
- The Five Stages of Illusion
- Defense System
- Feeling-Thinking-Behavior Chart
- Pyramid of Success

The Present You: This activity allows you to discover how you are in the present (Present Self) emotionally, mentally, spiritually, and physically according to how you respond to events and stresses.

Environment Activity: Through Environmental Activities, you discover how the past continues to affect your present and how *not* identifying past issues will cause emotional regression in the present.

Three Faces of Illusion: The Three Faces of Illusion (the 3 Rs) activity allows you to discover how resistance, resentment, and revenge keep you in illusion about life and stuck in situations where you operate on automatic pilot.

Automatic Pilot: Automatic Pilot shows how automatic feelings, thinking, and reactive behavior affect your life. Without intervention or knowledge learned from the Environment Activity, you will remain on Automatic Pilot.

The Five Stages of Illusion: This shows how the Five Stages of Illusion affect your life. These stages are the result of staying on Automatic Pilot.

Defense System: From this activity, you will learn what the defense system is, how it works, when you developed it, and how to become aware of when you use it. You will also learn how to make your defense system a choice, whether to use it or not.

Feeling-Thinking-Behavior Chart: This chart shows the flexibility you need amongst your four human components for them to become balanced.

Pyramid of Success: The Pyramid of Success allows you to quickly identify where you may be stuck in your process in any given situation and what activity you can do to get unstuck.

Interdependent

By being *interdependent*, you develop "give and take" relationships between interdependent entities (objects, individuals, or groups). When three of your four human components (emotional, mental, and spiritual) are brought into balance, they can work interdependently to assist you in achieving *impulse control* and choosing the right physical action in your life. What is impulse control? It's when you think about your response with good intention, before you actually respond, rather than responding automatically. We will be talking more about impulse control later in the book.

Listed below are the Power Model System™ informational components and activities that will bring forth interdependence:

- Five Stages of Maturity
- Discovering Internal Boundaries
- Life Spark
- Creating a Safe Spiritual Place
- My Internal System

Five Stages of Maturity: These are the five stages towards developing maturity. Maturity is how we function in daily life with internal balance and lowered stress.

Discovering Internal Boundaries: Internal boundaries—where *you* leave off and *I* begin—give us a sense of safety and identity. Here you'll discover what boundaries you want to change to become a healthier individual. This will give you a sense of self and allow you to learn the strengths and weaknesses of your boundary system.

Life Spark: We were all born with a Life Spark, a connection with our Higher Power (as we understand him or her to be). As you self-discover your authentic emotions, you will uncover and reveal your Life Spark. Once this happens, you will have a conscious relationship with your Higher Power.

Creating a Safe Spiritual Place: In this activity, you will create a self-relaxation tape and learn how to use it to go to a safe, spiritual place deep inside you.

My Internal System: Here you will discover what you need to function interdependently. A visual chart is created using the information you have gathered from your previous activities. This is where you will see how you can exercise impulse control over your life.

Independent

By being independent, you are free from the influence, guidance, or control of others. You are self-reliant and have an *independent mind*. This is where you achieve the ability to make independent decisions for yourself. You will be able to do this because you will have a functional interdependent system.

Activities include:

- Discovering External Boundaries
- Reality
- Gifts of Emotions
- My Personal Blueprint
- Five Steps to Centeredness
- Internal Shift
- Self Living in Reality

External Boundaries: In this activity, you will learn how external boundary systems work and how you can achieve a sense of self while successfully interacting with others.

Reality: In reality, you shift to your authentic emotions, have your defense system defined, establish your emotional boundaries, create your personal spiritual safe place, connect with your Higher Power, go through stages of spiritual growth, and know the right action for you at any given time. Your continued growth is reinforced.

Gifts of Emotions: Gifts are blessings. In this simple exercise, you will see how your authentic emotions reward you with internal gifts that strengthen each of your four human components. Emotional gifts reflect the perfection of the universe and have the ability to come around again and again throughout your life, demonstrating the amazing cycle of life.

My Personal Blueprint: In this activity, you will generate your personal blueprint by piecing together all the information you've been gathering through The Power Model System™ activities. This blueprint will show you a complete visual picture of your four human components and how they function and interact.

Five Steps to Centeredness: These five steps will enable you to be in a meditative state of mind, with your eyes wide open. You can go through all five steps in a matter of seconds, anywhere, with anyone, in any given situation. These Five Steps will reduce stress, keep your emotions from ruling your life, connect your internal power with your Higher Power, harmonize the use of both sides of your brain, calm and clear your thought patterns, and sharpen your intuitive abilities. The Five Steps to Centeredness will provide you with choices you never knew were possible and lead you to take the right actions in your life.

Internal Shift: When you perform the activities in this book, you will shift from having a desire to control others to being aware of yourself; from being dependent on your emotions to being self-empowered; and from behaving reactively to behaving proactively. The end result will be joy, joy, joy!

Self Living in Reality: In his activity, you'll be able to review what you've learned (how your four human components have become more balanced and interactive) and pinpoint what needs further review.

"Power" in The Power Model System™

When people hear the word "power", many times they think of power over a person, place, or thing. In the Power Model System™, the word "power" means a higher source that's available to all of us, in whatever form(s) each person perceives it (see Part 1 of this Chapter). There are often times in our lives where our burdens seem overwhelming. The Power Model System™ assists you in either tapping into your Higher Power in handling these situations and/or having the humility of simply letting go and turning burdens over that Higher Power.

If you perform the activities in this book, you will discover your *authentic self.* Yes, you can achieve this within these pages! With each and every activity, please know there are no wrong answers. That's right. Do each and every activity, but remember that all answers are right for you! They will always teach you something. One drop of learning a day makes an ocean of experiences in a lifetime.

As you go through The Power Model System™ and awaken to your personal blueprint, take your bows and know that you did the work of self-discovery. This will self-empower you to continue your journey of internal growth.

THE POWER MODEL SYSTEM CHART ™

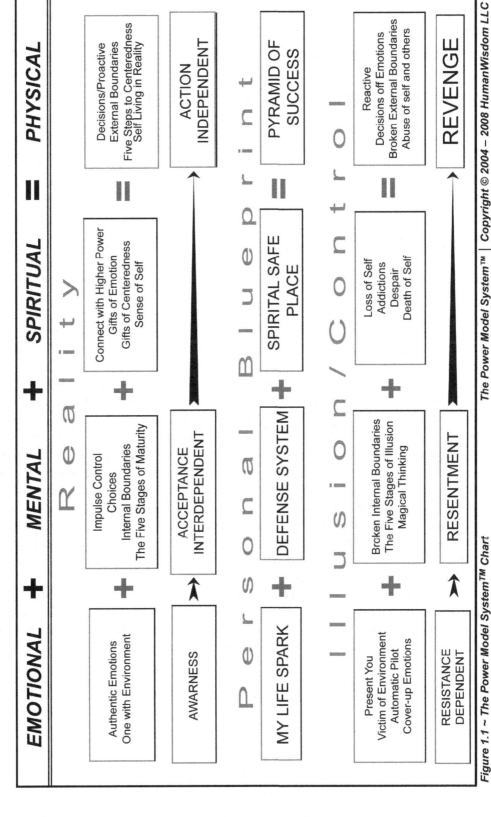

| EMOTIONAL | + | MENTAL | + | SPIRITUAL | = | PHYSICAL |

R e a l i t y

| Authentic Emotions
One with Environment | Impulse Control
Choices
Internal Boundaries
The Five Stages of Maturity | Connect with Higher Power
Gifts of Emotion
Gifts of Centeredness
Sense of Self | Decisions/Proactive
External Boundaries
Five Steps to Centeredness
Self Living in Reality |

AWARNESS + ACCEPTANCE INTERDEPENDENT + = ACTION INDEPENDENT

P e r s o n a l   B l u e p r i n t

MY LIFE SPARK + DEFENSE SYSTEM + SPIRITAL SAFE PLACE = PYRAMID OF SUCCESS

I l l u s i o n / C o n t r o l

| Present You
Victim of Environment
Automatic Pilot
Cover-up Emotions | Broken Internal Boundaries
The Five Stages of Illusion
Magical Thinking | Loss of Self
Addictions
Despair
Death of Self | Reactive
Decisions off Emotions
Broken External Boundaries
Abuse of self and others |

RESISTANCE DEPENDENT + RESENTMENT + = REVENGE

Figure 1.1 ~ The Power Model System™ Chart   *The Power Model System™ | Copyright © 2004 – 2008 HumanWisdom LLC*

Chapter 2

THE FOUR HUMAN COMPONENTS

Man can learn nothing except by going from the known to the unknown
          Claude Bernard

Human beings are given four components—emotional, mental, physical, and spiritual—to assist them in achieving balance in their lives. It's like having a state-of-the-art computer with all the options money can buy. The computer doesn't work properly unless all the components are wired correctly and electricity runs through them. Similarly, until all your four human components are aligned with each other to create brain patterns that control "fight-or-flight" responses (the primitive urge to fight or run when in actuality the situation doesn't call for such a response), you won't have the energy and wisdom that propels you to maturity, balance, and success. Once you form a pattern of fight-or-flight response to any kind of perceived danger at a young age, it could stay with you the rest of your life. In effect, you'd be on automatic pilot. Although you likely have no conscious awareness of these brain patterns, you can still learn to rewrite and recreate them so they're no longer on autopilot. Changing these brain patterns calls for a greater awareness of your internal blueprint and learning to re-pattern what you want to change.

When your four human components are balanced—they are completely aligned and in harmony with each other rather than being absent or in conflict with each other—they can help you become a "mature, balanced adult." This refers not to age but to the process of achieving peace and harmony within you.

Internal Blueprint

There are many self-help programs and books that teach you how to behave to become successful. But why is it so difficult to apply those teachings? As previously mentioned, it is because one or more of your four components is off balance, in conflict with another component, or completely missing. Your internal blueprint is based on these four internal components:

Emotional
- What you were taught about emotions;
- How you were taught to identify your emotions;
- How you were taught to express your emotions appropriately.

Mental
- How you were taught to identify your thoughts versus your feelings;
- How you were taught to identify your thoughts about yourself ;
- How you perceive the world around you;
- How you interact with the world around you;
- How you were taught to quiet your mind.

Spiritual
- What you were taught about power;
- What you were taught about a Higher Power;
- What you were taught about how you "fit" spiritually into the world.

Physical
- What your physical environment and behavior were like in your youth;
- How you were taught to keep your body safe in an unsafe world;
- How you re-act physically due to all the above.

Were you taught or do you believe that power is represented by money, career, and clothes? Is power reflected in who you know, what you know, what house you live in, or what kind of car you drive? Consciously or not, these connections with power exist subtly in your everyday life and affect your behavior.

This doesn't mean you shouldn't own nice things, drive new cars, earn college degrees, or have a great job. However, these possessions and achievements don't *define* who you are. You are much more than your degrees, car, job, money, or house. These things will help you get through life, but "who you are" goes much deeper. This is the part of yourself you want to connect with.

You may say that no one (even your parents) took time to teach you how to behave, but actually they did—by their actions and reactions toward you. You learned from their presence (or absence) in your life. Adults don't have to come out and say actual words to teach children; they teach through their actions. Children either follow the examples in front of them or go to opposite extremes to compensate. And you weren't influenced only by your parents. Your environment played a big role. In our society, television, magazines, and DVDs dictate what's cool (like wearing designer jeans) or how to have fun (like playing with the latest toys). Much of what you've learned also depends on where you received your education.

The combination of all these elements helped to mold your fight-or-flight response and your automatic reaction to the present.

Story Time

Gerry, a middle-aged man, held an executive position with the government. One day, the director of his department called me in and said, "I don't want to fire this employee or demote him, but I *do* want him to stop showing an attitude with others. He is unable to work under pressure, and we are under pressure a lot in this office." Then he looked me in the eye and said, "I heard that you could accomplish this."

I said, "I can't accomplish any of these things, but your employee can, given that he learns and applies the right tools." I interviewed Gerry and asked if he was willing to work with me. He said yes and then asked, "Does this mean I *have* to change?"

"No," I said. "You do not have to change. It is entirely your choice. You can change what you want and leave the rest alone. It's all up to you."

I shared with Gerry what his director had said about him and asked him if he had a hard time under pressure. He admitted he did. He let me know that his whole body tenses up, his mind goes a mile a minute, and no one can get anything done fast enough around him so he blows up at them. He let me know he has been known to yell and make inappropriate remarks at co-workers. He also shared with me how he then goes home on bad days from work and yells at his wife and children. Gerry seemed to be very aware of his behavior. He just didn't know how to stop yelling and reacting to the pressures at work.

We discussed things he would like to change about himself. He came up with yelling and losing his temper under stress and being able to take healthy criticism in the workplace. He let me know that he felt like he was a loser whenever he was told he needed to improve something about himself. Gerry said he got defensive and then wanted to rage. Gerry told me he had gone to anger management seminars, and what he learned was he was not to get angry or walk away. Gerry laughed and said, "I imagine myself talking to someone at work and I get angry. So the next thing they know, I am walking away from them. I can't tell them anything because I will start yelling." We both laughed because we knew that walking away did not help the situation.

By now I knew Gerry's coping skill was to go on autopilot and rage. He was also putting anger on top of all his emotions.

Gerry learned about his defense system, fight-or-flight (how he reacts in times of stress).

As Gerry went through the activities and learned how to use The Power Model System™, he was astonished at how much he was able to reveal to himself, including how his brain was wired for flight-or-fight situations. He self-discovered how he'd interpreted his environment in his youth—emotionally, mentally, physically, and spiritually—and how he was likely to react in certain situations. He said he'd always considered himself in total control, yet he found that when he was reacting on autopilot he was out of control.

As we worked to discover his unique personal blueprint, Gerry kept saying he was amazed by how simple the process was. "Just with the awareness of my four components and the logical process of The Power Model System™, I'm watching myself change."

The "amazing" change he experienced in himself went beyond the workplace. He saw his marriage improve as well as his relationships with his two children. He felt less stressed, and his productivity at work picked up as a result.

All in all, Gerry found himself behaving more openly and less defensively. He felt more relaxed. And because he had gained control over himself, he no longer felt a need to exercise control over others and his environment.

As we were completing our work together, I asked Gerry, "Have you ever gone to a workshop for success and liked the suggestions but found yourself unable to keep applying the behavior on a regular basis?"

"Oh, yes," he said and laughed. (He'd developed quite a sense of humor through his changing process.)

I encouraged him to integrate what he'd learned from The Power Model System™ with what he'd learned from other workshops. In doing so, he discovered he had the foundation he needed to move forward in any direction he wanted.

Gerry has since come back to my workshops on his own for a brush-up course, and he continues to be amazed at the simplicity of The Power Model System™. He doesn't need to carry around a book, memorize techniques, or behave a certain way. He's learned how everything is accomplished internally, anytime, anyplace, and with anyone.

Remember, like Gerry, your responses to your present environment and circumstances are due to past events or conditioning. Once you determine the patterns that make up your internal blueprint, you'll see that you have the choice to change, just as Gerry did. But as long as the patterns remain in your subconscious, they'll continue. You can't change what you're not consciously aware of.

Chapter 3

THE PRESENT SELF

A traveler am I and a navigator, and every day I discover a new region within my soul.
Khalil Gibran

For most of us, the condition of the "present self" in terms of our four human components (emotional, mental, spiritual, and physical) is currently unbalanced.

Have you taken workshop after workshop, read book after book, and said to yourself, *I know what to do, why aren't I doing it?* That seems to be the million-dollar question for all of us. Well, don't discard all the information you've gleaned from those other workshops and books. You'll be able to use all of it once you've created your own personal blueprint. It's not that you're incapable of doing and achieving all those wonderful things you've learned. You're just working against an invisible force that controls you internally and gets in your way.

So what are the consequences of this invisible force? The answer is simple: our four human components become in conflict with each other. This results in massive confusion in all aspects of our lives, including our relationships, careers, and spiritual life.

Here are some examples of internal human conflicts:

Emotional and Mental Conflict

When these two components aren't balanced your thoughts attack your feelings and split you in two—you *think* one thing and *feel* something totally different. As a result, you may constantly judge yourself or think you're going crazy.

Spiritual Conflict with the Emotional and Physical

You believe that your Higher Power wants you to stay pure in thought, but your body and emotions may never feel pure enough. For example, we humans have physical needs, one being sexual. We often have sexual desires, yet we feel guilty about this because of our spiritual beliefs. This leads to relationship problems within our selves and with others..

Mental and Physical Conflict

You know you should behave a certain way, and all of a sudden you observe yourself doing the opposite. You reap the consequences for not doing what you knew was right, and you can't figure out why you went against yourself.

Emotional and Spiritual Conflict

You feel angry at your Higher Power for an event that has happened in your life. Spiritually, you may believe that everything happens for a reason, but emotionally you cannot accept it. You feel a spiritual disconnection.

Mental and Spiritual Conflict

What you observe in the world doesn't coincide with your "spiritual book." You become confused about what is happening to you and/or in the world. This lowers your self-esteem and you begin to have illusions about life and what it's all about.

These are five examples of internal human conflict, but you and I know there are many more. Without having information about "who you are" internally, you keep working against yourself, unaware of exactly what you're working against and what affects you.

Now let's perform some activities that will assist you in becoming aware of where your conflicts lie in each of your four human components. You will first identify your conflict areas within each component. Then you will see how one component has affected the other three components. For example, if you have emotional stress, you'll see how it also affects you mentally, spiritually, and physically.

Activity: The Present Self

This activity requires four (4) colored pencils: Orange, Blue, Red, and Black.

Read through the instructions before beginning the activity.

Let's begin with exploring "where you are now" and "what you consciously know" about the present *you*. You are the human being in the middle of the chart in Figure 3.1 (next page). Notice that all four human components (emotional, mental, physical, and spiritual) are represented around your body. Each component is broken down into a set of human aspects including behaviors, reactions, physical symptoms, and beliefs. By learning which of these aspects relate to you, you will begin to become aware of the *invisible force,* making it less frightening and mysterious.

The Present Self (Part 1): The Discovery Process

Figures 3.1 and 3.2 (the example) relate to this activity.

1. Let's assign a colored pencil to each human component according to the table below:

Human Component	Pencil Color
Emotional	Red
Mental	Orange
Spiritual	Blue
Physical	Black

2. Go down the list of each component in Figure 3.1, and circle any item which relates to you.
3. With the *orange* pencil, color in the part of the body that any of the *mental* aspects affects. (The circled items in the mental box).

    Example: I get overwhelmed at times, so I circled Item 17. When I get overwhelmed my head feels dizzy, so I color in the head with the orange pencil.

4. Draw a line from each circled item in the mental list to the corresponding location in the body to remind yourself how you are affected.

    Example: Draw a line from Item 17 to the head.

5. Repeat Steps 3 and 4 above for the emotional with a red pencil.
6. Repeat Steps 3 and 4 above for the physical with a black pencil.
7. Repeat Steps 3 and 4 above for the spiritual with a blue pencil.

8. If you find yourself wanting to use more than one color for the same part of the body, then divide that section up so you can color it with multiple colors. Or, if a part of the body has already been colored in with a different color, simply draw a line to the body part using the correct color. You can also write down your own items (illusions) anywhere on the chart and then draw a line to the body from your new item.

ACTIVITY
THE PRESENT SELF
(Part 1)

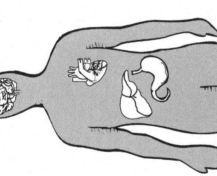

Emotional Illusions (red pencil)

1. Unable to identify emotions
2. Feel safest when I am angry
3. Fear other's anger
4. In fight-or-flight
5. Relationships are difficult for me
6. Feel crazy sometimes, not knowing the difference between thinking and feeling
7. Edgy
8. Easily startled
9. Go into crisis to finish a project
10. Do not know my emotional boundaries
11. Smile when I am angry
12. Feel like a victim in situations of life
13. Anxiety comes from nowhere
14. Try to control people, places, and things
15. Not aware of my emotional reactions
16. Yell more than I want to

Mental Illusions (orange pencil)

17. Overwhelmed
18. Anxious
19. Tense
20. Concentration problems
21. Depression
22. Difficulty in trusting
23. Do not know what I need
24. Lie to myself about what I really want in life
25. Judge myself harshly
26. Reactive to changes in my life
27. Magical thinking
28. Sleep problems
29. Unable to keep my mind quiet
30. Distorted perceptions of others and self
31. Compromise=win/lose=resentment
32. Sabotage thinking
33. Obsessive-compulsive thought patterns
34. Memory problems
35. Resistant towards looking inward
36. Difficulty in decision-making
37. Unable to state my boundaries and keep them

Spiritual Illusions (blue pencil)

38. Do not know my spiritual beliefs
39. Know my spiritual beliefs; do not apply them
40. Not enough quiet time
41. Unable to meet life on life's terms
42. Believe my Higher ower is responsible for my life
43. Do not allow time to grow spiritually
44. Try to control others' belief systems
45. Do not know the right action for myself
46. Believe I know the right action for others
47. Believe when something bad happens I am being punished by my Higher Power

Physical Illusions (black pencil)

48. Headaches
49. Fatigue
50. Overextended
51. Heart palpitations
52. Tense
53. Panic attacks (fight-or-flight)
54. Difficulty having fun
55. Isolate
56. Nervous system stressed
57. Reactive towards others
58. High blood pressure
59. Hold my breath when stressed
60. Tight muscles, when stressed
61. Tight jaw, grind teeth
62. Talk constantly, to feel comfortable
63. Gossip about others
64. Autoimmune problems
65. Muscle spasms
66. Do not care for physical needs, medical, etc.
67. Low pain tolerance
68. Unable to move (feet) forward towards goals
69. Have difficulty setting physical boundaries and keeping them

Figure 3.1 ~ The Present Self - Part 1

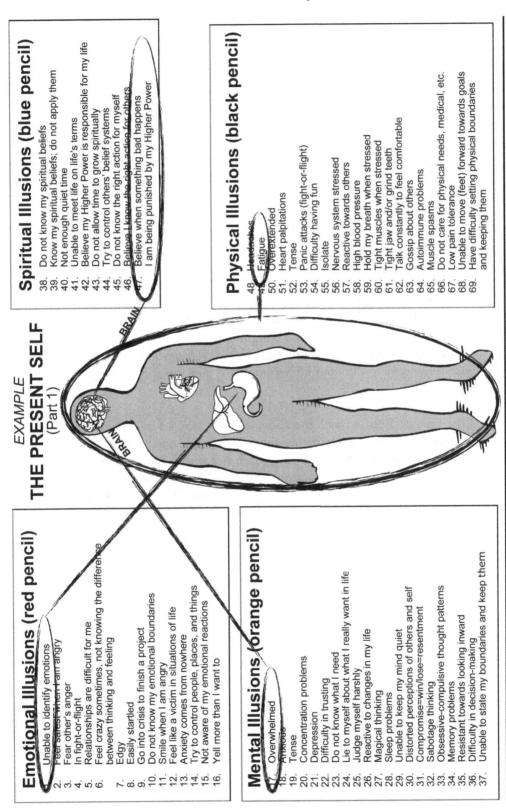

EXAMPLE
THE PRESENT SELF
(Part 1)

Emotional Illusions (red pencil)

1. Unable to identify emotions
2. Feel safest when I am angry
3. Fear other's anger
4. In fight-or-flight
5. Relationships are difficult for me
6. Feel crazy sometimes, not knowing the difference between thinking and feeling
7. Edgy
8. Easily startled
9. Go into crisis to finish a project
10. Do not know my emotional boundaries
11. Smile when I am angry
12. Feel like a victim in situations of life
13. Anxiety comes from nowhere
14. Try to control people, places, and things
15. Not aware of my emotional reactions
16. Yell more than I want to

Mental Illusions (orange pencil)

17. Overwhelmed
18. Anxious
19. Tense
20. Concentration problems
21. Depression
22. Difficulty in trusting
23. Do not know what I need
24. Lie to myself about what I really want in life
25. Judge myself harshly
26. Reactive to changes in my life
27. Magical thinking
28. Sleep problems
29. Unable to keep my mind quiet
30. Distorted perceptions of others and self
31. Compromise=win/lose=resentment
32. Sabotage thinking
33. Obsessive-compulsive thought patterns
34. Memory problems
35. Resistant towards looking inward
36. Difficulty in decision-making
37. Unable to state my boundaries and keep them

Spiritual Illusions (blue pencil)

38. Do not know my spiritual beliefs
39. Know my spiritual beliefs; do not apply them
40. Not enough quiet time
41. Unable to meet life on life's terms
42. Believe my Higher Power is responsible for my life
43. Do not allow time to grow spiritually
44. Try to control others' belief systems
45. Do not know the right action for myself
46. Believe I know the right action for others
47. Believe when something bad happens I am being punished by my Higher Power

Physical Illusions (black pencil)

48. Headaches
49. Fatigue
50. Overextended
51. Heart palpitations
52. Tense
53. Panic attacks (fight-or-flight)
54. Difficulty having fun
55. Isolate
56. Nervous system stressed
57. Reactive towards others
58. High blood pressure
59. Hold my breath when stressed
60. Tight muscles when stressed
61. Tight jaw and/or grind teeth
62. Talk constantly to feel comfortable
63. Gossip about others
64. Autoimmune problems
65. Muscle spasms
66. Do not care for physical needs, medical, etc.
67. Low pain tolerance
68. Unable to move (feet) forward towards goals
69. Have difficulty setting physical boundaries and keeping them

BRAIN

BRAIN

The Power Model System™ | *Copyright © 2007 – HumanWisdom LLC*

Figure 3.2 ~ Example: The Present Self - Part 1

The Present Self (Part 2): Consequences

Now that you have circled and marked what you are presently experiencing within your four human components, let's look at the imbalance in each component and how this affects the other three. Example: if you are unbalanced in your emotional component, your mental, spiritual, and physical components will be affected. (Remember, each of us is unique so our consequences may be different.). Becoming aware of these effects will enable you to become more conscious why some parts of your life may seem unmanageable.

Before doing this activity, look at the example in Figure 3.4 and then use the information that was revealed in Part 1.

1. On the following page (Figure 3.3), write down in the Illusion Column one item from each of the categories in Figure 3.1—mental, emotional, spiritual and physical—that you want to change. (You probably want to change all of them, but let's start with one from each component for now.)
2. With each of your choices, write down your thoughts about what having this illusion has cost you in your life emotionally, mentally, physically, and spiritually as in Figure 3.4.

When you are finished with the above activity, take a few minutes to review the activity. Most people who perform this activity are surprised to discover how much conflict they are carrying inside their body, mind, and spirit. We humans are amazing in our ability to walk through life in spite of overwhelming amounts of internal stress! Most of us truly believe this is a normal way of living our lives. Can you see how being off balance in one of your human components directly affects the other three?

ACTIVITY
THE PRESENT SELF
(Part 2)

Consequences for Present Self Illusions

Illusion	Emotional Consequences	Mental Consequences	Spiritual Consequences	Physical Consequences

EXAMPLE
THE PRESENT SELF
(Part 2)

Consequences for Present Self Illusions

Illusion	Emotional Consequences	Mental Consequences	Spiritual Consequences	Physical Consequences
MENTAL Overwhelmed	Constantly upset inside	My mind is never quiet. Hard to make a decision.	Unable to center myself.	I get all jumpy inside and feel like I am shaking.
EMOTIONAL Unable to identify my emotions	I yell a lot	My head feels like it's going to explode.	I feel disconnected to my belief system.	I feel exhausted with life, period.
SPIRITUAL When something bad happens, I am being punished by my Higher Power	I feel confused	I keep asking God why my life is this way and what did I do wrong?	I know what I believe, but I cannot apply it.	I do not have the energy to do anything fun. I drink alcohol to relax.
PHYSICAL Fatigue	Angry	My head feels like it's going to explode.	Unable to connect spiritually, because of the way my head feels.	I am getting a lot of muscle spasms and headaches. I just want to run away.

Chapter 4

THE ENVIRONMENT AROUND YOU

There is awareness and you can observe the whole mess. The whole mess shows you who you are, stay with it and it will take you to who you can be.
   Jack Ackerman

Ever since you were born, many aspects of life (positive and negative) have been teaching, forming, building up, and unfortunately often tearing down your mental, physical, emotional, and spiritual components.

The following are examples of what has affected our four human components and our internal blueprint since conception:

- Social environment
- Educational environment
- Religious conditioning
- Family environment
- Genetics
- Brain functions (chemistry)
- Generations of drugs and alcohol use
- Thinking disorders
- Challenges in learning
- And many more. The list is endless.

This list gives you an idea of how external and internal environmental factors can affect our coping abilities. Our internal coping system is based on how we perceived our environment and chose to cope with those perceptions at a young age.

Some people try to balance one component at a time before moving on to the next component, believing that eventually all four components will be aligned and developed. Or they work on some components and completely ignore others based on their comfort level or defense system. For example, if they think that believing something makes it so, they might first want to work on developing positive thoughts. "Believe it and it's so!" or "Say it and claim it!" or "Think positive thoughts" would represent this mental process. Although we'd all like it to be that easy, it's not. When you work with just your mind, you ignore your other three human components. You need to treat yourself as a whole person, integrating your body, mind, and spirit with your emotions. Balancing all our four components is crucial, because it's the only thing that will bring us internal peace. *Balancing your entire being brings out your internal power, your true self.*

For many of us, the emotional component is either the weakest or the most dominant component. Even if you worked on your emotional issues all your life, you would most likely still not have the results you want. Why? Because in your youth, your over-reactive emotional response to the environment (or complete lack thereof) became part of your unconscious mind and you created a belief system with an unbalanced emotional component in place. The same thing would happen with your other three components. Your behavior would reflect the influences that have patterned your brain. Do you want to live the rest of your life from the level of knowledge and unchecked behavior you obtained as a young child? Not if you want peace and joy in your life!

But there's good news! The fact that the human brain forms patterns in the early years doesn't mean it has to stay that way. Over time and with practice, you can re-pattern your brain with awareness, acceptance, and action. As noted earlier, doing this may sound simple, but it's certainly not easy. For example, your fight-or-flight response is firmly in place, which means when you sense danger you'll react a certain way automatically until you change this response.

Have you ever asked yourself, *why can't I change? Why do I always revert back to my old habits?* That's precisely what The Power Model System™ addresses.

Have you ever said to yourself, *"I'm an adult! I should be able to handle whatever comes my way in life in an adult manner.* I know I have. But when the stress of a situation hits me, guess what? I sometimes find myself overwhelmed. I don't act like an adult. I react like a child would, and I feel pretty silly afterwards. I then look back and say to myself, *why did I feel and act the way I did?* I think of all the things I could have done differently. So, as much as I'd like to say, "I'm an adult. I should be able to handle whatever life throws my way in an adult manner," I can't always say this is true.

> *Being an adult doesn't mean being internally balanced. Just because we're physically grown doesn't mean we won't revert to childish behavior. Size and age mean nothing. It's knowing ourselves and maturing to become a balanced human being that really matters.*

Being an adult doesn't automatically mean *being mature*.

To understand why, let's consider these scenarios:

- Have you ever felt like a kid asking your parents for money when you went into your boss's office to ask for a raise?
- Have you ever let the disciplinary action get out of hand while disciplining your child? And when you looked back at the incident, were you aware that you got involved in a power struggle with your child and acted his/her age instead of staying the adult?
- Have you ever been in a discussion with your partner and disagreed with him/her, started to get angry, and begun raging (like a two-year-old), perhaps bringing up an incident from a year ago? Did you find yourself sounding like your dad or mom?
- Have you found yourself acting childishly with friends or co-workers? (By this I mean "immature" behavior, not "child-like" or playful behavior.) You could hear and see how foolish you were being, but for some reason you couldn't stop yourself.

If you answered "yes" to any of these questions, you've experienced *self-regression*.

So, if you can hear and see yourself acting out, why can't you stop the behavior?

Reverting to Childhood Behavior

"Regression" refers to acting from the subconscious part of the mind with no awareness of the reason why.

Regression: *1) relapse to a less perfect or developed state; 2) psychology: reversion to an earlier or less-mature pattern of feeling or behavior; a relapse of symptoms; a defense mechanism in which one flees from reality by assuming a more infantile state; returning to a former state.*
The Merriam-Webster Dictionary

Subconscious: *existing in the mind but not immediately available to consciousness; affecting thought, feeling, and behavior without entering awareness.*
Conscious: *the part of the mind that's keenly aware of something and attaches importance to it.*
The Merriam-Webster Dictionary

How do you prevent regression? To put it simply, you bring the information in the subconscious part of your mind to your conscious mind with the help of The

Power Model System™. This is not wishful thinking; it is fact. You are the expert on you. You hold all the answers about you, within you, in the subconscious part of your mind. This is good news!

Regression can make you feel like an eleven-year-old when you're asking your boss for a raise. If you react with the fight-or-flight response under stress, you're in a regressive state. (This happens more often than people realize!)

While some of the stress you experience in life can't be changed, much of it can be. What you can certainly change is how you *respond* to stressful situations. Compounding stress on top of stress isn't the answer. Constant self-regression is stressful on the body, can cause many diseases, and much "dis-ease" within your life.

Wouldn't it be wonderful if:
1. You no longer needed to experience self-regression stress in your body;
2. You could live with events in your life (no matter how stressful they are) and be able to stay in the present;
3. You could learn to recognize regressive behavior, change it and remain in the present?

All of these are entirely possible!

How Stress Affects the Body

You don't need a degree to understand what happens to you if you continue to experience stress in your body and mind. But you will only take full responsibility and accountability for your behavior if you understand how your mind, body, and spirit work together. So let's take a walk down stress lane.

This next section is a little technical, so hang in there! I'll highlight the main points for you. The information comes from a book entitled *Affective Neuroscience* by Jaak Panksepp[1], Ph.D, a well-known research professor in psychology and psychiatry at the Medical College of Ohio in Toledo. I'll walk you through Dr. Panksepp's findings on what stress does to our bodies and minds.

> The fight-or-flight response is a biochemical reaction that, when you sense danger, prepares you to either remove yourself from the situation (flight) or defend yourself (fight). When you're under stress, the body becomes alarmed through a sense of impending danger and your body chemistry changes. According to Panksepp, "Stress is anything that activates the pituitary-adrenal system (the ACTH-cortisol axis). Everything that is typically considered to be a stressor in humans generates this brain response." To put it another way, when neuro-emotional influences reach a certain part of the hypothalamus, neurons travel through axons toward the pituitary that triggers the release of

ACTH (the abbreviation for adrenocorticotrophin hormone). ACTH is released into the bloodstream and travels to the adrenal cortex, where it triggers the release of cortisol. Cortisol regulates the intensity of the stress response to promote energy utilization in the body under stressful situations.

Panksepp also confirms that "sustained stress can kill certain brain cells" because "if cortisol secretion is sustained at excessive levels, the metabolic resources of hippocampal neurons become depleted and die prematurely." To simplify, research has shown that enormous tension and stressful conditions force the human endocrine system to become overloaded in our bodies. This triggers chemistry in the body, which, in turn, affects the nervous system. This change weakens the auto-immune system. It's no wonder that without awareness of automatic fight-or-flight patterns, we can become physically ill.

A group of hormones triggers an internal alarm system that will cause some of the following body reactions: rapid breathing, increased heart rate, sweaty or dry palms, edginess, digestive problems, blood vessel and pupil constriction, dry throat, hyper-alertness, inability to sleep, poor concentration, and memory lapses. When the stressful situation is over, you may be very hyper and then move into exhaustion.

If you have prolonged periods of stress, the condition becomes chronic and you start believing this is a natural way of life for you or it's the way everyone lives and feels. Sometimes people with this behavior will put themselves in dangerous situations or create situations that elicit the fight-or-flight response because it seems normal. However, that feeling is the body's dependency on the adrenal rush and the sense of power that accompanies it. Although this is a false sense of power, it's the closest these people get to feeling powerful. If you are one of these people, you don't have to live this way. In fact, I encourage you *not* to live this way.

Think of a time when you were stressed and your mind, body and spirit reacted in a negative way. You found yourself handling the situation with behavior you didn't like. In this state, your mind took you back to a time when you felt young and helpless. You reacted with the same behavior you used in the past, with no conscious awareness. Most likely, you blamed your reaction on whomever or whatever was in front of you at the time.

If the body, mind, and spirit could stay in the present instead of reverting to the past, there would be less destruction of your nervous system, which could lengthen your life span. And that's just one of the benefits.

Do you see how a present situation can trigger reactions from the past and force your body and mind to go on autopilot? This is how you become *reactive to* your immediate environment instead of *interacting with* your environment. You perceive the environment as having manipulated you into feelings and behavior instead of recognizing that you have choices at all times. (Lack of awareness of yourself leaves you thinking you have no choices.)

Easy to Recognize Regression, Hard to Change It

Those who have had temporary success in halting regression in their lives have said they had to put all their energy into the new behavior, even when they knew how tiring it would be. Many have said, "I felt like I was working against myself." Later they found out they were. They couldn't change their behavior permanently. That was before they implemented The Power Model System™.

Just being aware of where a behavior comes from doesn't make it easier to stop it. You still have to learn how your four human components—emotional, mental, spiritual, and physical—influence that behavior. This knowledge will set the stage for lasting change.

Story Time

Ed, thirty-six years old, was still putting his fists through the walls of his kitchen every time he became angry. "I saw my dad do that when I was young," he said. "Why would I do it now, knowing how much it scared me? I know I scare my wife a lot when I do it. I don't want to, but before I know it, I'm putting my fist through the wall."

Ed attended a Power Model System workshop. He took home his internal blueprint plus a five-step exercise. He called me two weeks later to tell me he'd gone through The Power Model System™ twice and had been working the activities daily. In fact, both he and his wife were doing them. Amazingly, Ed hadn't lost his temper once during that time, and he felt great about himself. He had the confidence to keep practicing The Power Model System™ and each time he worked the model, he saw changes in his behavior. This, in turn, gave him the encouragement to continue to apply the model internally.

During the workshop, Ed had become aware of how much he'd damaged his body with his subconscious self-regressive behavior, in addition to damaging his kitchen wall and his marriage. Through an activity called The Life Spark, Ed became aware that he'd used anger to cover his feelings of fear and sadness, which to him meant death as a child. Since he saw his dad put anger on top of his emotions and survive, Ed had integrated the same system internally—emotionally, mentally, physically and spiritually.

With this insightful awareness came more authenticity. Incorporating this piece of knowledge, he now realized his anger was only a cover-up for other emotions. Whenever he felt himself starting to get angry, he stopped and asked himself what emotions he was really feeling *inside*. By embracing the true answer, he was able to deal with his *authentic* emotions, which were fear and sadness. As Ed used his new knowledge, he was able to identify the full range of his emotions. He stopped punishing himself for being afraid or sad. As a result, the walls in his house were mended and so was his marriage.

He also started working with his children and helping them through The Power Model System™ so they would learn at a young age in life to identify their emotions and express them appropriately.

Ed's experience demonstrates how an imbalance of the emotional component can cause severe mental, emotional, and spiritual problems in a person's life, internally and externally.

When You Regress

Let's review step-by-step what happens when you regress:

1. Environmental stress triggers a subconscious memory from your past;
2. This memory causes you to react to your present situation using past emotions, thoughts, and behavior directly in accordance with your fight-or-flight patterns formed in your youth;
3. Now you've gone on automatic pilot in your present situation, just as you did (or would like to have done) in the past.

You may recognize the folly of youth in the past and be surprised by your automatic behavior in the present. You may ask yourself, *where did that response come from?* Since you don't know, you look around at the present situation and find something or someone to blame (the "reason"). There, it's done. Finished! You get rid of that something or judge that someone. Now you believe you will never act that way again.

But it's not true! Soon you realize that those old coping skills are no longer working for you. They're not getting you the results you want in your adult life, your career, partnership, or relationships with family members and friends. Of course they're not working—you're an adult but you're responding to stress as if you were still a child!

This is only one example of the invisible energy forces you're working against.

Confusing Relaxation with Exhaustion

In the past, one of my favorite fight-or-flight responses was yelling. Today I laugh at the old me who thought that if I could yell and vent my anger I was resolving the issue at hand. My body and mind felt better and I'd say, "Glad I got that out of my system." But it wasn't out of my system! I would go into an adrenalin rush, tear up my body internally with my yelling, *and then interpret my exhaustion as relaxation and resolution.* Those responses might have worked when I was young, but they don't work now. Rather they leave me at the mercy of my environment, never knowing what will trigger me.

The following activity taps into the subconscious part of your brain so you can understand how regression works. What you stored through your sensory system and recorded in your subconscious mind when you were young will be brought forward into your conscious mind. As information about your fight-or-flight responses comes to a conscious level, you'll have a new awareness of your belief system. Once you bring a past event into your conscious awareness, you can work with it and either keep the same belief system or change it—but this time with conscious awareness. By changing your belief system, you automatically change your behavior and the choices you have in your life. Simple, yes! Easy, yes—*if* you first have the information or internal blueprint to work with.

Activity: How the Environment Affects You

Figures 4.1, 4.2, and 4.3 relate to this activity.

Before starting this activity in Figure 4.1, read through the instructions and look at the example activity shown in Figure 4.2.

1. Environment Event Column (Figure 4.1)

In the column headed "Environment Event," write down a *recent* event that produced a lot of stress and anxiety in you. It could be a situation at work, with your partner, with your children, or a friend.

2. Sensory System Column (Figure 4.1)

Go over the "Sensory System" list and circle which sensory system took this event in. The following descriptions will help you pinpoint which of the senses you used at the time.

Sound: What was the tone of voice someone used to convey something to you? Was there music? Was the music fast or slow? Did you hear the lyrics of a song? You can even note silence (the absence of sound has an effect on people.) Determine what sounds were occurring and what sounds were not.

Sight: If you saw people, note their facial expressions. Were you in a room, in a car, outdoors? What colors did you see in that space? What kind of furniture (if any) was there? Were friends or family in the room? What were they wearing?

Taste: While this event was taking place, did you sense a taste in your mouth? Were you eating, chewing gum, or smoking? Did your mouth react with a bitter taste, a sweet taste? Did your mouth get dry?

Touch: Were you slapped, hit, caressed, or touched in any way? Did you touch anything (clothing, furniture, blanket, stuffed animal, etc.)?

Smell: Did you smell anything (sweat, cologne, perfume, and/or food)?

3. Body Sensations Column (Figure 4.1)

In your mind's eye, visualize the *recent* event as if you were there. How does your body feel? Are you tense anywhere? Does your head feel tight or full of pressure? Do you feel pain or numbness anywhere? Is there pressure behind your eyes, neck, or shoulders? Write these sensations into the Body Sensations column.

4. Emotions Column (Figure 4.1)

In this column, circle the emotions you felt throughout the event.

You probably understand what most of the listed emotions are but I'll explain two of the less common ones listed.

Shutdown: This is sometimes looked upon as a negative reaction to an event in your life. There are two ways to exercise shutdown and, depending on your intention, you will get two different results.

Unhealthy Shutdown: When you're in a stressful situation, you freeze and shut down. You go on automatic pilot. You don't feel anything; you can't think or move. In this situation, you become very vulnerable to your environment. You feel fear and flip the switch to cut off all emotion and thinking. With unhealthy shutdown, you don't identify or process your emotions.

Healthy Shutdown: You're in a stressful situation but able to recognize that you're feeling fear. You then choose to shut down and think your way through the situation. You make a commitment to yourself that you'll go back to this event later and process your fear. But for now, you need to keep yourself safe, shut down all emotions, and think through your choices about how to get yourself out of the situation. *Learning to choose and how to use healthy shutdown is the key.*

Power: I list power as an emotion because I believe we seek a sense of power over ourselves, situations, people, places, and things. When we don't have that sense of power over these things, we feel out of control. Thinking we can control people, places, and things gives us a false sense of power. Some people gain a sense of power from being angry. Others gain a sense of power by staying in shutdown all their lives and never dealing with their emotional side. Usually these people have a belief system that tells them emotions are too messy to learn about, process, or resolve. We also use money, work, drugs, alcohol, gambling, food, etc. to feel a sense of power. If you're in a human body, you exercise some false sense of power. It starts when we're very young. What and how we're taught about self-empowerment determines what gives us our personal sense of power.

Circle each feeling you can identify in your body—it's okay if you have more than one. Keep the picture(s) in your mind. This makes it much easier to bring your emotions to the forefront of your experience.

5. Age Line (Figure 4.1)

After you've finished filling in the four columns, go to the "Age" line. Put down your pencil or pen. Take some deep breaths *in* through your nose and *out* through your mouth. Check for any tense parts of your body. Stand up and stretch. Sit down and just relax. Continue deep breathing.

Visualize numbers from 1 to 30 passing through your mind. 1, 2, 3, 4 . . . Just let the numbers pass through. When one number lingers longer than the rest or jumps out, write it on the Age line. This gives you an important reference point. *Picture yourself at the age of the number you've written down.* When at the age you recorded did you feel the same emotions or body sensations you experienced in the *recent* event? What happened in that year that patterned your present fight-or-flight response? (Your mind might lie to you, but your body will not.) You'll find that once you've pictured your past event in your mind's eye, you'll experience some of the same sensations in your body.

When you reacted to the *recent* event, how old did you feel? You might even go back to the *past* event in your mind's eye. It could be when you were in your childhood, teen years, young adulthood, or recent years. Ask yourself some of these questions: Where was I living? Did anything happen to my parents, friends, or relatives? Did anything stressful happen in or at my school, at home, or with my peers? Did I have a pet?

6. Fog Column (Figure 4.1)

Under the "Fog" heading, write down the *past* childhood event you've uncovered. You might discover some similarities between the *recent* and *past* environments. The past event might be an abusive situation, a move to another house, attending a new school, or your dad or mom going away for a while. It could be a smell, a person's tone of voice, or the gesture of a familiar authority figure from your past. As you visualize your past event, you'll notice that your body starts feeling the same or similar to the way it did in the *recent* event. This is why I call this column "fog." The information you are bringing forward comes from your subconscious mind.

Other Events

At the end of this chapter, I have included an extra blank Environmental Activity Chart, Figure 4.3. Make as many copies as you need for other events. The more you practice this activity, the more awareness you'll have through self-discovery. If something in your environment triggers a response from you, do this activity so you'll know exactly where the reaction originated.

After charting a few events in the Environmental Activity, rest for a while. You've done well.

You Can't Change What You Aren't Aware Of.

ENVIRONMENTAL ACTIVITY

Date: _____   Age: _____

ENVIRONMENTAL EVENT	SENSORY SYSTEM	BODY SENSATIONS NERVOUS SYSTEM	FOG	EMOTIONS
	Sounds			Anger
				Hurt/Pain
	Sight			Shame
				Guilt
	Taste			Shutdown
				Saddness
	Touch			Fear
				Power
	Smell			Loneliness
				Happiness

Figure 4.1 ~ Environmental Activity

EXAMPLE
ENVIRONMENTAL ACTIVITY

Date: 9-3-04   Age: 8

ENVIRONMENTAL EVENT	SENSORY SYSTEM	BODY SENSATIONS NERVOUS SYSTEM	FOG	EMOTIONS
I went to talk to my partner about changing my job. I did not like the people I worked with. The new job offer is better money and a higher position.	(Sounds)	My mouth was dry. The palms of my hands were sweating. My stomach was tight.	When I was 8 years old, my father and mother were fighting all the time. The fighting was about Dad always changing jobs and never staying in one very long. He always said, when he lost his job, "I did not like them anyway."	(Anger)
	(Sight)			Hurt/Pain
			I discovered that my body felt the same way it did when I heard my Dad and Mom fight. I can still remember the smell of my Dad's after shave, the sight and sounds of them yelling at each other. I felt so alone and kept thinking I must have done something wrong, along with feeling afraid they both would leave me. My biggest fear is, am I becoming like my Dad?	(Shame)
	Taste			Guilt
				Shutdown
	Touch			Saddness
				(Fear)
			My partner never even said anything, but only asked, why I was so upset about making this change.	Power
	(Smell)			(Loneliness)
				Happiness

Figure 4.2 ~ Example: Environmental Activity

ENVIRONMENTAL ACTIVITY

Date: _____   Age: _____

ENVIRONMENTAL EVENT	SENSORY SYSTEM	BODY SENSATIONS NERVOUS SYSTEM	FOG	EMOTIONS
	Sounds			Anger
				Hurt/Pain
	Sight			Shame
				Guilt
	Taste			Shutdown
				Saddness
	Touch			Fear
				Power
	Smell			Loneliness
				Happiness

Figure 4.3 ~ Environmental Activity

Chapter 5

THE THREE FACES OF ILLUSION

Resentment is like taking poison and waiting for the other person to die
      Malacky

Illusion: *1) an erroneous perception of reality. 2) an erroneous concept or belief; the condition of being deceived by a false perception or belief. 3) something, such as a fantastic plan or desire, that causes an erroneous belief or perception.*

The Merriam-Webster Dictionary

Many great teachers have spoken about illusion and how human beings have a tendency to stay in illusion yet think they are in reality. Do we humans have a natural desire to grow and become balanced spiritual human beings? No, we do not. It's a choice. We either grow or stay in illusion of what we think life is about.

We generally want to see ourselves and the world through our illusive state. Of course these two go hand in hand—if we are into the illusion of who we think we are, we perceive the world through that illusive state of being. We project what we think the world is. It follows then that we would perceive others, events, and so forth in a similar way.

Of course, reality often breaks our illusions wide open. This ultimately leads to what I call the "Three Faces of Illusion" or the 3 Rs, *Resistance, Resentment,* and *Revenge,* which is our way of fighting back in order to stay in denial and illusion. Why do I call them Faces of Illusion? Because they are the illusionary persona we enact in order to hide from reality or fit the world into our limited level of understanding and perception.

We are born with so many possibilities! It is our responsibility to become all we can be, to become aware of our purpose in life and fulfill it. But our illusions keep us from fulfilling our dreams. In my case, knowing why I'm here allows me to work through many challenges and still fulfill my purpose. It also gives me passion for all areas of my life. It allows me to overcome the greatest of odds and fulfill my purpose according to my Higher Power. I am certain that if I hadn't come out of my illusive state of being, I wouldn't be writing this book today.

> *The years from conception to age ten represent the period when you were influenced the most and you developed your belief system, including your patterned reactions that can affect the rest of your life. It's the territory of childhood issues.*

If you came from a household where your childhood needs weren't met, you likely grew up carrying abandonment issues or having low self-esteem. These will continue to affect you in subtle ways throughout your life until you address them and bring them to closure.

People develop ways of coping with losses and other events as best they can. Their coping skills are based on many factors: personal perception, the behavior of those around them, and how they internalize what they see, hear, touch, and feel during a specific event. What did others say to them after the event? What did they come away with—emotionally, mentally, spiritually, and physically—from that event?

Our uniqueness ensures that if five people experience the same event, each will have a different interpretation of what took place. Each would utilize a different coping skill, based on the internal fight-or-flight responses that are programmed into their brains. We all have the same four human components but interact with them differently.

> *Listening to two people who've been through the same situation give their interpretations has always amazed me because those interpretations will be totally different from one another. It's never about who's right or who's wrong. Both people are right according to their perception and interpretation at the time.*

Because of our widely differing perceptions, the Power Model System™ assists you in resolving your own experience of an event using your own interpretation and perception. A common factor that contributes to our perception is the fact that one or more of our human components is dominating over the others. We perceive the environment through our physical, emotional, mental, and spiritual selves. How an experience of an event gets processed and/or distorted by each of our human components will determine our perception of the event.

Thus, I recommend you begin working from your own perceptions of events, and then become aware and understand why you have certain patterns in your perception of these events. Only then, can you re-pattern yourself successfully.

So let's see how having imbalance in our human components affects our perception of events and ourselves.

Being Dominant In One of Your Components

People sometimes get stuck in a growing-up stage and aren't mature in one or more of the four human components. Often one or two of these components dominate while the others simply get left behind. This imbalance governs our perception and usually leads to "The Three Faces of Illusions," or the 3 Rs—Resistance, Resentment, and Revenge—which cause major and often hidden conflicts within yourself and others. Let's see how these conflicts can manifest when one of the components becomes dominant over the others.

> *The truth of the matter is that any person dominated by only one human component is immature.*

Dominant Feeler

We have all met people who are emotional about everything in their lives and have difficulty thinking through any situation. Have you ever found yourself in so much emotional pain that you were paralyzed, unable to think or take action? Do you find yourself in this position more than you want to be? This is a clear definition of a "feeler."

Feelers find it difficult to recognize others who aren't emoting all the time as kind human beings. They believe that people who aren't emotional all the time don't care. Feelers find such people cold, uncaring, and insensitive to their emotional blow-ups. They make decisions in their life according to how they *feel*, not what they think.

Dominant Thinker

Perhaps you are someone or know people who never truly feel and think through everything analytically without considering their or others' feelings. These people are unable to identify with their emotions. Most of the time, they appear calm and reserved. This persona gives the impression that they're more adult than the Feelers, but this isn't the case. Dominant Thinkers keep their emotions buried, and when an emotion does surface, it is usually anger. Thinkers attempt to control others by their statements, which are usually orders for how others should act. They look upon Feelers as childish and immature and have very little tolerance for emotions of any kind.

Dominant Physically

There are others who say, "I don't want to talk about feelings or thoughts. I'll just do something and it will all be okay." They allow their physical component to dominate their behavior. They don't have discussions with others before making a decision, even though this decision may affect the people around them; they decide and take action. Sometimes this action is inappropriate for the situation. Whatever the damage, they truly think everything will work out fine. They justify their behavior. While it's good for people to have an exercise program, physically dominant people exercise when they're uptight, when there's a problem, and/or when a stressful situation presents itself. Once they're through with the exercise, they don't discuss or soul-search to resolve the issue.

Dominant Spiritually

Some people believe they should just "pray and wait for an answer." They don't want to listen to their feelings, thoughts, or choices. Prayer or their spiritual book is always the answer. Once they perceive or interpret an answer, no one is allowed to disagree. They say, "God is guiding me." Spiritually-dominant people use their spiritual knowledge as a means to get someone to do exactly what they want. As in the other dominant behavior types, they all believe others should be like them. Their lack of internal balance makes them closed-minded. These people not only hold strong religious or spiritual beliefs but also believe theirs is the only path for everyone to follow.

How These Imbalances Affect Us

When we as individuals function from only one or two of our human components, we have a difficult time being flexible with anyone who is different from us. *This inability to tolerate differences is due to immaturity.*

Everyone can find a common ground if they choose. Choice and maturity require the use of balanced physical, mental, emotional, and spiritual abilities. Without this common ground, we inevitably run into the Three Faces of Illusion (Resistance, Resentment, and Revenge). We *resist* the fact that the world and other people behave differently than we do or want. We *resent* that the world and other people refuse to convert to our point of view. And if the resentment becomes strong enough, we enact *revenge*.

Story Time

A forty-year-old man named Alan came to my office and said in our first discussion that no matter what happened in his fifteen-year marriage, he was always "waiting for the other shoe to drop." He said he felt the same way about his career—he'd always had a feeling of dread in the back of his mind that something would go wrong.

While Alan talked, he was smiling. When I asked about the smile, he said, "Even while I'm saying this, I'm thinking how crazy I must sound. But my wife and I talked it over and she told me I've had this fear all the years she's known me. My pattern is to always point to something outside myself to blame, like the economy is slowing down so that's why I'm laid off. If my wife points out something that I need to improve I get mad and say, 'If you don't like it, leave.' Of course, I feel sorry for saying that as soon as it comes out of my mouth. But the next time we disagree on anything, I hear myself say, 'If you don't like it, you can leave.'" (Notice that statement has resistance, resentment, and revenge all rolled up into one.)

"What brought all this to a head was something that happened a month ago. My wife wanted to visit some of her childhood friends who'd moved to Germany. I felt okay with the visit at first, but then I started to be afraid she wasn't coming back. After two weeks of visiting her friends, she told me she wanted to stay there one more week. That's when I blew up and started yelling into the phone. I felt like I was having a heart attack. After our conversation, she flew directly home and made a doctor's appointment for me. The doctor told me I was having anxiety attacks. I've always been an anxious person, but I'd never experienced anything like I felt on the phone that day. The doctor suggested I see a specialist on stress, so here I am."

I let Alan know he was the expert on *him* and that he needed to do the self-discovery work to learn where this anxiety was coming from. "If I was the expert on me, I would already know what this was about," he said. "Either that or I would never have experienced this in the beginning." I let him know he just needed the right tools for self-discovery and that we'd be working together with The Power Model System™. "I'm so glad you said 'system,'" he said. "I don't want to just start poking around my life with no system of where we're going or how to get there."

We started with the environmental activity. We used Alan's experience of talking to his wife on the phone about her staying longer with her friends. Here's what we discovered:

When Alan was two years old, his mother had to go to the hospital. She was away from home for two weeks. That sounds innocent enough, but, as we shall see, how Alan *perceived and interpreted* that event was critical to the patterning of his reactions to later events.

Story Intermission

One of the developmental stages from conception to two years of age is building a sense of trust and dependence on your mother and father, establishing awareness that Mom and Dad respond with love and make you feel safe. This allows you to go out into the world with an example of trust and how it works. Let's say you're two years old and your mother has to be in the hospital for a week or two. How this event is handled will determine whether you continue to be affected by it. You could become irritable and unresponsive. You could cry excessively over the littlest thing. You could keep waking up during the night crying. You'd likely experience some symptoms of disturbance.

What if the people around you don't respond to your need for extra attention or don't' reassure you that you're okay and that Mama will be home soon? Perhaps they feel stressed and worried because she's sick. Perhaps they aren't coping well themselves with the situation.

How many people would be aware of your developmental stage at this time of your life? How many people take a child-development class before they have a child? How many even take parenting classes? Most people raise kids the best they can, usually by imitating the way their parents raised them. Or they decide to avoid mistakes they think their parents made with them by going in the totally opposite direction.

A two-year-old boy whose mother goes into the hospital for two weeks would likely think his mom had disappeared for good. Because a child has no sense of time at this age, a day could seem like forever. If you were that child feeling anxious inside, you'd look for a way to stop your fear of loss and feel safer. You'd need some form of control. In this case, you're feeling hurt and afraid. You cry and cry but don't get the extra attention or reassurance you need. So you cover the fear and hurt with something like anger or anything else that gets you more attention. More importantly, it gives your two-year-old personality a sense of power and control. And it sets a pattern for the future when any situation that remotely seems like abandonment comes up. You cover up your authentic feelings with other feelings or behavior you are more comfortable with.

As you grow into adulthood, every time you experience fear and hurt internally, you avoid it. Because it's patterned in your subconscious, you're not aware that you're covering up other emotions. You find something in your environment to excuse your reactive behavior. You might be told over and over that you have an anger problem, but you never get to the root cause. Consequently, you keep going on autopilot and getting stuck in that cycle of behavior while the original reason for your anger stays buried in your subconscious.

Let's assume anger is your favorite reaction response.

Possible loss equals fear → fear equals anger → anger gives you a sense of control/power to be able to change the present situation, even if you can't.

Years of these internal chain reactions cause you to feel more and more anxious. As a result, you go from feeling anxious to having anxiety attacks, then from having anxiety attacks to panic attacks.

Here's a possible progression: Stress → fear → anger → anxiety attacks → panic attacks.

This pattern becomes a fight-or-flight response in your subconscious mind. You go from your emotions to an illusionary mental belief system to your defense system that puts you in a reactive mode. This means you are *resisting* the reality of the situation. It means you will *resent* those you believe are responsible for the situation. And if the resentment becomes strong enough, you will start enacting *revenge* in various ways.

Being stuck can be a creative place to be. Why? Because being stuck gets your attention! With stress come feelings. With feelings come thoughts and then action (such as yelling, raging, and panic attacks). You may not be consciously aware of your emotions and thoughts, but your reactive behavior will eventually get your attention or someone else's. Hopefully, this is the first step towards awareness.

Story Time Continued

Alan went through The Power Model System™ and arrived at several self-discoveries that improved his relationship with his wife. But the most important thing that happened was that he had a better relationship with *himself*, which then extended to better relationships with others in all areas of his life. As Alan did the environmental activity, he was able to immediately see one of his issues and recognize where it had originated in his past. As he continued working through The Power Model System ™, he made further self-discoveries and noticed he was having fewer panic attacks. The last time I heard from him, he told me he continues to use this system whenever an issue comes up for him in any area of his life so that he can self-discover what it is and how to resolve it.

Alan found that by going straight to his childhood and finding where his belief systems started, which he did very quickly with The Power Model System™, he was able to change those patterns he became aware of. He treated The Power Model System ™ process as "his mysteries to be solved." It became a game with him. The more he could find out about himself and what he and his Higher Power had created together in his childhood, the more he could recreate in himself to become a more balanced person. His wife joined in and learned a lot about her self as well. Self-discovery became a family affair.

Over the years, I've seen how just *having awareness* can spark active motion toward achieving balance. As individuals become aware of their personal blueprints, they move closer toward maturity in all four of their components. Consequently, one area does not dominate their life.

The Illusion of Life

As I've said, our system of emotional, mental, physical, and spiritual components is integrated and established at a young age. As we grow up, we view the world from our established system. Unless we encounter a life-changing event or have a strong desire to grow internally, we will continue through life with these same patterns. Perceiving the world from this knowledge base is not realistic. I call it "living in illusion."

Living an illusive life is the foundation of immaturity.

Here are just a few characteristics of living in illusion—where you see the world through the lens of your immaturity and believe you are in reality:

- Dependency on something or someone to motivate you to take action in your life
- Thinking you actually have control over people, places, and things
- Procrastination
- Problem-oriented
- Blaming others
- Making excuses
- Over- or under-inflated ego strength
- Self-centeredness
- Scarcity mentality; you believe there is not enough for you to succeed
- Reacting to life with your emotions
- Inflexibility within yourself and with others

I used to think life was this way. It is not. It's how *I saw life through my illusions.* As I moved from illusion to reality in my life, it was as if someone had lifted a veil from my eyes, mind, and spirit. I woke up, and so can you!

Now let's look at each of your four human components in illusion. See if you recognize behaviors you are exhibiting. Knowing where you are enables you to make changes. If you don't see your illusions, you won't be able to move into the reality of life.

> *As I moved from illusion to reality in my life, it was as if someone had lifted a veil from my eyes, mind, and spirit. I awoke, and so can you!*

The Illusion of Emotional Power

Emotion: *1) the affective aspect of consciousness: feeling 2) a state of feeling 3) a psychic and physical reaction (as anger or fear) subjectively experienced as strong feeling and physiologically involving changes that prepare the body for immediate vigorous action.*

The Merriam-Webster Dictionary

What is Emotional Power in Illusion? It is reactive, emotional behavior you developed at a very young age.

You use emotions to get what you want or get out of what you don't want. Let's look at how this works.

A two-year-old acts out, trying to express his or her emotions. At the age of two, part of your development involves learning how to communicate what you want and discovering your many emotions. You try to communicate with others, which is a positive thing in a functional family. You try different ways to get what you want, when you want it. At this age, you become upset if you're not understood. Unfortunately not all of us (even as adults) have gotten past these young stages.

Here are some emotional human behaviors (illusions) that people commonly find themselves stuck in.

<u>I-Want-What-I-Want-When-I-Want-It Mode</u>

Some people get stuck reacting to life whenever it doesn't immediately hand them what they want, when they want it.

Story Time

Tommy is a two-year-old who is with his mom in a store. He spots a toy plane and points to it. Mom says, "No." Tommy gets angry and yells and kicks his legs in the shopping cart. Mom says, "No" again. Tommy starts crying and pointing to the toy plane and lets Mom know he still wants that plane. Mom says, "No" again. Tommy stops crying and smiles at Mom. Then he puts his arms up in the air, which is a sign from Tommy that he wants to hug Mom. Mom leans over the shopping cart and hugs him. He then smiles again, points to the toy plane, and says, "Please?" Mom says, "Okay, we will get it this time, but this is the only toy you are getting today."

Let's examine what just happened to Tommy. He wanted something and he let Mom know. Mom would not give it to him. He tried anger, but that did not work. He tried yelling and kicking, but that didn't work either. Even crying didn't get him what he wanted. But guess what? A hug, a smile, and a "please" got him what he wanted when he wanted it. Well, what do you think he will do the next time he hears "No"? You got it. Usually parents pass their own emotional illusion programming on to their children. If this happens repeatedly, Tommy will learn what gets him what he wants when he wants it, and he will take this into his adult world. If it doesn't work, he will quickly blame the other person, whoever it is, for not treating him appropriately because he smiled, said please, gave them a hug, and was nice to them. To Tommy, this means he should automatically get what he wants. Tommy has now learned to use his emotions to get what he wants, depending on whomever he is with. Tommy will demand instant gratification in his adult life and think this is normal. When asked how he feels, he will try to anticipate what you want him to feel so he can please you. He is unable to identify his emotions so they build up. Do you see how this will inevitably lead to resistance, resentment, and perhaps revenge? He *resists* the reality that people simply won't give him everything he wants. He will *resent* the fact that all his emotions have not changed the situation or others. And he may even enact *revenge* because he sincerely believes he deserves better.

Defensive Mode

Some people are always defending themselves. No matter what you say, they take it wrong. They go into fight-or-flight survival mode in which everything is taken *personally*. They suffer from fear and living in a "me" world. Everything is about them. Since they have a fear of being attacked, they attack first by defending themselves. They feel better as soon as the person they are *defending* themselves against agrees with them. The agreement of the other party quiets their fears. This person is functioning in *emotional illusion*, which is now affecting their *mental illusion*.

This is a stressful position to be in all the time. Their fear is aging their bodies and minds. They only hear portions of conversations because of their fear, and they believe these portions are about them. They also believe that if others have a different opinion from theirs, they're being personally attacked. The feel a need to defend themselves until you agree with them. They also believe that if you really understood what they were saying, you'd agree with them. This means they have to find a way to explain the issue so you can understand their position, assuming that once you understand you'll agree with them. All of this is connected with childhood issues. Remember, we built our perceptions, our belief system, and our fight-or-flight responses way back then. The fight-or-flight response comes from *fear* and *anger*. This defensive mode often leads to revenge very quickly, because attacking is a key defensive tactic.

Victim Role

In many cases, generations of families fail to identify and work with their emotions. People in these families feel victimized by the world. Each generation supports the next in their "emotional victim" role.

Some people in emotional illusion are unable to say no, or they say no all the time. This is the "martyr" role. Hidden beneath their fear is anger. They're angry because they perceive that people want them to do so much. People in this victim role harbor huge amounts of *resentment* that literally eats them from the inside out. Often, this will lead to one final *vengeful* act that destroys their life and that of others.

From victimization, you slide down to "poor me." Then you go from "poor me" to self-pity. From self-pity, it's downhill all the way. Before you realize it, you're in a self-destruction mode, invoking all the justification and rationalization you need to behave any way you want, potentially harming yourself and others.

Cover-Up Emotions

Cover-up emotions are one of the most popular means of staying in illusion. I have devoted an entire chapter in this book (Chapter 13) to assist you in discovering your cover-up emotions. For now, let me just say that a cover-up emotion is an emotion you use in place of your authentic emotions. For example, if you are sad or hurt, you may express anger instead. This can lead to a lot of resentment and even revenge because the real you is constantly being suppressed.

The Illusion of Mental Power

Mental: *1) of or relating to the mind; specifically: of or relating to the total emotional and intellectual response of an individual to external reality, "mental health." 2) of or relating to intellectual as contrasted with emotional activity. 3) of relating to, or being intellectual as contrasted with overt physical activity. 4) occurring or experienced in the mind.*

The Merriam-Webster Dictionary

Most problems that occur in Mental Power Illusion are due to unresolved emotional issues and an inability to identify your emotions. Instead of identifying and resolving your emotions, you adapt a thought process to justify your emotions and your reactive behavior to them. Mental illusion is the bridge to your other three human component illusions. It creates justification for staying in your emotional, spiritual, and physical illusions. Mental illusions are thoughts and beliefs that keep you with the familiar in your life.

Here are some mental illusions people find themselves stuck in:

- Can't hear choices due to defenses
- Become mentally judgmental and overwhelmed
- Controlling
- False ego strength
- Magical thinking
- Act as everyone's counselor
- Worrying most of the time

Limited Choices

Mental illusions affect how you think. You are unable to look at all the possibilities of choice in any given situation in your life. You are either confused with your choices and can't make a decision, or you are very rigid and narrow-minded in your decision-making. You continue to see only your childhood choices in life.

Judgmental and Overwhelmed

Some of us have mental tapes that play in our head. Have you ever heard yourself saying the same phrases your parents said to you, despite the fact that you couldn't stand it when you heard it from them? (And now you're saying them yourself and you still don't like it!). You may have such thoughts as "I'm not good enough," "I'm not smart enough," "I don't have the right to be rich/successful/happy", "I do not have the right to my own thoughts".

These messages stem from what you think about yourself. What you think about yourself comes from some of the things you were taught by others in your childhood. You don't know who to trust, because you feel uncertain about your own thought process. Due to your uncertainty, you're always comparing yourself against your own thoughts, or are forever trying to ignore them or fight against them. This ultimately leaves you overwhelmed in handing the most basic tasks in life because you are constantly battling yourself.

Controlling

Controlling usually comes from the sub-conscious need to feel safe. When it comes to relationships with others, you would be the one who keeps trying to change the other person. Even if you see a red flag that screams, "Let it go!" You don't listen, and you keep trying to get them to change or understand your point of view. You believe that if they understood you, they'll change, and everything will be okay. So your thought process in mental illusions would be "He/She will change, because they love me," or "Once I have gotten them to understand my point of view, then…" "If they don't, something is wrong with me," "I am so stupid," or "Something is wrong with them." "They are stupid". These are some of the tapes that play in your head.

To see people for who they are in reality—the good, bad, and ugly—is wise.

Healthy Ego Strength versus False Ego

Ego: *the self especially as contrasted with another self or the world.*
Strength: *the quality or state of being strong, capacity for exertion or endurance.*
Healthy: *the condition of being sound in body, mind, or spirit.*
Weak: *1) mentally or intellectually deficient. 2) not firmly decided: vacillating.*
3) resulting from or indicating lack of judgment or discernment. 4) not able to withstand temptation or persuasion.

The Merriam-Webster Dictionary

One of the toughest things you might experience when in the illusion of your Mental Power is not being able to handle healthy criticism. If someone tries to help you by giving you feedback about yourself, you might perceive it as a put-down for not knowing what he or she knows. Others might say you're overly sensitive. In reality, your negative reaction is due to under- or over-inflated *ego strength* (false ego).

I hear a lot about healthy self-esteem in our society. I'd prefer to hear more about healthy "ego strength," which covers more diverse parts of us as human beings. There's nothing wrong with having a healthy ego and knowing your own weaknesses and strengths. People with healthy ego strength are flexible in life. They can take criticism and are able to learn from their past and present in order to change their future. Healthy ego strength starts from within.

Problems arise when you have a *false ego,* which is often the case if you have any underdeveloped childhood stages or unresolved issues. You develop a false ego by identifying yourself from negative past experiences and/or by pretending to be something your not - rather than who you really are. When critiqued, you will often protect this false ego at all costs, because you believe your very identity is being attacked. This usually results in arrogance, being too self assured, pretending to know what you don't know, etc.

If you're unable to take healthy criticism in your life, you stay in survival mode and are constantly defending your position rather than being open-minded and flexible. You view change in any area of your life as negative. Your inability to handle healthy criticism that might result in improving yourself often results in not taking advantage of new opportunities that may come your way. This affects your perceptions of success.

You lie to yourself about what you really want because subconsciously you believe you can't have it anyway. What a way to sabotage your career and your life!

Magical Thinking

Unexpected consequences occur when "magical thinking" kicks in, which is a belief that problems will just disappear if you ignore them. If the problem doesn't go away, you eliminate the person, place, or thing in your life that you think is causing it. Do you remember when you first started to date someone you liked? After the "honeymoon" period ended, you probably felt or said that he/she had changed. In the beginning, you saw that person as you *wanted* to see him/her. Gradually you woke up, as if from a dream and saw the "real" person. The period before the waking-up is what I refer to as *magical thinking*.

Magical thinking can be problematic, even dangerous, especially in the case of an abusive relationship. In this case, you choose to not wake up and you see the harmful person only the way you want him or her to be. Despite the abusive behavior, you keep making excuses for the person and continue to believe that everything will be okay.

Counselor to Everyone

When trapped in the illusion of your Mental Power, you may also see yourself as everyone's counselor. Despite being unaware of your own needs, you presume to know those of other people. (I'm very familiar with this one. When I went into the counseling field, I had to learn when to put my counselor hat on and when to take it off. It took practice. My mental illusion thinking was that others' needs were more important than mine.)

If you're stuck in this stage of mental illusion, you're basing your decisions on an immature perception. You think others should know your needs and fulfill them without your having to voice them. Even if you do know some of your needs, you might not know how to express them, or you feel you don't have the right to express them.

Story Time

One day, a forty-two-year-old woman named Brenda came into my office. When I asked why she was there, she said, "I'm a mess. I'm a successful lawyer and I have a good private practice. But all I do is work, work, and work. I've been married three times. My first husband was an alcoholic, the second one was a recovering alcoholic who started drinking again after the first year of our marriage, and the last one refused to work after we got married. I ask you, how can I have such success in my work and fail so much in my private life?"

Then Brenda evaluated herself by saying, "I'm attractive and well-dressed. I have good taste and I like to go to nice places. I'm praised for my work and I can go on and on about how wonderful it is. Yes, I work about sixty hours a week, but it makes me happy. Nothing else does. I heard you can get to the bottom of this and fix my problems with bad relationships so I can have a good one."

I looked her in the eyes and said slowly and gently, "*I* can't do anything, but *you* can do a lot."

Brenda threw her head back and laughed. Her laughter filled the room in an open and joyful way. She said, "Oh, my. Do you have any idea *how* I'm going to do this?"

"Yes, I do." I then said, "You have a beautiful song. It's joyful, light, and pure music."

"I don't know how to carry a note," she said, "and I don't like hearing my own voice." When I said I was talking about her laughter, she just sat and stared at me. "I don't laugh much anymore," she said sadly.

"Laughter is healing," I said. "You have a joyful laugh that comes from the depths of your heart."

We started with this question: "If you could create anything in your life, Brenda, what would it look like?" Brenda wrote out her answer. Then we did the Environmental Activity from Chapter 4, Figure 4.1.

We talked about a present situation that stressed her and then identified an event that happened when she was nine years old.

Story Intermission

Let's climb into Brenda's story as if you were her.

You're nine years old, and one day you come home from school at three in the afternoon. You rush to get all your homework done because that night Dad has promised you dinner out at a special restaurant with him—just you and Daddy for the first time ever. This is a Thursday evening and your birthday is the following Saturday. The dinner with Daddy is his birthday gift to you. You and Mommy went shopping together. You picked out a special green dress and green ribbons for your long, golden brown hair.

After you finished your homework at four o'clock, you started to get ready for your evening out with Daddy and by five o'clock, right on time, you were ready to go. Daddy and Mommy had agreed you had to keep your bedtime at nine-thirty on a school night, so they planned for the two of you to arrive at the restaurant between five-thirty and six o'clock. If you were served by seven-thirty at the latest, you'd have plenty of time to eat, talk, and leave by eight-thirty to get home by nine o'clock and in bed by nine-thirty.

As you wait for Daddy, you wonder what the restaurant will look like, what you'll eat, how the food will taste, and of course, how Daddy will think you look. When six o'clock comes and goes, you start to feel scared. What could have happened to Daddy? You know he comes home regularly after you've gone to bed during the week. Tonight, though, you just know something has happened to him, or he'd be here by now. You sit down with the most normal look on your face because you don't want to worry Mommy, but inside you feel so scared you can taste the fear in your mouth. By seven o'clock, you look over at her and ask her to call Daddy. "Make sure he's okay," you say.

She says she will and goes to the phone. Soon you hear her yelling, "You never make time for us. All you do is work. How can you do this on her celebration birthday night?"

Hearing those words, your stomach is turning into knots and you're feeling sick. You're afraid of what will happen next. What if Daddy gets mad at you? What if Daddy says it's your fault? What if, what if... The questions swirl in your head. You don't know what will happen next, but you know it will be something bad. When Mommy gets off the phone, she says, "Daddy's coming home soon. He should be here in just a little while. Do you want a snack while you wait?" As she asks you this, she pours herself a glass of wine. You say, "No, I want to wait for Daddy." She just smiles, downs her first glass of wine and pours another.

You sit on the couch as if you're frozen, not wanting to wrinkle your dress or mess up your hair. You aren't aware of it, but you keep holding your breath. At eight-thirty, the phone rings and Mommy answers it. After listening for a minute, she says, "You can tell her yourself." She hands you the phone and you're thinking all the time, *I hope Daddy's not mad.*

Then Daddy says, "Sugar, I know it's eight-thirty. I'm ready to come home, but honey, I can't take you out this late because you have to go to school tomorrow. You have to be in bed at nine-thirty. If you weren't so young and could stay out later, we could have gone, even now. So Daddy will make it up to you next week, I promise. You be a good girl for your mama because she thinks this is upsetting you. But I know you're a big girl and you understand that Daddy has to work. I have to work so you can have your big birthday party, a nice house to live in, and new clothes. You understand, don't you?"

As tears roll down your cheeks and your chest feels ready to burst, you whisper, "Yes, Daddy, I understand. I'm a big girl." At that moment, you assume in your child's mind that it was your fault that you and Daddy couldn't go to dinner. You weren't old enough to stay up late. Daddy wanted to take you out but couldn't because you were too young. And if you want to live in your nice house and have your big birthday party, then poor Daddy has to keep working.

As you hang up the phone, you look over at your mother. She has the bottle of wine on the table beside her and pours herself another glass. So you go over to her and give her a hug. You tell her you love her. She says, "I know, baby," and continues to drink.

You go up to your room, take out your scissors, and cut your long hair. You put on your pajamas and go to bed. In what seems like the middle of the night, you hear Mommy yelling at Daddy and Daddy yelling back. He says, "How can you say I work too much? Where would all of you be if I didn't work? At least I'm not running around. I'm working sixty hours a week. And look at you. You're drunk again! Why don't you stop drinking and take care of the house or join a club or do what other wives do? I'm better off working all the time than being home with you and your bottle." You hear Mommy yell, "What is there for me to do? You drive me to drink. You're never home; you're always working; you never have time for family stuff. You couldn't even make it for her birthday dinner."

As you listen to this fight, you're developing a belief system as to what a marriage is about. You love both of them, but you hate the fighting. After this evening, you never ask Daddy to make any promises. If he makes any, you don't expect him to keep them. If he does, you're surprised and pleased, but you know in the back of your mind that he usually doesn't keep a promise and soon you just accept it. The same goes for Mommy. You know not to plan anything with her in the evening, only in the morning or early afternoon because if she does promise to do something, she'll start drinking and forget all about it. You'll have to take care of it yourself. You learned early in life that you take care of the drinker. And you learned not to expect anything from the men in your life because they're doing the best they can.

Remember, parents do the best they know how. Because these parents are both unhappy, they "fix" their emotions by forming an addiction—one to alcohol and one to work—while all the time saying that the other makes them do it. It's called the Blame Game. They both *resist* each other's call to change. They *resent* each other for drinking or failing to come home. And they both are enacting *revenge* when they fight, ignore each other's needs, and practice their addictions.

<u>Story Continued</u>

Over time, Brenda underwent great emotional pain and developed a thought process that became a part of her: "I have a choice to be like Daddy or like Mommy, so I'll work hard and Daddy will love me." She married men who were drinkers so she could take care of them just like she took care of her mother. When she self-discovered her internal profile, Brenda realized that her parents had demonstrated two behaviors to cover up their feelings: 1) not identifying or expressing emotions, and 2) turning to work or drink to keep the pain down.

As much as she resented her dad, Brenda internalized that resentment and went into her own addiction. Indeed, she resented the fact that she couldn't work hard enough for her dad (as she perceived he'd done for her) to make him love her. Deep down, she believed this was *her* fault, not his. Consequently, she focused on schoolwork at a young age and went on to law school, following in her father's footsteps. She went on to marry men who were similar to her mother. She eventually resisted all emotions and then fell into resentment toward herself. She buried the resentment deeper through her work addiction. The revenge she heaped upon herself was severe. Consequently, she had no good relationships and an unhappy life.

In our sessions, Brenda started remembering remarks she'd made to her partners when they commented about her long hours at work. She was amazed to realize they were the same things she'd heard her father say. She also realized she always felt responsible for not being able to keep her partners from drinking.

Brenda's story has a happy ending. She worked through and identified her emotions and went into recovery for work addiction. What a different life she lives now! She's far more productive in less time because she's put her life in balance. At first she went through withdrawal, not knowing how she would spend her spare time, but she soon developed new interests and friendships unrelated to her work. She learned a lot about gardening and told me one day, "I never thought I would ever just sit and watch the flowers grow or see life in such a humorous way." Then she laughed in her unique, joyful, deep tone. This time, it came straight from her soul.

The Illusion of Physical Power

Physical: *having material existence: perceptible especially through the senses and subject to the laws of nature.*

The Merriam-Webster Dictionary

Physical Power Illusions are reactive behaviors you developed when you were young to cover up the pain of your emotions and the thoughts that accompany them. You may bounce back and forth between different behaviors based on fight-or-flight responses. Some of these behaviors/conditions are:

- Internal physical reactions of stress
- Tensing your muscles without even being aware of it
- Headaches
- Addictions
- Inconsistent behavior
- Abusive behavior (internally or externally)

As you become more entrenched in physical illusion, you find yourself using alcohol to excess, overworking, overeating, staying in relationships that don't work, or not being present to work out issues with others (you're always leaving and/or shutting down). Physical illusion breeds physical abuse of yourself and others.

If you go through life in illusion, you'll choose behaviors that will numb you (in body, mind, and spirit) and keep you in the "barely functioning" mode. At first, this numbing behavior will work for you—it will keep you in your physical illusion and allow you to function for a while. But in time, it will overtake you and you'll be in an addiction of your choice (alcohol, working, gambling, etc). As you go along this path, you'll think, *This is life. This is all there is. This is normal. Everyone feels this way inside. I just need to accept it.* But eventually you'll start to dislike the consequences. That's when you'll be forced to look at what's behind the behavior.

> *Having an addiction removes all purpose to your life—all except feeding your addiction, of course.*
>
> *Addictions rob you of having a relationship with your soul.*

My work-addicted clients laugh and say, "Wow! Work did it for me." "I just kept working and stayed numb." "I worked long hours. I now know I wasn't in touch with myself at all. I would work till my body was numb and then work some more. My reactive behavior was work addiction, which was covering up all my emotions, thoughts, hopes, and dreams. And finally I suffered burnout."

Addictions take time away from your life and family—years you can't get back. I know from personal experience that work addiction is easy to fall into. In fact, society loves us for it. It encourages us to work, work, and work until burnout occurs. I never had to look at myself. I thought I'd worked through my issues. If problems occurred around me, I just worked harder. Does any of this sound familiar? This is Illusive Physical Power.

Some people who reach their goals of success with career, family, and possessions still feel unhappy but don't know why. They think, *Here we go again.* They assume their present situation must be causing the problem so they file for divorce, spend more money, change jobs, get a new car, take a vacation, or buy an expensive piece of jewelry. But when they're through reacting to their unhappiness, they're still not happy! The divorce rate speaks volumes about the level of unhappiness in our society today. Many divorces occur because people decide not to deal with their issues.

When people's actions are restricted by childhood belief systems, most of which remain subconscious, they simply react on autopilot without thinking. If people were fully aware of their feelings, thoughts, and actions, wouldn't they make better choices?

> *Happiness comes from within. Happiness has nothing to do with what you own, where you live, where you work, or what car you drive. It has everything to do with what goes on inside of you.*

Story Time

Let's look at Joe, a twenty-seven-year-old man who couldn't keep a job. He came with his girlfriend to a Power Model System™ workshop and told the group, "I'm here for her." At the same time, she kept telling people, "I'm here for Joe. He needed to come because he keeps losing jobs." I said, "Glad you're here for each other." They both laughed.

Typically over three-day workshops we do a lot of group activities and role-playing. I let everyone know ahead of time that the workshop isn't therapy. Rather, it's designed so each person can leave with his or her personal blueprint profile. If people feel they need special help, they should see a therapist, coach, or counselor outside the workshop.

Joe and his girlfriend sat next to each other the first day. Joe acted happy, laughing and joking with everyone. He said he could relate to some of the information but affirmed that he'd had a good childhood. He loved both his dad and mom and had received love from them too.

The second day of the workshop Joe sat apart from his girlfriend. Joe wasn't as loud and didn't laugh as much as the first day. He quietly walked up to me during lunch break and asked if he could talk to me about what he had learned so far about himself. We sat down at a table in the back of the room. His girlfriend had gone to lunch with some new friends, so we were alone. He had a look of realization in his sad eyes. He was mad at himself because, as he said, "I should have figured this out a long time ago."

He went on to say that he could suddenly see how he kept doing things that would get him fired from his jobs. He had a deep-rooted belief: "If I work too hard, I'll die young." Lets see what he self-discovered by imagining that you are "little Joe."

Story Intermission

Let's climb into Joe's story as if you were him.

You love your dad. You both do everything together except go to Dad's work. A truck driver, Dad sometimes takes you on short runs. On the days when he brings the truck home so he can leave for work early the next morning, you hear him in the kitchen asking your mom, "Is dinner ready yet? Do I have time to take 'you-know-who' for a ride around the block?" Even if dinner is ready, Mom says, "You know we can always make time for a ride. See you both when you get back."

Your dad started taking you for rides when you were only a year old. It became your favorite thing to do together. So anytime you see the truck coming home, you know the odds of going for a ride are great. Even the days when Dad looks awfully tired, you know you'll still ride around the block together with both of you laughing.

As you get older—four, five, six years old—you brag to other kids about what your dad does for work. You tell them about your rides with him in the big truck, how many gears this truck has, and how great it is to be up high looking over all the cars on the road. The kids who hear your stories in kindergarten and first grade say they wish they had a dad like yours. Anyone watching can see the closeness and love between you and your dad. It's also great being with Mom when Dad goes out for days on long hauls. She plays kid card games with you—Crazy 8's, Steal the Pack, and many others. All is well in your life. You have two parents who love you and love each other.

Then one day, in one second, your whole life changes. At the age of eight, you come home from school to find your aunt in the kitchen, crying. You ask her where Mom is. Auntie keeps crying and finally says, "Oh, honey, she's in the hospital. Your mom is sick." You ask to see her. "Oh, no, little kids can't go into hospitals, but she'll be home soon." Auntie stays at your house for five days. Then one day, you come home from school and seemingly out of the blue, Mom's there sitting in a kitchen chair. As she opens her arms, you run across the room and fall into them. She tells you she has a sickness called cancer, but she's glad to be home and it's all going to be okay.

Dad calls home every night. He tells you he has to take long hauls so he can get Mom well again. The nights he finally gets home are heaven. You can hear Mom and Dad laughing like old times. Mom still plays cards with you in the evenings and laughs with delight when you let her win. You love your parents deeply.

As the medical bills soar, Dad starts driving more and more, not sleeping much. Mom is having treatments and doing okay as far as you know. No one talks about it much. One time, you hear Mom on the phone telling Dad, "You're working yourself to death. Please rest on the road. We love you and want you to be safe." Then you hear Mom laughing about something Dad says. After she hangs up, she turns to you and asks if you finished your homework. You tell her "Yes" and she says, "Then let's play cards."

You remember this evening particularly well because four hours into the dark night when you're sound asleep, the phone rings and soon you hear Mom yell, "Oh No-o-o!" She starts crying and yelling "No!" at the same time. You run into the kitchen where the phone is and see Mom on the floor, crying. You just stare at her, but in your gut you know. Your mother only cries if it's really, really bad. Something terribly bad just happened.

People start coming over to your house to help Mom and you. You hear your aunt tell your uncle, "He died instantly when he hit the cement wall. I kept telling him he was working himself to death trying to pay all the medical bills. But you know how he was. He was a working fool."

As an eight-year-old, you make some decisions. Emotionally, you decide to stay strong. Mentally, you decide that work kills and if you're smart, you won't let it kill *you*. You file those lessons away in your mental belief system. Your feelings of loss take over and the belief system gets buried in your subconscious mind. All you remember over time is the year your dad died and that he was in a truck accident. Your resentment about the loss turns inward. You hold onto the belief that work will kill you. You subconsciously decide to never work hard.

Story Continued

In the present, Joe is a person who's willing to look at himself; otherwise, this issue wouldn't have come up for him. As much as he laughed and joked at the workshop, a part of him wanted to grow beyond his limitations and honestly find out what was blocking him.

By articulating the eight-year-old boy's issue, the thoughts that went with it, and his subconscious reaction (how he'd behaved to get fired from his jobs), Joe understood his behavior. In his mind, it enabled him to stay alive. Although this conclusion came from a child's mind, it still held power over his present-day life. Joe linked the emotion (fear of death), the thought (work kills), and the reactive behavior (sabotage his jobs) so he could continue to support his belief system, which also supported his thoughts and reactive behavior.

After Joe finished the workshop, he shared his relief that he knew where his issue about work came from and how it fit in with his experience. He said, "Now I know that I'm not lazy, stupid, or any of the other stuff I was telling myself."

Later in the year, Joe and his girlfriend came to another three-day Power Model System™ workshop. I was surprised and pleased to see them again. They said they'd learned so much in the first workshop they wanted to come again and discover more about themselves. They had recently become engaged. Joe had been in the same job for a full year. For the first time, he was enjoying internal balance and felt eager to climb the career ladder. He also said he felt less fear about taking career risks in his life.

The Illusion of Spiritual Power

Spiritual: *relating to, consisting of, or having the nature of spirit; not tangible or material; concerned with, or affecting the soul.*

The Merriam-Webster Dictionary

People in Spiritual Power Illusion have little or no spiritual knowledge, conflicting spiritual beliefs, or believe they have all spiritual knowledge without actually knowing themselves. They have no wisdom or firm foundation on which to base this knowledge.

Here are the most common spiritual illusions:

- My spiritual belief can replace knowledge of self;
- Everyone should have my belief system because it's the only true one;
- I am unsure of my spiritual belief system;
- My Higher Power punishes me when bad things happen in my life;
- I am angry at my Higher Power.

My Spiritual Belief Can Replace Knowledge of Self

If you have no knowledge of self, you are sleeping. How can you know what is real when you are sleeping?

You're the only one who can wake yourself up from your illusive dream world. You're the only one who can bring yourself to an awakened state. No one else can do it for you. By reading about and doing these activities, you're awakening yourself through self-discovery. Give yourself a pat on the back!

When you know yourself, you have a passion for personal growth. You don't rely on a belief system to shape your identity. In awakening, you realize that your spiritual beliefs are a part of you but they don't define all of you. Your spiritual beliefs *guide* you.

My Belief is the Only Belief

As a child, I was told that the religion my parents believed in was what my family practiced and it was the only true religion. My parents didn't exactly say this, but the religionist leaders did. I was confused by that statement. At age thirteen, I believed that a Higher Power was for all people of all religions. At that time, I remember being told by my religious teachers that I would understand more when I was older, that other religions were to be tolerated but ours was the only *right* way. Now that I'm older, my belief is the same as it was when I was thirteen: we all have souls, and our Higher Power-given right is the freedom to choose any of the spiritual paths available to us.

If you believe in a Higher Power, it's important that you choose and connect to your Higher Power belief system. If you don't choose this from your own heart, how can it truly be your belief system? How could you integrate it into your life? This personal choice is what makes each one of us unique. It's also why each one of us needs to decide for ourselves what spiritual path to follow. The path each human takes depends on what his or her soul needs to learn.

The illusion about spiritual power comes when people pass judgments on those with spiritual beliefs that are different from their own. For example, if you were born Catholic and believe in its principles and live within the tenets of the Catholic Church, then Catholicism becomes your Higher Power belief system. When you state that the world should see a Higher Power the same way you do, you're operating in Spiritual Illusion—you want to be in control and force other people to believe as you do. This is judging others and their spiritual beliefs. While you certainly don't have to agree with what is being taught in other religions, a little respect wouldn't hurt!

When you behave reactively in spiritual illusions, you aren't connected to your Higher Power in that moment. This also means that while you are judging others for their religions and/or spiritual beliefs, you are not connected to your Higher Power, which takes you right into spiritual illusion.

It's important that each of us make it a choice to choose and connect to a Higher Power belief system.

My Higher Power is Punishing Me or Others When Bad Things Happen

Have you ever become emotional about your belief in your Higher Power or feel loved when something good comes your way? How do you feel when you think something that comes your way *isn't* good? Are you as grateful then as you are for the good events? Or do you believe you are being punished for not being a good follower? In my view, changing your perception of your Higher Power or doubting your relationship with your Higher Power just because something good or bad happens is a spiritual illusion. I don't mean to imply that when something cruel or horrible happens in my life I immediately accept it. I know that within these events are pain and suffering, but once I'm able to process my emotions, thoughts, and the spiritual reality, I know I'll receive a gift from the event.

Can you, as a soul, take that pain and suffering and allow your Higher Power to help you though it? I know this isn't easy to do. But it's important to find a way to connect with your Higher Power at all times. I promise you that in *every* event in your childhood and adulthood—good or bad—there's a reward in the form of knowledge and wisdom from your Higher Power. So you'll want to connect with your Higher Power throughout every day, not just when something happens that stresses you.

The 3 R's

You're probably wondering why I focus so much on the 3 Rs—Resistance, Resentment and Revenge. I do it because they're a big red flag that signifies you are in illusion, and they can keep you there for a very long time—sometimes an entire lifetime! While exercising these 3 Rs *internally*, you also exercise them *externally*. In fact, that's how you create and recreate your life. You tap into the universal law of "like attracts like," which means two things: 1) what happens to you internally will be drawn to you externally, and 2) what isn't happening internally will be repelled from you externally.

Resistance leads to *resentment*, which leads to *revenge*. When you continue to resist learning about who you are inside emotionally, your emotions take you to resentment, or thought patterns of you and others. In resentment, you have a tendency to hang on to your mistakes of the past along with any mistakes others have made involving you. You also mentally justify your resistance. This brings us to the third R, revenge. Revenge is where you pursue behaviors that numb you and stop any feelings and thoughts from surfacing. Addictions and unhealthy relationships are forms of self-revenge. We are all familiar with revenge that can be inflicted on others.

Now let's look at the 3 Rs in another way.

The 3 Rs can keep you from resolving your past childhood issues. When you continue to resist looking at your childhood, you continue to resent events that happened in the past that caused you pain (involving your parents, relatives, etc.) This can lead you to take revenge on yourself and/or people from your past or whoever reminds you of your past. In the end, resistance is almost always futile. It's like holding your breath till you get your way. It will only make you sick.

It's not always a matter of functional or dysfunctional childhoods but rather childhood developmental stages that we all go through, regardless of what type of family we have. The emotions, thoughts, beliefs, and behaviors we developed from conception until we were ten years old aren't always what we want to feel, think, believe, and act upon when we reach adulthood. This is why each person should become accountable and responsible for his or her own life. I'm not saying there aren't childhood issues of abuse, neglect, abandonment, and so on. But if you don't move through them, you won't become mature and balanced. (I strongly suggest you find a therapist to assist you through issues such as abuse.)

As you grow in awareness of yourself, you grow in awareness of others. That's the way it works. Many times we don't see others for who they are because we don't want to look at ourselves for who we are. We try to avoid recognizing what we need to change in ourselves.

You might think that others should teach you how to trust, make the right decisions, and how to live. But that's not true. You need to go within and become aware of who you are so you can know your own truth. The sooner you come out of illusion with yourself, the sooner you'll be living in reality with others.

Now let's piece together all four of your human components in illusion to bring forth awareness of some of your illusions.

Activity: The Three Faces of Illusion

Figures 5.1A, 5.1B, 5.2A, and 5.2B relate to this activity.

In the following activity, you'll be connecting your emotional, mental, spiritual, and physical illusions. The goal is to bring your illusions to the surface so you become aware of the effect your human components have on each other. With this awareness, you can begin to build a bridge to reality.

Read through the activity, look at the example, and then start the activity.

1. On The Three Faces of Illusion charts, Figures 5.1A and 5.1B, take a moment to review each column. If you've ever had a single emotion, thought, or action that refers to the descriptions in the lists, circle them. If you have any unique illusions you would like to add, do so at the end of the corresponding list in Figure 5.1B. See Examples: Figures 5.2A and 5.2B illustrate an example.
2. Look at the circled illusions. What do you think? How do you feel about them?
3. Go back and read the chart on The Present Self, Chapter 3 (Figure 3.1).
4. Check the circled items in each component on The Present Self Activity, and see the similarities between the two charts. You can almost match your symptoms (The Present Self Figure 3.1) with the circled thoughts and feelings in The Three Faces of Illusion Figures 5.1A and 5.1B.

<u>Example</u>

Let's look at how someone named Sue might fill out Figure 5.2A.

On the chart, Sue circled the items that applied to her for the following reasons:

Emotional Power in Illusions (circled items)
I have been victimized

> Sue states she has felt like a victim all her life. She has ended up in abusive relationships and has a hard time getting out of them. At her workplace, she seems to be the person people yell at when they find an error.

Mental Power in Illusions (circled items)
I can't hear my choices due to defenses
I have illusions/magical thinking

> Since Sue found one of her defenses to be "constantly talking when she is stressed," she realized she cannot quiet her mind enough to hear her choices. She also found that if she avoids the situation, it will go away by itself (magical thinking).

Spiritual Power in Illusions (circled items)
I believe my Higher Power punishes me when bad things happen in my life.

Sue learned very young that if she was good, all good things would come to her. So when something wrong happens, she automatically believes she is being punished.

Physical Power in Illusions (circled items)
I decide/act based on how I feel
I have no boundaries

Sue realized that the reason it was so hard for her to leave an abusive relationship was because she was basing her decisions on the emotion of love. So she stayed and took the abuse because she loved him.

Sue came to realize her relationship problems were due to the fact that she does not know her boundaries and that she does not apply any boundaries with anyone else in her life. Note: Boundaries will be discussed later in the book. Boundaries are required in order for you to respect yourself, respect others, and ensure that others respect you.

Reflecting Back to the Present Self

Sue reflected back to her Present Self chart (Figure 3.2) on what she marked at that time. She was amazed to find how her illusions affected her present self. In other words, she was able to connect the items she circled in The Present Self chart (Figure 3.2) to the items she circled in The Three Faces of Illusions chart (Figure 5.2A). This is what she found.

Present Self – Emotional: Being *unable to identify her emotions*, she played the *victim role* and did not speak up for herself. She never even realized she was angry about what was happening.

Present Self – Mental: *Being overwhelmed mentally* explained her *inability to think through her choices* in any given situation. So *magical thinking* took hold and she just figured the situations would work themselves out.

Present Self – Spiritual: Sue realized she sunk even deeper into the *victim role* from her belief that *when something bad happens in her life she is being punished.*

Present Self – Physical: Sue connected her physical illusions to her Present Self chart by realizing her constant *fatigue* was caused by *making decisions off her emotions* and by *having no boundaries.*

THE THREE FACES OF ILLUSION

Situation

SPIRITUAL POWER

Kind - Loving - Gentle   CENTERED   Firm - Honest

Spiritual Illusion (not connected)
- I believe my Higher Power punishes me when bad things happen in my life
- I am unsure of my spiritual belief system • I am angry at my Higher Power

EMOTIONAL POWER	MENTAL POWER	PHYSICAL POWER
Illusion	Illusion	Illusion
What are my emotions?	*What am I telling myself?*	*What is my reactive behavior?*
• I have been victimized	• I have false ego strength	• I decide/act based on how I feel
• I feel helpless	• I can't identify my emotions	• I have physical body reactions
• I want instant gratification	• I have no tolerance for my feelings	• I have addictive behaviors
• I have no emotional boundaries	• No tolerance for human characteristics	• I have no physical boundaries
• I want what I want, and I want it now!	• I am critical of others	• I have inconsistent behavior
• I am stuck in the past	• I can't hear my choices due to defenses	• I get headaches and fatigue
• Fight - or -Flight – I am on survival mode	• I have no mental boundaries	• I have poor communication
• Don't know what/how to feel	• I have self-hatred	• I don't look at the consequences
• I fear anger in others	• I don't know who I am	• I overextend myself physically
• I feel others' emotions	• I have a distorted perception of myself	• I am frequently off work
• Feel responsible for others' emotions	• I am overwhelmed	• I have difficulty having fun
• I feel everything	• I don't know my own needs	• I get stuck and do nothing
• I feel nothing	• I over-react to changes	
• I overreact towards others	• I worry a lot	
• I cannot contain my emotions	• I have illusions/magical thinking	
	• I have concentration problems	
RESISTANCE	**RESENTMENT**	**REVENGE**

Figure 5.1A ~ The Three Faces of Illusion   *The Power Model System™ | Copyright © 2007 – HumanWisdom LLC*

THE THREE FACES OF ILLUSION cont..

Situation _____

SPIRITUAL POWER

Kind - Loving - Gentle   CENTERED   Firm - Honest

Spiritual Illusion (not connected)
- I believe my Higher Power punishes me when bad things happen in my life
- I am unsure of my spiritual belief system • I am angry at my Higher Power

EMOTIONAL POWER		MENTAL POWER		PHYSICAL POWER	
Illusion		Illusion		Illusion	
What are my emotions?		*What am I telling myself?*		*What is my reactive behavior?*	
• I get too close too fast with others • I laugh when I want to cry • I put anger on top of hurt • I am unable to say No • I say No all the time • I experience prolonged resentment • I experience prolonged resistance • Change is a punishment to me • I rage • I feel guilty when setting boundaries • I get angry when others don't know what I want without my telling them		• I judge myself harshly • I believe in scarcity • I take constructive criticism personally • I am problem-oriented • For me, change equals problems • I think problems will disappear • I don't know who to trust • I assume what others think • Others should know my needs • Give me solutions to personal problems • I am responsible for the whole company • I make excuses about my behavior • I daydream too much • I lie to myself about what I want in life • I get bored or tired and give up • I procrastinate • I don't have anything to offer		• I get anxious and tense • I freak out after a presentation • I have tension in my body • I am inflexible • I isolate myself • I'm unable to reach personal/career goals • I talk too much and gossip • I keep busy all the time • I become physically abusive when angry • I yell when I am angry	
RESISTANCE		RESENTMENT		REVENGE	

Figure 5.1B ~ The Three Faces of Illusion Cont..
Add more items at the end of each list as needed.

The Power Model System™ | Copyright © 2007 – HumanWisdom LLC

EXAMPLE:
THE THREE FACES OF ILLUSION

Situation _____

SPIRITUAL POWER

Kind - Loving - Gentle   CENTERED   Firm - Honest

Spiritual Illusion (not connected)
- I believe my Higher Power punishes me when bad things happen in my life
- I am unsure of spiritual belief system • I am angry at my Higher Power

EMOTIONAL POWER	MENTAL POWER	PHYSICAL POWER
Illusion	Illusion	
What are my emotions?	*What am I telling myself?*	*What is my reactive behavior?*
• I have been victimized	• I have false ego strength	• I decide/act based on how I feel
• I feel helpless	• I can't identify my emotions	• I have physical body reactions
• I want instant gratification	• I have no tolerance for my feelings	• I have addictive behaviors
• I have no emotional boundaries	• No tolerance for human characteristics	• I have no physical boundaries
• I want what I want, and I want it now!	• I am critical of others	• I have inconsistent behavior
• I am stuck in the past	• I can't hear my choices due to defenses	• I get headaches and fatigue
• Fight-or-Flight – I am on survival mode	• I have no mental boundaries	• I have poor communication
• Don't know what/how to feel	• I have self-hatred	• I don't look at the consequences
• I fear anger in others	• I don't know who I am	• I overextend myself physically
• I feel others' emotions	• I have a distorted perception of myself	• I am frequently off work
• Feel responsible for others' emotions	• I am overwhelmed	• I have difficulty having fun
• I feel everything	• I don't know my own needs	• I get stuck and do nothing
• I feel nothing	• I over-react to changes	
• I overreact towards others	• I worry a lot	
• I cannot contain my emotions	• I have illusions/magical thinking	
	• I have concentration problems	
RESISTANCE	**RESENTMENT**	**REVENGE**

Figure 5.2A ~ Example: The Three Faces of Illusion   *The Power Model System™ | Copyright © 2007 – HumanWisdom LLC*

EXAMPLE:
THE THREE FACES
OF ILLUSION Cont..

Situation _____

SPIRITUAL POWER

Kind - Loving - Gentle | CENTERED | Firm - Honest

Spiritual Illusion (not connected)
- I believe my Higher Power punishes me when bad things happen in my life
- I am unsure of my spiritual belief system • I am angry at my Higher Power

EMOTIONAL POWER	MENTAL POWER	PHYSICAL POWER
Illusion	Illusion	Illusion
What are my emotions?	*What am I telling myself?*	*What is my reactive behavior?*
• I get too close too fast with others • I laugh when I want to cry • I put anger on top of hurt • I am unable to say No • I say No all the time • I experience prolonged resentment • I experience prolonged resistance • Change is a punishment to me • I rage • I feel guilty when setting boundaries • I get angry when others don't know what I want without my telling them	• I judge myself harshly • I believe in scarcity • I take constructive criticism personally • I am problem-oriented • For me, change equals problems • I think problems will disappear • I don't know who to trust • I assume what others think • Others should know my needs • Give me solutions to personal problems • I am responsible for the whole company • I make excuses about my behavior • I daydream too much • I lie to myself about what I want in life • I get bored or tired and give up • I procrastinate • I don't have anything to offer	• I get anxious and tense • I freak out after a presentation • I have tension in my body • I am inflexible • I isolate myself • I'm unable to reach personal/career goals • I talk too much and gossip • I keep busy all the time • I become physically abusive when angry • I yell when I am angry
	I have panic attacks.	I'm afraid to take action in my life
RESISTANCE	**RESENTMENT**	**REVENGE**

Figure 5.2B ~ The Three Faces of Illusion Cont..   *The Power Model System™ | Copyright © 2007 – HumanWisdom LLC*
Add more items at the end of each list as needed.

Chapter 6

AUTOMATIC PILOT

If those who lead you say to you, "See, the Kingdom is in the sky," then the birds of the sky will precede you.
If they say to you, "It is in the sea," then the fish will precede you.
Rather, the Kingdom is inside of you, and it is outside of you.
When you come to know yourself, then you will become known, and you will realize that it is you who are of the sons of the living Father.
But if you will not know yourself, you dwell in poverty and you are that poverty.
Sayings of Jesus, Compiled by Ricky Alan Mayotta[2]

Automatic pilot: *1) acting or done spontaneously or subconsciously; 2) done or produced as if by machine (mechanical).*
The Merriam-Webster Dictionary

Automatic pilot is like a chain reaction—once begun, it becomes a habit to be observed and predicted by yourself and others. Simply stated, you don't like the results this behavior produces in your life, but you don't know how to stop it. Many times you don't even realize you are on autopilot. The behavior comes from your *subconscious*. (There's that word again!) Behaving from your subconscious is being asleep, in illusion. Being conscious is being awake, in reality.

For example, if a pilot flying a plane puts the controls on "automatic pilot," he can take a short break from the constant alert state of flying. It's as if he's gone unconscious for a while to rest his mind. But what happens if the plane is left on autopilot too long? What if the pilot gets careless and doesn't eventually take responsibility for flying the plane? Of course you know the answer! If left on autopilot too long, the plane could crash into something or run out of fuel, crash, and burn.

This is also true of humans. We develop a system by the age of ten and then leave it alone to run on autopilot the rest of our lives. Not taking responsibility for how each of our four components affects our lives can lead to a nervous breakdown, burnout, or change-of-life syndrome (defined as people wanting to change everything and everyone in their lives, hoping to feel better inside). This is important to know because of its effect on individuals, families, communities, and society in general.

Your "patterning"—how you consistently respond or react to events—stems from how your four human components are connected, which affects your defense system (based on fight-or-flight). If you experience an event today that's similar to a stressful past experience, a "button gets pressed" and you go on autopilot. That means you're no longer "in the driver's seat" of your life in a conscious way. If you continue resorting to or falling back on the same coping behaviors for stressful situations you used when you were young, you'll react to similar situations in ways that are inappropriate for an adult and suffer the consequences that come from childish behavior.

You may stop undesirable behavior and succeed for a while. But without true awareness of the cause, this change of behavior will work against your emotional, mental, and physical energies because of your past internal conflicts and patterning. That's part of the *invisible force*. People who continually work at stopping certain behaviors they want to change often tell me how exhausting it is. Some express that they feel controlled by others who are telling them to stop the behavior. Some maintain the new behavior for one or two weeks and then revert back to their old behavior. *To change anything internally, it's critical that you use all four components at the same time.* Only then can the change come from within, which then results in true human wisdom.

When you go on autopilot, you put stress on your internal system. For example, when a close relationship breaks up and you feel threatened by a sense of abandonment, it's easy to fall into a reactive behavior and become automatically defensive or abusive. Of course, this behavior comes with consequences. If the stress you feel stays bottled up inside, you can damage your internal organs or your nervous system. You are unable to think straight, your muscles tighten, your auto-immune system weakens, you start catching a lot of colds, etc. Chronic stress can damage your mind and body and lead to burnout.

I know people may look at burnout as something awful, possibly even an illness. But what if I suggested that there may be important messages—hidden blessings— within each and every situation? What we refer to as burnout symptoms—a midlife crisis, depression, and so on—are actually signals that something isn't right. The body and mind are telling you to stop because something internally is "off." Rather than ignoring these vital signs, regard them as indicators that you're doing something that's not working. If you keep going in the same direction, you'll get more of the same body, mind, and spirit messages. If you pay attention to these signals, you are wise indeed!

There is no spiritual component in autopilot. Why? Because even though you may have strong spiritual beliefs, you're unable to apply them consistently. You find yourself habitually relying on automatic pilot reactions. When you are in any kind of reactive behavior, you're not connected to your spiritual power in reality.

Now that you know how important it is to disengage from autopilot, let's perform an activity that will help you recognize when you are on autopilot.

Activity: Being on Automatic Pilot

Figures 6.1 and 6.2 relate to this activity.
See the example in Figure 6.2 before filling out Figure 6.1.

It's a good idea to make copies of Figure 6.1, so you can redo this activity whenever you feel it's necessary.

1. In the upper right corner of the page in Figure 6.1 next to "Situation," write a recent event where you felt out of control and went on autopilot.
2. Take some timeout to remember what behaviors you exhibited during the event.
3. Under the heading "Physical Power," write the behavior remembered.
4. In the column "Mental Power," write the thoughts that were going on in your head at the time. There's some reasoning behind your reactive behavior that usually comes from our emotions. Recall the event in your mind's eye and watch the mental movie. What are you telling yourself? Example: "He/she is a fool" or "They deserve how I am acting" or "They make me act this way." Allow these thoughts to surface and write them down.
5. In the column "Emotional Power," write any emotions you were experiencing at the time.
6. Carefully examine your emotions, thoughts, and reactive behavior relating to this situation.

This activity helps identify your automatic pilot responses. If the environment triggers unresolved issues, you will go into reaction. All this comes from your fight-or-flight system. By observing and writing, you become aware of automatic behaviors sabotaging your life and how your emotions determine your reactions. As you look back on "The Present Self" Activity (Figure 3.1) and your illusions circled in Figures 5.1A and 5.1B, you are able to relate them to your autopilot responses.

AUTOMATIC PILOT

Situation:

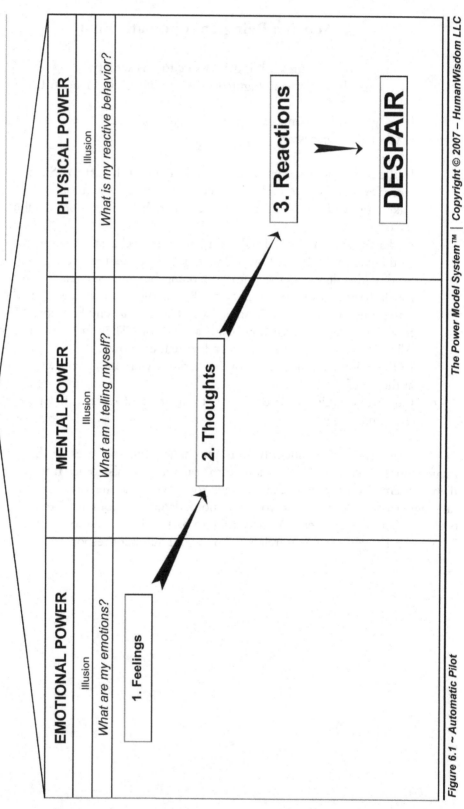

EMOTIONAL POWER	MENTAL POWER	PHYSICAL POWER
Illusion	Illusion	Illusion
What are my emotions?	What am I telling myself?	What is my reactive behavior?

1. Feelings

2. Thoughts

3. Reactions

DESPAIR

EXAMPLE
AUTOMATIC PILOT

Situation: I went to talk to my partner about changing my job. I did not like the people I worked with and this new job offer is better money and a higher position.

EMOTIONAL POWER	MENTAL POWER	PHYSICAL POWER
Illusion	Illusion	Illusion
What are my emotions?	*What am I telling myself?*	*What is my reactive behavior?*

1. Feelings

Anger

Lonely

Fear

Shame

2. Thoughts

I must be doing something wrong.

I'm becoming like my Dad. Never staying in one job very long

3. Reactions

I told my partner not to yell before I told him/her my decision.

I was fearful and on the defensive.

DESPAIR

Figure 6.2 ~ Example: Automatic Pilot

The Power Model System™ | *Copyright © 2007 – HumanWisdom LLC*

Chapter 7

FIVE STAGES OF ILLUSION

And then the day came when the risk to remain tight in a bud was more painful then the risk it took to blossom.
          Anais Nin

        We covered the illusions you live with in Chapter 5. Now we're going to learn about the Five Stages within these illusions and combine them with The Three Faces of Illusion (the 3 Rs). This is the cycle that leads to addiction in our lives. You'll continue to go through the Five Stages of Illusion in various orders until you take action to stop yourself. When I talk about "addiction," remember that I'm not just addressing alcohol, drugs, and food. Humans can also become addicted to anger, work, fast cars, money, power, possessions, and so on. An addiction is anything we connect with that gives us a sense of power, albeit a *false* sense of power.

The Five Stages of Illusion are:

1. Honeymoon in Resistance
2. Resentment of Reality
3. Power Struggle in Illusion
4. Commitment to Addiction
5. Co-Creation in Despair

Anything we put in place of our Higher Power connection will make our lives unmanageable.

FIVE STAGES OF ILLUSION

Honeymoon Period in Resistance

Resentment of Reality

Power Struggle in Illusion

Commitment to Addiction

Co-Creation in Despair

Stage One: Honeymoon in Resistance

Do you remember how wonderful you felt when you first met your life partner, got a new job, or went on an exciting vacation? You thought it would be wonderful and never considered that you might have to face obstacles. Welcome to the honeymoon stage of illusion! This is when you see a person, situation, or place as *ideal*. What could be wrong with that, you ask?

Here's what can be wrong. You can get stuck in the honeymoon period and stop growing, learning, and maintaining balance. In a relationship, getting stuck commonly occurs if it is abusive physically, mentally, or emotionally. One partner believes the other is going to change. "He/she really didn't mean to hurt me. He/she got upset," says the victim. The abused and abuser believe that this will never happen again. Both of these individuals have a *resistance* to seeking help and looking at themselves individually. The truth is that the abusive behavior in the relationship is covering up other issues from both parties' childhoods and belief systems.

Resistance in the honeymoon period occurs when people refuse to examine what's going on within, even when they discover that things, events, people, or relationships aren't what they thought they were. Humans don't like to be wrong about anything and have a tendency to think they're right all the time.

How do you know if you're in the Honeymoon in Resistance period with yourself and others? Consider the following questions and write down your answers.

- Do you and your partner show respect to each other?
- Do you know your higher purpose in life?
- Do you have a Higher Power belief system and apply it daily?
- Is your life as stress-free as you'd like it to be?
- Do you think you're at your full potential in your life?
- Do you get anxiety attacks?
- Do you experience debilitative fear when you have to learn something new?
- Is your family life the way you would like it to be?
- Have you been doing the same thing in your life and expecting different results?
- Do you find that no matter how hard you try, your life still doesn't change?
- Are you able to find peace within yourself?

Here's an example: Let's say you're driving your car down the road and it gets stuck in the mud. What do you do? First, you get out of the car and look at each wheel to see which one is stuck, or if they all are. Once you figure out which wheel is stuck in the mud, you put a board or rock under the stuck wheel. You may get a little muddy doing this, but staying clean isn't a priority. What's important is balancing your four wheels so you can drive your car out of the mud.

Now imagine that each of the wheels on the car is one of your four human components. Just as you need all four wheels pulling together to get out of the mud, you need all four of your human components working at the same time to get "unstuck" in your life. You need to examine each component individually and then see how the four of them can work together in balance and harmony to get you on the road again. And just as you would get muddy examining the car, examining yourself can get quite messy in the beginning.

In the honeymoon period, you believe the mud is normal and you stay stuck. If anyone suggests you look at yourself, you go into resistance. Is this worthwhile? Many people admit that their honeymoon period was very costly to them.

> *Whatever happened in your past (however you perceived it) needs to be faced in your present. Failing to do so will cost you your future.*

Story Time

Miriam, an attractive forty-year-old woman who was nicely dressed, came into my office looking very tired, and immediately sat down in a recliner. I sat directly across from her, also in a recliner. A few minutes went by while I watched her practice deep breathing to get relaxed. Silence hung between us as she continued to compose herself. After she had relaxed as best she could, she said, "I'm always feeling tired and bored. I can't seem to feel good about my life. I have a good family. My children, who are ten and fifteen, don't have any kind of problems. My husband's a good man who doesn't run around or go to bars. He works hard and puts in long hours. We've been married for seventeen years and I still love him very much." I asked her what she loved about her husband. Miriam smiled and said, "His joy. He laughs a lot and is happy over the littlest things. I wish I could be like him."

Then she began to look sad and said, "What's wrong with me? I know I should be happy. I can't see a reason to go to any more workshops that deal with emotional problems. I feel like I've tried them all. When I finish them, I feel great. Then three weeks later, I'm back where I started. I know what I *should* do, but it's so hard for me to change my behavior." As she spoke, I could hear the despair in her voice. I could also sense the tiredness down to her soul.

"Knowing me, I'm never going to change. But I need to keep looking because I know deep down inside me this is not how I want to live. I believe in God and go to church every Sunday. I think I just need to pull myself together and straighten up. God, my father, promises me everything, including happiness, so I know it's mine to have. I just haven't found the way to get it yet. It's all so confusing to me."

"It sounds like you've made many attempts to change," I said.

She sighed and said, "Oh, yes. I've read all the books and done all the workbooks because I want to grow. But it hasn't done any good. Maybe I'm just supposed to be this way. Maybe this is normal and I'm not yet used to being normal. I should be happy that I don't have some of the problems other women have. I feel blessed with my husband, children, and my life in general, but honestly I don't feel happy. How can that be, feeling blessed but not happy?"

As she went on with her story, she mentioned that her husband had his moods, but nothing too serious. "When he walks in the door at night, I can tell he's angry so I keep quiet and let the children know Dad's not in a good mood. If I don't stay quiet enough he explodes, but it's my own fault for being noisy." I asked her what she meant by noisy. "I make noise moving the dishes instead of staying quiet. Or sometimes the kids will be playing and they start laughing too loud or even fighting, the way kids do."

When I asked Miriam what her husband did when she was noisy, she became rigid in her chair, and in the quietest voice said, "He starts yelling at me to keep the kids quiet and tells me how hard he works. He wants to come home and have some peace, but it's too noisy for him. I know he's not asking for much. He's a good man, works hard, and goes to church every Sunday, even when he's tired. The least I can do is keep the house quiet."

"Have you spoken to your husband about his yelling?" I asked.

"Yes," she said, while tears filled her eyes. "But he says he is who he is and this is how he's always been, so I'd better get used to it. This statement ends the discussion. Then he's usually in a bad mood the rest of the day. But the kids have gotten better at being quiet. As soon as he comes home, they go to their rooms until dinnertime. During dinner, they've learned not to make noise. After dinner, they take their baths and go to bed. And in the morning, they stay quiet until he leaves for work. After that, we talk freely. So things are going very well at home now." Then her feelings of despair surfaced again as she said, "Maybe it's just me. I don't know why I can't seem to be happy."

From this conversation, I surmised that Miriam resists becoming aware of her home situation. She covers it over with her stories about what's going on that avoid the truth about her marriage, embracing an illusion of how things are in her relationship with her husband and making excuses for him. She knows she's unhappy, but in reality is she looking for a solution? Yes, she is, as long as it allows her to stay in resistance about the real issues. So she stays in the honeymoon period, telling herself everything is okay and resists looking at the part she's playing in this situation.

When I asked her about her childhood, she said, "Oh, no. Not that again. I'm forty years old and I left my childhood behind." While she said this, Miriam's face turned pale, her jaws tightened, and her foot started tapping on the floor. Her body language and her words didn't match. When I asked if she was feeling upset, she said, "Feeling? I'm feeling nothing. And, no, I'm not upset. Well, maybe just a little." Then she said, "I'm tired of people asking me about my childhood."

I noticed that when I asked about her feelings, she answered with a thought. When I pointed this out, she again went into resistance and said, "Oh, well. What's the difference—thought or feeling? Anyway, my childhood is over and done with."

Miriam's situation exemplifies what I call the honeymoon period of illusion, when people say they want to "figure it out" yet won't explore any avenues that are painful to examine. Because she resists looking at herself, Miriam could stay in this stage of not knowing for the rest of her life.

Miriam is not even aware of experiencing fear from past experiences, which is why she has trouble identifying emotions other than her unhappiness. She clearly doesn't want to explore where her unhappiness is coming from. Indeed, she simply might not have the coping skills to work with reality. To her, not knowing is better then knowing because knowing would disturb her present situation. It would also change how she sees herself.

Miriam wants to stay in the Honeymoon Period and resist learning what the reality is in her marriage, with herself and her husband. This way, she can always say to herself, "Someday he will change" or "I love him; he's a good man" or "Why am I so fussy? Why can't I accept him the way he is?" or "My childhood has no effect on my present life."

You'll notice that I'm calling it Honeymoon Period in Resistance, not spiritual thinking. Wanting some situations to be what you want them to be is not to your benefit. By just letting life happen and flowing with it, you'll continue to believe everything will work out and won't discover where the problem lies, within yourself or others. You'll continue to get the same results and then say, "Oh well, that's how life is." You'll believe you don't have to take a chance or take any action to change your life.

Miriam does not believe she has the right to confront her husband about his behavior. By finding something in her life to blame, like herself for being bored, she continues to avoid the real problem, which is her husband verbally abusing her and the children. She needs to work through her childhood issues. Facing her childhood issues will help her to understand why she puts up with her husband's behavior.

Eventually, Miriam attended one of my three-day workshops with the intention of just having fun, but the results she achieved were amazing. She successfully came through her resistance and denial. For example, in a group session, we were working through the Five Stages of Illusion in The Power Model System™ and she felt thrilled that she could recognize herself and laughed about her behavior of avoiding reality.

During the workshop, she uncovered some childhood issues that were keeping her stuck. Another group member shared in one of her groups about how she kept picking unhealthy relationships due to her belief system from her childhood. As she was sharing, a bell went off in Miriam's head. She remembered how her mother and father interacted when she was a child. Dad raged and mom made excuses for him. She would not say anything to him because if she did, he would go from being verbally abusive to physically abusive with her. Miriam was taught to stay quiet and not upset her father.

So much had changed! She wrote me a thank-you letter praising The Power Model System™, saying it made sense to her logically. She also wrote that her changes had positively affected her marriage. Her husband was learning new ways to communicate to her and learning that his past behavior was abusive. She also began learning more about her own childhood issues. And now her family was having family meetings once a week to discuss how everyone felt and how they could improve their communication with each other. She was feeling excited about life.

What had happened? Miriam had become aware of characteristics common to both her dad and her husband. She also saw how her behavior was similar to that of her mom. (As in her own marriage, her mother had never really talked with her father.) She had been raised in a verbally and physically abusive home and thought this was normal. Because of her awareness, she was able to stop the next generation of her family (her children) from believing that yelling and screaming were normal means of communication.

What I know is this:

Internal growth brings happiness and joy into the soul of a human being. It comes from deep inside. Everything else is frosting on the cake.

Those who tend to "stay stuck" refuse to look inward. If they continue to resist change, they will digress to Stage Two.

> *You do have choices to change your perception and interpretation of yourself.*
> *These choices come from within.*

Stage Two: Resentment of Reality

The Resentment of Reality stage is characterized by *resentment* (from the 3 Rs). Resentment of Reality in the illusion stage is thinking that "I don't like the way life is" or "I don't like this particular situation", and I don't want to look at how I can change to make it better. The belief, that "I shouldn't have to look at myself or look at my contribution to the situation" breeds resentment. A little voice says, "I'm not going to look any further into myself, but I resent that this is all there is." It's a mental illusion based on the past and employs a belief system that was created years before. Resentment occurs when you think it's your *right* to have had a particular learning experience before becoming an adult. You resent that you have to grow up and/or you're not aware that you're stuck in illusion. While you are in this stage of Resentment of Reality, you really believe you're in true *reality* and not in *illusion*. In your mind you believe you don't have to look in the mirror because it's really about *other* people.

If you're stuck in this stage, you feel unhappy about not getting what you want but have already decided not to investigate yourself. You conclude that *others* are responsible for your life not being the way you want it to be. Between the resistance and the resentment, your body gets locked into a chemical chain reaction that affects your mind and spirit, resulting in stress. This is the *blame* stage.

Story Time

It was a bright sunny day, when a large man came through the doorway of my office. I remember looking up and seeing how his body took up the entire doorway. He had to bend his head down as he came through it. I introduced myself and shook his hand. He had a smile on his face as he sat in the recliner.

"I sure am glad you have a big chair," he said. "I get tired of these small things most people call a chair." We both laughed. Then there was silence. He looked at me and then looked away. This went on for about three minutes. He finally asked, "Aren't you going to ask me any questions?"

When I said, "What do you want me to ask?" he laughed out loud—a big, hearty laugh. "I guess I need to talk, right?"

I smiled and said, "Right."

He then told me his wife had died a year earlier. He talked about how much he loved her over the thirty-five years they'd been together. He'd thought he was doing well since her death, but as the year went on, he started to feel angry almost all of the time. When she was alive, they both used to laugh a lot, and he missed that. He said his three grown children were concerned about how much he'd changed since their mom had died. As he was talking to me, I noticed he was tensing up, looking more and more stressed. Angry, yet sad at the same time.

I sat and listened. He talked for an entire hour about his marriage, family, parents, and thoughts on death. He was amazed when he looked at his watch and said, "I can't believe it. This is the most I've talked in a year." I told him that was good and asked him how he was feeling. He looked me straight in the eye and said with relief, "Maybe I've become more closed-up and angry since May died."

We had one hour left in our two-hour session. I told him I wanted to hear a little more about what happened when *his* mother died and left him and his father. He causally sat back and said, "Oh, my dad died a year later. He said life wasn't worth living anymore."

I asked, "Have you had any thoughts along those lines?"

"No, I don't think I do. I know it was hard on me being seventeen when they died. I went to live with my aunt, and she was great to me."

"How did your mom die?" I asked.

"She had cancer. Now that I think of it, my dad was never sick until after my mom died. Then he developed a heart condition and died of a heart attack." I watched the wheels go around in Bob's head as he thought about his parents' deaths. I asked him if he saw any similarities between his parents' situation and his and May's.

"Some," replied. "That Mom died first and then Father. May died first and I'm still alive."

Then I asked the big question. "*Are* you still alive, Bob*?*"

He broke down and cried. Finally he said, "No, I haven't been since May died." He sobbed for a long while. When he stopped, he said, "I feel like a house has just been lifted off me." His eyes were bright. His face shined. He smiled, and a look of amazement filled his face.

"Your mother died, and he joined her," I said. "I suppose your father faced that choice, even if he was unaware he was making one. It's time for you to make *your* choice. You don't have to believe and choose the same as your dad."

Bob said, "I see the connection, but I need to understand this better."

"The first stage is when May died, but you kept your life with her, burying the reality of the situation," I said. "You resisted dealing with your loss. In the second stage, you developed resentments about having this loss in your life. You continued to resist experiencing the emotions, thoughts, and spiritual beliefs that go with any loss. This is where you were when you first walked in here."

Bob had a smile on his face and said, "Good. I needed to understand what I was doing along with the feelings."

I then suggested he visit May's grave, give her some flowers, and say goodbye. "Also let her know it's okay with you that she left. She needed to go. And be sure to thank God for the years you had together and the beautiful children that came from your marriage."

Our time was up so I asked him if there was more he wanted to talk about. He said, "No, I'm okay now." He stood up to leave, but before he did he gave me a big bear hug and thanked me. I never heard from Bob again.

If you choose to stay in the illusion with resistance and resentment, there's little anyone else can do for you. It's your choice. Making no decision is the same as making a decision—you've made a decision to *not* make a decision. Choosing to *not* make a decision to change will lead you to Stage Three, Power Struggle in Illusion.

Stage Three: Power Struggle in Illusion

Power: *possession of control, authority, or influence over others.*
Struggle: *to make strenuous or violent efforts against opposition.*

Merriam-Webster Dictionary

This stage is characterized by confusion and anger that occurs when you get into an internal power struggle with yourself, emotionally and mentally. In this Power Struggle stage, your emotional state is in constant conflict with your mental state. Your emotions are telling you one thing, and your thoughts are saying another.

Let me put it another way: you say one thing to someone but do another. Or, as the saying goes, you're not "walking your talk." When you tell someone you will change, you might mean it at the time, but when it comes time to follow through with actions, you don't do what it takes.

Beware of this stage. You're not likely to welcome the consequences!

In this stage, you shut down from your neck down. In other words, you operate from your mind only. You have a difficult time identifying your emotions unless they're extremely strong. This means that you react off them without knowing they are there. In fact, you might not even realize the difference between one emotion and another. For example, you may experience only anger when you're actually hurt, or vice versa. You might become terrified that if you start to identify your emotions or deal with any of them, they'll overpower you and you'll get out of control. Ironically, you're already out of control! You are under the illusion that by not feeling your emotions, you'll stay in control. Because making changes is new and scary, you often struggle to maintain what's familiar, even if this means you're confused, feel miserable, and are angry most of the time. This familiar state of mind becomes your comfort zone and reinforces your subconscious belief system that life is hard.

If you're in a relationship with someone you truly love, you're unable to make an emotional or mental connection. A spiritual union is really out of the question without this connection. Consequently, you deliver double messages to yourself and others because what you say differs from what you do. You still believe you're in reality, while you are really in illusion. At this stage, you don't have much love for yourself. Love starts with loving ourselves. Only then can we express love for others.

If someone asks if you are angry, you might say "no" in a loud voice, indicating that you are angry but don't want to acknowledge it. With anger, you have two choices: pull the anger inward or push it outward. You can't seem to identify or express your emotions or justify your thoughts, so you conclude that everyone else is wrong or, at the opposite extreme, that the situation is entirely your fault. There's no in-between thinking; it's all black or white.

I have seen a lot of men and women in this stage so unhappy with who they are that they decide to change everything *outwardly* in their lives. They start all over with a new career, family, and friends. Marital affairs are common at this stage. People think their partners are their enemies and believe that with a new partner, everything will be better. What they don't realize is that nothing will improve until they look at themselves *internally*.

There are only two ways to go when you are in the Power Struggle of Illusion: inward or outward. Outwardly, you overwork and feel stressed all the time. You rage over little things. You start drinking to relax and eating past the point of enjoying the food. You work past the point of enjoying your career. If you power-struggle internally, you will find yourself power-struggling externally with others in your life. You hold onto resentments and blame your past for what you're experiencing in the present, unaware that when you do this, you set the stage for experiencing the same resentment-filled future. All of these robot-like behaviors create chemical reactions that can damage your nervous system and deplete your body of vitamins (especially B-complex). Thus, you feel constantly overwhelmed and stressed.

Story Time

Janette is a beautiful woman in her thirties with an above-average IQ and lots of ambition. She came to see me about her boyfriend and let me know in the first two-hour visit all the things that were wrong with him.

On her second visit, she started by saying, "He doesn't know how to make a commitment; he doesn't know how to treat women or how to communicate; he doesn't know how to share money; he just doesn't *know* . . ."

After the first fifteen minutes, I said, "I don't want to hear about him any longer. I want to hear about you."

So she went from being angry at him to being angry at me. "This isn't about me. This is about him," she said. "Don't you get that?"

"Oh! Well, then, we need him here so you can tell him all these things directly."

"I told him to come. I tell him all the time. We're on the phone for hours." I sat in silence. She looked at me and said, "Well, what should I do?"

"Keep doing what you're doing," I said.

"I could do that without coming here."

"Yes, you could. But I'd like you to keep a pad by the phone. Record the time you start the phone call with your boyfriend and the time you end it. Write down the way your body feels while you're on the phone with him, and just be aware."

She laughed and said, "I could do that easily."

"Great," I said. "I'm going to call this visit over. Come back next week with your records."

Being the responsible person she was, she walked into our next session and handed me a tablet. Then she sat down, not looking very happy. She had logged a total of thirteen hours for the week in conversations with this man. She'd written down words like "angry," "mad," "tense," "hang-ups," and "call-backs." When I asked, "What do you think about this?" she said, "It's crazy."

She had three children at home who were overhearing these calls, and they told her not to speak to him. I laughed and said, "You need to see the humor in this. Your children are wiser than you are in this situation." She relaxed and said, "I guess so."

As we worked on her Power Model System™ personal blueprint, not surprisingly we discovered that her whole fight-or-flight defense system was based on anger. She was a woman with a lot of mistrust toward men due to experiences in her younger years. She'd learned to express all of her anger at everyone. The extent to which she lived her whole life in "fight" mode was amazing. She'd seen many therapists, so she knew all the right words. She let me know that most of the therapists told her how knowledgeable she was.

I told her on the third visit not to count me among them. I said, "I'm concerned about you continuingly doing damage to your body internally." This got Janette's attention. She looked at the various activities we'd done within the model and realized that the answers didn't lie.

"What's wrong with me? Why can't I just walk away?"

Janette didn't drink, take drugs, overwork, or embrace any of the most common addictions. (Although she considered herself squeaky clean from addictions, she had family members who were damaged from alcohol and drugs.) I told her, "Your addiction may be the adrenalin rush of anger, and your body could be strung out. That means you have to have a "hit" of anger and rage daily. Tell me, how do you communicate with your children?"

"I yell."

"How do you deal with problems at work?" I asked.

"I keep my temper outwardly, but inwardly I'm a mess."

With this awareness, Janette looked at the Five Stages of Illusion and accepted the nature of her problem. Then, looking at the Power Struggle stage, she said, "Gosh, this is me. I promise myself I'm not going to blow up. The next thing I know, I'm on the phone, blowing up."

Janette and I set up a program in which she'd call her boyfriend only once a week. As a result, she started going through withdrawal and found herself blowing up more often at her children. By the time we finished her Power Model System™ personal blueprint, she'd started practicing impulse control and was learning when to use it, i.e., refraining from using the phone. In the meantime, she focused on developing a strong spiritual belief system. During this process, she experienced symptoms of physical withdrawal such as exhaustion, headaches, anxiety, and sleeplessness.

It took Janette about six months before she could go a week without blowing up about something. I would like to say this is an easy habit to break, but it's not. Janette had to come to awareness about herself in many areas. The process allowed her to see how she used anger to have a sense of control and safety in the world, and how she picked people to be in her life at whom she could justify being angry. As we worked on the power struggles within her, she was able to slowly conquer the power struggles outwardly in her life too.

Even if you have no awareness of what you're doing to yourself, you're still responsible for the results.

Unfortunately, it is easy to become accustomed to this stage and believe that life in this war zone is normal. You struggle to hold onto the familiar while continuing to get more and more diseased with life and within yourself, believing that's "all there is." The stress leads you to find a way to relieve this reality, which takes you to the next stage of illusion, Addiction.

Stage Four: Commitment to Addiction

Commitment: *1) a pledge to do. 2) the act of pledging or engaging; the act of exposing, endangering, or compromising; also, the state of being pledged or engaged.*
Addiction: *1) compulsive need for a habit-forming substance. 2) the condition of being habitually or compulsively occupied with or involved in something. 3) habitual psychological and physiological dependence on a substance or practice beyond one's voluntary control.*

The Merriam-Webster Dictionary

Addiction refers to behavior that allows you to avoid dealing with your life issues or internal struggles. It works by seeming to take away all the pain, doubt, and emptiness you feel. That's what makes whatever addiction you choose so seductive. It does its job well.

This stage is characterized by relieving the pain of your internal power struggles in illusion through addictions that numb you so the reality of life can't get through to you. At this stage, you make a commitment to continue cycling through the 3 Rs: *Resistance*, *Resentment*, and *Revenge*. Because you're familiar with these reactions, you know what to expect. In the Commitment stage, you are well aware of how to relieve the stress that builds up inside you. Affection from loved ones doesn't get through because your addiction doesn't allow them to get close to you or you to them. This gives you even more reason to numb yourself.

Addictions are the way you seek revenge on yourself. Use of your addiction numbs your mind, body, and spirit.

In effect, you become committed to a false sense of power, which is better than no sense of power at all. Your addiction is your way of coping with the turmoil you feel inside, taking away the pain of stress and problems. What could be more powerful than that? Alcohol and drugs are the most common addictive agents, but work, gambling, eating, acquiring money or possessions, anger, crises, and danger can all be addictive. Genetics also plays a part here, so often there's a pattern of the same addiction in families.

Various addictions have different effects chemically on our body, mind, and spirit. For example, you might not click with alcohol or drugs, but overworking does the job for you. You might not overdo gambling, eating, or acquiring money, but you can get high on racing, rock climbing, or sky diving and then engage in them to excess. Doing these activities isn't a problem in itself. The problem occurs when you engage in them *to avoid facing yourself*, and before you realize it, you become dependent on them.

Let's face it, if addictions didn't ease despair in the short term, they wouldn't be so prevalent. But in truth they cause even more despair in the long run.

Story Time

James and his partner Larva came to a workshop because he was stressed. His partner had agreed to come because she felt she could also learn something and then they could talk about what they'd learned. James was the silent one and wasn't very interactive through the days of the workshop. When he did talk, he spoke words of wisdom and said he was enjoying learning about himself and hoped he could relieve some of the stress in his life. Larva was the expressive one. She shared openly and had a great sense of humor. As both of them went through the system, I noticed James starting to withdraw from the group. By the third day of the workshop, James and Larva asked if I could talk with them alone.

Larva began. "Kay, James and I have been talking and want to get your feedback." James started to stand up and then relaxed and sat back down in the chair. I said, "James, go ahead and walk around if you need to." He then stood, sat right back down, and as he did so, he looked at Larva and said, "I need to do this for me." Larva sat back in her chair and said, "Okay."

James started out by explaining what the activities had taught him about himself. He also said he'd been extremely stressed the past year in his career as a lawyer. He looked at me and said, "Larva and I have been together for ten years. Last year we started having a lot of trouble. And last year I also had the career stress and my mom died, which was very hard for me. We're a tight-knit family, so I needed to help my dad through the loss. I'm aware now that I hadn't processed the loss of my mom or the stress of my career, and that's when the troubles started in our relationship."

I said, "James, have you become aware how you coped with the stress?" Tears came to his eyes and he said, "Yes, I've gone drinking at least three times a week with my friends from work. They've invited me over the years—six years to be exact. But I never went, except on special occasions like someone's birthday or when someone received a promotion. Then I would call Larva and invite her to join us if she could, or I'd be home at a certain time.

"What I've discovered so far is that I've done the changing in this relationship, not Larva. I've been accusing her of changing. But I've been drinking after work nearly every day, not calling home to let her know where I am or when I'll be home, getting home at late hours, and becoming angry if she says anything. In fact, I defend myself by saying this is my relaxation. Kay, I'm very concerned that I may have a drinking problem. Do you think I'm an alcoholic? Now I know that my behavior demonstrates I'm more committed to drinking with my office buddies than communicating with Larva. I don't exercise anymore because I'm too tired. And I'm angrier than I've ever been."

Larva sat silently and listened while James talked. Then I asked, "What do you think, James? Do you think you have a drinking problem?" He said, "I don't know."

I said, "That's a good answer." I then suggested they go to an addiction counselor together and see what they could figure out, along with attending some 12-Step AA meetings. They both started to relax as they looked at each other. Larva said it was a good start. James agreed.

As we came to the close of the workshop, Larva and James shared with others how much this workshop had helped both of them become aware of how they handled life's stresses. Also, they said becoming aware of stage four of the Five Stages to Illusions had created a major breakthrough for them. I heard from both of them about three months later. Due to James' self-discovery, he was in recovery for alcohol and they were both enjoying their participation in the 12-Step program.

If you stay in your addition too long, you enter the final stage of Co-Creation in Despair.

> *A spiritual belief connection and a commitment to an addiction*
> *cannot exist in a human being at the same time.*

Stage Five: Co-Creation in Despair

Co: *to appoint as a colleague or assistant.*
Create: *to produce or bring about by a course of action or behavior.*
Despair: *to lose all hope or confidence; to produce or bring about by a course of action or behavior.*

The Merriam-Webster Dictionary

We have discussed how you and your Higher Power co-created your internal system together for handling stress when you were young. Co-creation also occurs when you're committed to an addiction. You and your addiction become co-creators in leading you into a life of misery. This state of illusion is characterized by despair and death of self. *It is your responsibility to become fully aware of this co-creation and take full responsibility for the results.*

Once you're in this stage, you'll continue to repeat all the previous stages internally and recreate them in your life externally. Unsuccessful relationships, family turmoil, communication breakdown, and legal problems appear as recurring themes in your life. Even when you think you're going to have a different result, you encounter the same problems again. In the beginning of this stage, you think you have control over yourself, your life, and your addiction of choice—including when, why, and how much you use. In the end, however, your addiction controls you and your life. Your emotional and mental pain snowballs. You lose your ability to make choices because you constantly need to feed your addiction.

You find yourself in a downward spiral, playing the "victim role" and experiencing pity, despair and then the death of "self." Once you're on a roll covering up your emotions, thoughts, and spiritual beliefs, you go further into the victim role. You pity yourself because you believe you're at the mercy of your environment. Then you shift from feeling pity to feeling despair. If you stay in this victim role for too long, you justify doing anything you want when it comes to your addiction. And if you're feeling miserable long enough, death might even begin to look appealing.

> *You never stand still. You're either learning and growing or you're on a downward spiral.*

Before you realize it, you're in a self-destructive mode, embracing all the justification and rationalization you need to behave anyway you want, potentially harming yourself and others. Throughout this process, you'll most likely blame others for your life. You'll expect that someone other than yourself can make you happy or change your life. Of course this is impossible. The only person who can stop this downward spiral is you!

Most often, a life-changing event suddenly makes you realize how unmanageable your life is. Such an event might be a divorce, death, illness, job loss, financial problems, legal problems, or intervention from loved ones. A catalyst could even be acknowledging that you want to have a meaningful love relationship but don't know how. The turnaround occurs when you decide that "enough is enough."

Story Time

Jim was thirty-four years old, 5'11" tall, and 175 lbs, with sandy-colored hair that never looked combed, steel gray-green eyes and tanned skin. He worked as a foreman in construction crews and had a smile that could light up the room. Along with all this, Jim had a great personality, had come through a very tough childhood, and took pride in himself. He was self-educated and could hold a conversation about almost any subject. Jim enjoyed reading and learning new information, kept up on current events, and loved a good debate on any topic.

My first encounter with Jim was about eighteen years ago when he attended one of my one-day workshops. He let me know he was attempting to clean up from a ten-year heroin addiction. After attending the workshop, Jim joined a weekly men's group I was conducting at that time. As long as he continued with his recovery, attended Narcotics Anonymous meetings, and stayed in the weekly men's group, he did well. His marriage improved, and he was able to return as a foreman on his crew. (Due to his past drug use, he'd been demoted to working as a crew member.) As he said in the group one night, "I have it all—money, marriage, recovery, and health." I told him that the order in which he listed his "having it all" was disconcerting to me. Jim smiled his best smile and casually said, "Oh, you know what I mean." The other men in the group were also concerned about Jim's priorities.

One night in the group, the topic was Higher Power. The others in the group could see that Jim was getting too confident about being clean and sober for nine months. He had stopped his 12-Step meetings and was hanging out with some of his old friends who drank. He told the group this wasn't a problem since they only used alcohol, not drugs. He'd also gotten a promotion at work and a big raise—his life was going great. One of the men in the group started talking about the Five Stages of Illusion and how he found himself power-struggling between his addiction and his Higher Power. Jim told them he'd be all right.

"Look at me," he said, and all eyes turned to him. "I don't even have a Higher Power and I'm doing great. Look at all the good things that are happening in my life. I'm not drinking or drugging; I'm on my way." There was silence in the group of eleven men. No one said a word, including me. I let the statement that came out of Jim's mouth fall on his ears. I just thought about what he'd said and what we'd all seen from him during the last three weeks.

Jim looked at me and said, "I *am* doing well. Don't you think so?"

I asked, "Do you want an answer from around the block or straight between the eyes?"

With a big smile, Jim said, "Let's go between the eyes."

"All right," I said. "This is where I see you in the Five Stages of Illusion. In the *Honeymoon* period, you're just thinking everything is wonderful. You went into resistance when told to attend more 12-Step meetings. In the *Resentment of Reality* stage, you were resentful about group members pointing out that you needed to stop hanging out with your buddies in bars. In the *Power Struggle* stage, you became arrogant about being clean and sober, as if that was all you had to do to be in recovery. In the *Commitment in Despair* stage, you told us you have no Higher Power connection. I would say you may be heading for a relapse. What do you think?"

The room was silent again. Jim looked at me and said, "Kay, I'm going to think about what you said and what the rest of the group has given me as feedback over these last three weeks."

Next week Jim didn't come to group. Instead, he called and booked an appointment with me. I knew the minute I saw Jim coming through my office doorway that the *Power Struggle* stage was over, and so was the commitment stage. He had on his black leather jacket, a dark shirt, his hair was tousled, and he was smiling. Nothing about him looked unusual, but there was an air about him. I was happy to see him and let him know we had all missed him in the group.

He sat down and in a very low voice said, "I'm not coming to group any more. I really don't need it. I feel great and really can't see any more groups or meetings being of use to me. I know you don't agree with me." When he was through talking, I let the silence dance between us. Jim started to feel uncomfortable and asked if I was mad at him.

I said, "Oh, no, I'm sad. For you to be so close and yet so far concerns me."

Jim smiled and said, "I know what I'm doing. I promise I'll work at developing a Higher Power, and I can do that on my own. I've even been able to drink socially with my buddies lately and be fine. Don't be concerned for me." As he was talking and telling me how great everything was in his life, his eyes filled with tears and he said, "I'm going to miss you." I let him know that I'd miss him too and he could come back anytime—I was just a phone call away. He gave me a hug and left the room.

I would like this story to end here, but it doesn't. Three weeks later I received a phone call from his wife, who was also in recovery. "Jim moved out a week ago, due to us arguing over his drinking and him hanging out with his old friends. Last night he died from a heroin overdose. I wanted to call you and let you know. Three weeks ago when he stopped coming to your office, he kept saying, 'I know Kay means well, but I'm going to prove her wrong. I don't believe this Higher Power thing, and I can beat this disease without one.' He told me about the last night in the men's group, and I said I hoped he'd think long and hard about what they said to him, but he just got angry with me."

I let her know that she'd done everything she could. After we talked for about thirty minutes, I wished her well in her recovery and hung up the phone.

That evening I grieved for Jim at home. Knowing that how he lived and how he'd died was his choice still didn't stop the pain of his dying. He was a bright, personable young man who had lived his life without ever self-discovering what a beautiful soul he was. I knew that nothing in the whole world could have given him greater happiness than making a connection with his Higher Power. Jim's story illustrates the death of "the self" that I speak of. And yes, it can also lead to death of the body.

Rather than ending this Chapter on such a sad note, let's look at someone who made a different choice.

Story Time

I had the good fortune of having a gentleman named Howard in one of my three-day workshops. Howard was fifty-four years old and came to my workshop because he thought it would help him with his career. Howard had been in the banking business for thirty years. He brought two of his employees with him, all three of whom had a great sense of humor and were looking forward to the three days.

When introducing himself to the group, Howard stated he had had a heart attack two months earlier. His doctor had told him he was addicted to working. He told us that he had worked since he was thirteen years old and felt work was good for everyone. He told his doctor he couldn't take time off work because they needed him. He did the best he could while in the hospital and worked at changing his diet, etc. but did not understand why he had to cut back from sixty hours a week at work. He had heard about HumanWisdom's workshops and had decided to come. We all welcomed him.

By the time we got to the fifth stage of the Five Stages of Illusion, Co-Creation in Despair, he was sharing that he understood what the doctor meant by him working sixty hours a week. Howard came to an agreement with the other members in the group that he would cut back to forty hours and would have to decide on a hobby to keep busy. Howard later told us that the big question in his mind was, "How could I have been abusing myself for so long and think it was normal?"

Howard was a gift to all of us. This was a man who had been close to death two months earlier and was now overjoyed at what he was learning about himself.

Hopefully, not all people who overwork, overeat, gamble, etc. require such a drastic event in their life to know something is wrong. A lot of us can learn from Howard by taking a look at our lifestyle earlier on in life.

It takes whatever it takes to wake up.

Help is available to assist you in gaining control of your life instead of spiraling down through these stages!

Chapter 8

YOUR DEFENSE SYSTEM

Nothing is good or bad, but thinking makes it so.
William Shakespeare

In Chapters 1 and 2, I explained how you and your Higher Power created your internal fight-or-flight behavior when you were young. We all have a fight-or-flight defense system—it's built into our human bodies. But do we all know what we've established internally as a result of having it? No. That's part of the invisible force that continues to keep us stuck in our lives.

Here's Steven K. Baum's, Ph.D. definition of defense mechanisms from his book *Growing Up at Any Age: How to Know when Adulthood Arrives*[4]

> "Emotional defense mechanisms may be the biggest wild card in determining who becomes an adult. Defenses are our protection against perceived threats. Although we don't have a complete understanding of defense mechanisms, we know that they help us maintain a sense of balance between what we can cope with and what we cannot, and that they enable us to manage stress and marshal resources against a particular problem. Some of us, however, create too many defenses and use them to disguise inner needs."

You might have created your defense system behavior from watching your parents and imitating the way they reacted to stress. At a young age, you figured out how to deal with your environment. You established a defense system—a way of dealing with stressful events and feeling safe in the big, wide world out there.

Any situation you perceive as dangerous will flag an automatic fight-or-flight response in your being. As a child, you perceived these as life or death situations. I believe a High Power gave us perfect internal systems to cope with life, including a defense system to keep us alive. I've heard stories from people that could easily inspire others to say, "This person has to be lying. No child could live through such abuse or such dangerous situations." Not true. The human spirit takes over in life-or-death situations and survives against great odds. Thanks to our connection with a Higher Power in these situations, we can learn how to keep ourselves alive in overwhelming life-or-death situations in our youth—even if we aren't aware of the connection. We somehow take action and live through the event. The strength to survive resides deep inside our body, mind, and soul. How else would a child who has little experience with the outside world know how to stay alive in an abusive or dangerous situation?

Later in life, when you are in a dangerous situation, you go into the automatic survival behavior. This defense system (the behavior you choose) gives you a sense of control, which allows you to cope with events that overwhelm you. You may have never been aware or seen your survival behavior before, but deep down you have knowledge of it. This keeps you alive. So the next time you perceive a stressful situation and think that what happened before could happen again (abuse or other dangerous situation), you're ready to enact your past survival behavior.

So how does your Higher Power come into all this? Well, the first time the abusive or dangerous event occurs it is my belief that you go deep inside and connect with your soul in an effort to stay alive. The connection between you and your Higher Power creates the behavior that enables you to survive through the painful situation. This creates the patterning. Remember the concept of automatic pilot? It means that in any given stressful situation, you react the way you're patterned to react. As you get older, however, this same automatic behavior that helped you as a child can and will work against you. It keeps you in the past, not the present (which is regression, as you learned from doing the Environment activity).

Once a behavior has sunk into your subconscious mind, you tend to repeat that behavior without realizing it. For example, if you want to stop yelling, you may say to yourself over and over, "I'm not going to yell." But then something stressful happens and you automatically start yelling again. This same behavior can spill over into your relationships, workplace, and family, causing great damage.

> *Your defense system is a large part of you, an invisible force of energy you're working against when you want to apply new behaviors.*
>
> *Defense systems aren't bad. They helped give you a sense of safety when you were young. You don't want to throw away your defense system or any other part of yourself. You only want to bring it to your conscious mind, so you can make clear choices about whether to put defense mechanisms into action or not.*

When you become conscious of your defense system, you'll be rewarded with more control over yourself and a higher tolerance for stressful situations. Along with that, you'll be closer to your spiritual self as you develop a close relationship with who you really are.

When I look at other self-help or counseling programs designed to assist people in growing and maturing, I find the subject of "behavior" to be too generalized. These methods take time and usually result in someone pointing out your defense system. I don't believe this is effective. You are capable of self-discovering your own unique defense systems if given a choice. This leaves you in control. *You are the expert on you.*

Initially, you may recognize only a few of your defenses, but the more often you look at your list, the more you'll recognize. Let's suppose you've learned some things at a self-growth workshop and you know how you want to behave and the goals you want to achieve. Why can't you accomplish them? The answer to this question lies in how your emotional, mental, spiritual, and physical components work together internally. Part of this profile is your defense system, which you'll identify at the end of this chapter by doing an activity.

The more you know about your defense system, the more control you'll have over the choices in your life and the decisions you make. There are only two emotions connected with our defense system: fight (anger) and flight (fear). *Your automatic defenses bypass the rational mind when you perceive danger.* Once you are in defense mode, everything is exaggerated and distorted. You then go from crisis to crisis in your life.

In looking at other self-help or counseling programs, I found these methods take time and usually result in the new behaviors not holding after 35 to 45 days. If all self awareness comes from within through self-discovery, then you can have permanent changes from within. This leaves you in control. You're the expert on you.

I'd like to say it's easy to identify when you're feeling fear or anger, but it isn't. Why? Because throughout our childhood we learned to pile other emotions on top of our anger and fear. So it becomes like a mystery novel, researching the system we've created. Fortunately, the mystery can be solved!

Let's look at an example of how the fight-or-flight responses of anger and fear are formed.

As a child, a situation occurs that you perceive as "life or death." Let's say that due to some event, you no longer feel safe around a particular adult. This triggers a fight-or-flight response in you. First you feel angry and you want to fight the adult in front of you. You decide this is not a good idea because the adult is bigger than you, so your next response is flight (fear) You think about running away but decide this isn't a good choice either because there's nowhere to run. So now your body has recorded anger, stuffed it, then recorded fear and stuffed that. There has to be a third choice if you're going to survive: whatever this adult will accept from you. It could be smiling, acting happy, crying, or acting sad. So you pretend to be happy, for example, and keep down your defense system emotions of anger and fear. Now "happy" becomes programmed into your subconscious mind and will be automatically activated all throughout your life when this button is pressed. You're unaware that every time you do this automatically, you're affecting your body, mind, and spirit. (Failure to identify buried fight-or-flight responses can overwhelm our body, mind, and spirit.)

In past stories you learned what emotions will work to get what you want when you're two years old. Well, the truth is you don't stop at the age of two. You continue throughout your life, trying out different emotions and behaviors to see which one will give you what you want at that time. For example, let's say you're ten years old and your parents said they would take you to see a movie. You're told that tomorrow will be the day all of you are going, but guess what? You want to go right now, or at least in a few hours. Your parents say no. You scream and they say no. You cry and they still say no. Well, since the first two emotions and behaviors didn't work, you try another approach. You become "the victim" and tell your parents how all the other kids have seen the movie already and you're the only one in your class who hasn't seen the movie. Your parents give in and take you to the movie. You now know what works—at least with your parents.

> *Develop your own internal observer. Start by monitoring yourself. As an observer, you can learn how to identify what emotions and thoughts go with a particular behavior. This is the core of change, which comes from within you. Changes that come from within are more likely to become permanent.*

This is a good example of how each of us experiments with different emotions and behaviors when we are young to see which one gives us what we want at the time. It's amazing how we carry these behaviors into adulthood in our subconscious mind and then act off them. We don't normally address "instant gratification" in our childhood, so we carry it into adulthood.

To help you identify how you react under stress, I have put together a list of some of our normal responses to perceived stressful situations.

Fight: Anger-Driven Defense

Anger: Yell, scream, and threaten

Sarcasm: Use a form of wit marked by the use of sarcastic language intended to make its victim the butt of contempt or ridicule. Instead of telling others you're angry about the way they treated you, you make a joke to put them down. If they say anything about the put-down, you tell them you were only kidding.

Defying: Do the opposite of what someone suggested just to let him/her know you don't do what anyone says. Exhibit bold resistance to an opposing force or authority.

Blame: Take no responsibility for a situation. Instead, you find someone or something to blame for the results you get.

Judging: Behind words, your attitude lets other people know that whatever it is, they did it wrong. If they'd done it differently, then everything would be okay. You give an opinion with an attitude behind it.

Projecting: Project attitudes, feelings, or desires to someone else as a unconscious defense against anxiety or guilt. Tell others what they're doing wrong, while you're doing the behavior you're accusing them of doing.

Rationalizing: Devise self-satisfying but incorrect reasons for behavior. Give justification for everything that happens.

Intellectualizing: Don't want to gain any insight into an emotional problem. Instead, you use intelligence to provide an intellectual analysis of any given situation. Lecture without emotion and give all the intellectual reasons for the behavior. Don't connect with emotions and aren't able to identify them.

Resenting: Continue to hold a grudge against someone or something. Harbor a feeling of deep and bitter anger and ill will.

Raging: Act out all anger from the past by yelling, throwing things, calling others names, hitting, etc.

Flight: Fear-Driven Defense

Distancing: Move away from another person emotionally, mentally, and spiritually, even if not physically walking away.

Dismissing: Walk away and ignore what others are saying.

Detaching: In the mind, emotionally separate from the situation at hand. Separate, disunite, disengage, and sever.

Denying: Keep doing the same things while wanting different results. Refuse to face a situation that's painful. Avoid reality, and refuse to believe, recognize, or acknowledge. Reject.

Avoiding: Don't address something that's happened. Will do anything to avoid a situation.

Victimization: Have a "poor me" belief that perpetually makes you see yourself as a victim of circumstance.

Martyrdom: Continue to support others who don't support you. Knowing you'll be abused, you keep going back for more.

Pretending: Live in a dream world and pretend everything is okay. Even when told a situation is negative, you continue to pretend it's the way you want it to be.

Weeping: Instead of identifying fears and other emotions, you cry.

Laughing: Laugh when you want to cry or when you're angry.

Smiling: No matter how you really feel, you smile through everything.

Fainting: The brain doesn't get enough oxygen due to holding your breath or dizziness from not being able to handle the reality of a situation. You pass out.

Shutting down: Shut down your body, mind, and spirit, and yet don't move away physically from a situation.

Forgetting: You feel safer during those times you don't remember because you've pushed the facts to the back of your mind.

Depression: Have a lot of inverted anger about certain situations in your life and don't express it. Your angry emotions take you into a depressed state of mind.

Complying: Never disagree and always complain.

Fantasizing: Live in a world that's far removed from reality. Spend a lot of time daydreaming.

Suppressing: Keep your feelings from being revealed, even to yourself.

Disassociating: Disassociate yourself from a given situation. You aren't "present" at all.

Insulating: Isolate yourself to keep from feeling emotions.

Grandiosity: Think and talk about great things you can do, but most of the time they're unreachable goals.

Shame: Experience of this painful emotion caused by a strong sense of guilt, embarrassment, unworthiness, or disgrace. You may use this emotion to cover most of your other emotions.

Silence: Don't talk when someone disagrees with you or tries to express a difference of opinion. Would rather stay silent than disagree with someone.

Compensating: Compensate for others' feelings of stress, often trying to calm people down, feed them, care for them, etc. Adjust or make up for others' problems while avoiding your own.

Verbosity: The more nervous you get in a situation, the more you talk. The more you talk, the less you actually say. People make excuses and walk away while you're still talking. You keep talking even while your mind is saying, "Be quiet." Talking has become a defense system.

Sadness: You put sadness on top of any stressful situation, even though you may have other emotions going on. You feel safest when you're sad.

Pain: Use emotional, mental, or physical pain as a way of blocking out a situation.

Fear is a crucial emotion we need for survival. But when fear is continually cycled in the human body, it can cause a series of problems. Similarly, anger expressed appropriately is useful—you need to be able to express how you feel. But constant anger and/or fear can also cause a series of physical problems.

Consequences of Fear or Anger

- Anxiety
- Autoimmune problems
- Autonomic nervous system problems
- Depression
- Edginess
- Glandular damage (adrenal glands)
- Headaches
- Isolation from others

- Racing thoughts
- Accelerated respiration
- Constricting blood vessels
- Fine motor skills deterioration
- Altered state of perception
- Distorted perception of time
- Tunnel vision
- Hearing and vision problems
- Feelings of sleep-walking
- Memory loss
- Exhaustion
- Confusion
- Muscle spasms, trembling of limbs
- Panic attacks
- Passive-aggressive behavior
- Phobias, fear of fears (Examples: inability to leave the house, constantly washing the hands, fear of socializing, fear of driving, flying, etc.). The person has no control over the fear and may feel he/she will die if they don't give in to the compulsion.
- Rapid heart rate
- Release of dopamine (puts your muscles on alert)
- Rise in blood pressure
- Shallow breathing or holding the breath
- Startled easily
- Staying frozen in movement
- Thoughts canceled out in the brain
- Painful tightening of muscles around neck and shoulders
- Tightness in gut
- Stomach problems
- Other physical problems that come and go during stressful times
- Sweating

Do you see how a fight and/or flight response can affect the aging process?

> *Stress is not the issue; it is how you perceive and respond to stress that causes problems in health and aging.*

Here's what Ellissa S. Epel, Ph.D[5]., a professor of psychiatry at the University of California at San Francisco (UCSF) has to say about stress:

> "People who are stressed over long periods tend to look haggard,
> and it is commonly thought that psychological stress leads to
> premature aging and other ...diseases of aging."

Numerous studies have shown that stress is related to poor health, heart disease, and a compromised immune system. Dr. Epel researched chronic stress with fifty-eight healthy mothers. Some had healthy children and some were "care-giving mothers" of a chronically ill child. The main factor in this study was how these mothers perceived stress and how the stress affected them. The results demonstrated that care-giving mothers had higher stress levels than did mothers of healthy children.

I'm sure you have your own list of what happens to you under stress. Your goal should be to readjust your system so it's in balance. As internal balance takes over, many of these symptoms will gradually disappear. And the amazing thing, the miracle of it all, is that your perception of what you call stress will change!

Everyone walking this earth has a defense system.
If you exist in a physical body, you have a defense system.

You Are the Observer

As you continue with this system and discover many parts of you, you'll start looking at yourself more objectively. You'll become more excited about the discovery process because you'll be able to choose what to change. You'll be able to observe your life as if it were a movie.

Simple Guidelines to Be a Good Observer

- Observe all aspects of your physical, emotional, mental, and spiritual components without judgment;
- If you find that you're judging yourself, don't judge the "judger" part of you;
- If you do judge a part of you, accept it and move on;
- As you create your inner observer, you'll notice your awareness level increasing with all four of your human components;
- Most important, keep your sense of humor through all of this!

You've done a great job of self-discovering so far. Give yourself a pat on the back! Relax, and reward yourself with something positive!

Now let's perform an activity to help you discover your own unique defense system.

> *The ability to achieve balance doesn't depend on your age, sex, race, culture, occupation, level of education, religion, addiction, and so on. Rather, it depends on your commitment to practice being aware of what you're thinking, feeling, and doing. Most important, it depends on connecting with your Higher Power belief system.*

Activity: Discovering Your Defense System

Figures 8.1, 8.2, 8.3 and 8.4 relate to this activity.

In this activity, you will uncover how your fight-or-flight responses were patterned in your youth when your environments didn't feel safe or when you perceived danger. You adapted different responses until you found one that made you feel internally safe (not necessarily physically safe). It may have been a false sense of safety, but it felt real to you at the time. After your emotional, mental, spiritual, and physical patterns were created, they became automatic and remained that way. When you begin the self discovery process, you will be able to see your defense patterns. Only then will you have choices of what to change.

Step 1: Check Defenses That Apply to You

1. Look at the list of defenses (Figure 8.1) under the category headings "Fight" and "Flight."
2. Check all the items that apply to you.

See example in Figure 8.2.

Step 2: Write Down Your Top Ten Defenses

1. In the area marked My Defense System in Figure 8.1, write down the top ten defenses from the items you checked in Step 1 that you employ the most.
2. Put them in order of importance.

See example in Figure 8.2.

Step 3: Consequences of Defenses

1. Choose five to seven defenses from the top ten and list them under the Defense column in Consequences of Defenses in Figure 8.3.

2. In the remaining columns of Figure 8.3, list the consequences you've experienced as a result of each defense behavior.

See example in Figure 8.4.

DEFENSE SHEET

FIGHT   total:____   *FLIGHT*   total:____

- ☐ Anger
- ☐ Blaming
- ☐ Defiance
- ☐ Dismissing
- ☐ Judging
- ☐ Intellectualizing
- ☐ Projecting
- ☐ Raging
- ☐ Rationalizing
- ☐ Resenting
- ☐ Sarcasm

- ☐ Avoiding
- ☐ Can't Remember
- ☐ Compliance
- ☐ Compensating
- ☐ Denial
- ☐ Depression
- ☐ Detaching
- ☐ Disassociating
- ☐ Distancing
- ☐ Fainting
- ☐ Fantasizing
- ☐ Grandiosity
- ☐ Insulation

- ☐ Laughing
- ☐ Martyr
- ☐ Pain
- ☐ Pretending
- ☐ Sad
- ☐ Shame
- ☐ Shutting down
- ☐ Silence
- ☐ Smiling
- ☐ Suppression
- ☐ Talking
- ☐ Victim
- ☐ Weeping

MY DEFENSE SYSTEM

1. _____
2. _____
3. _____
4. _____
5. _____
6. _____
7. _____
8. _____
9. _____
10. _____

EXAMPLE
DEFENSE SHEET

FIGHT   total: 6

- ☒ Anger
- ☒ Blaming
- ☐ Defiance
- ☐ Dismissing
- ☒ Judging
- ☐ Intellectualizing
- ☒ Projecting
- ☐ Raging
- ☐ Rationalizing
- ☒ Resenting
- ☒ Sarcasm

FLIGHT   total: 4

- ☒ Avoiding
- ☐ Can't Remember
- ☐ Compliance
- ☐ Compensating
- ☐ Denial
- ☐ Depression
- ☐ Detaching
- ☐ Disassociating
- ☐ Distancing
- ☐ Fainting
- ☐ Fantasizing
- ☐ Grandiosity
- ☐ Insulation

- ☐ Laughing
- ☐ Martyr
- ☐ Pain
- ☐ Pretending
- ☐ Sad
- ☒ Shame
- ☐ Shutting down
- ☒ Silence
- ☐ Smiling
- ☐ Suppression
- ☐ Talking
- ☒ Victim
- ☐ Weeping

MY DEFENSE SYSTEM

1.	Anger	6.	Resenting
2.	Blaming	7.	Avoiding
3.	Judging	8.	Shame
4.	Projecting	9.	Silence
5.	Sarcasm	10.	Victim

Figure 8.2 ~ Example: Defense Sheet   *The Power Model System™ | Copyright © 2007 – HumanWisdom LLC*

CONSEQUENCES OF DEFENSES

Defense	Emotional Result	Mental Result	Spiritual Result	Physical Result

Figure 8.3 ~ Consequences of Defenses   *The Power Model System™ | Copyright © 2004 – HumanWisdom LLC*

EXAMPLE
CONSEQUENCES OF DEFENSES

Defense	Emotional Result	Mental Result	Spiritual Result	Physical Result
Avoid	I felt shame from avoiding subjects.	I worry and have constant stress.	I feel numb	Headaches, body aches, shaking. Lasts for at least 30 minutes.
Judge	When pointed out to me, I rage.	I have to go over and over it in my mind. Fear sets in.	I feel separated from my Higher Power.	Upset stomach.
Sarcasm	Anger at myself when I hear my words.	I keep trying to tell myself it was a joke until my head hurts.	I feel shame and separated from my Higher Power.	My head hurts, and I feel stressed.

Step 4: Which One Are You?

1. Go back and look at Figure 8.1, Step 1. In what category do you belong, Fight or Flight? Go down the list of defenses under *fight* and add them up. Now go down the list of defenses under *flight* and add them up. Write the total for each category next to the title of Fight or Flight. Then circle Fight or Flight, depending on which one has the largest total.
2. Fight is driven by anger, so if you've marked more boxes in the Fight category, examine your anger issues and note that you've developed a defense system around anger.
3. If you marked most of your defenses in the fear-driven Flight area, look at your issues of fear.

Quick Review

So far you have self-discovered the following:

- How events stemming from your past continue to cause problems in your present life and leave you at the mercy of your environment;
- How your four components (emotional, mental, physical, and spiritual) are interacting internally to cause certain internal situations in the present for you;
- How you can go on automatic pilot in your life without a second thought;
- How you can stay in illusion in your life without knowing you're doing so;
- How addiction plays a part in your life;
- How your personal defense system serves and/or hinders you;
- How coping skills developed when you were young are acted out in your life today;
- How effortless it is to fall into the 3 Rs (Resistance, Resentment, and Revenge) with yourself and others.

> *Bathe in the center of sound, as in the continuous sound of a waterfall.*
> *Or, by putting fingers in the ears, hear the sound of sounds.*

Looking at yourself at such a deep level is difficult and takes courage and a lot of love and patience, so keep going slowly through the activities. Stay in the present with your process, rather than focus on future results.

Chapter 9

REALITY CHECK

Joy isn't the absence of pain; it's the presence of God
    Thackeray

As I've said many times, we often get stuck in life and can't seem to move forward. Each of us gets stuck in different ways in one or more of our human components. Part of getting back into reality is finding out where and how you are stuck.

Have you ever wondered why at times it doesn't work when you try to change your behavior, feelings, or perception? To change your *outward* behavior (physical component) you also need to change your three other human components (emotional, mental, and spiritual).

Look at each component in the Feeling, Thinking, Behavior Chart in Figure 9.1. This chart shows how the emotional, mental, spiritual, and physical are parts of the whole and work together. If any one of these is neglected there will always be a void in the whole, in you. *The four components must be working together for us to create permanent changes within.*

You are already a spiritual human being. You are already everything you want to be.
All you have to do is self-discover Reality

Getting Stuck in the Feeling Component

Have you ever tried to change a certain emotional reaction but soon reverted to your old behavior and then felt guilt or shame? What do you suspect happened? Did you believe you hadn't worked hard enough to control your anger (or whatever emotion you felt)? Did you not take your commitment seriously?

In all likelihood, you did work hard to control your anger and you did take your commitment seriously. But because you were unaware of how your defense system worked, you used one or more emotions as a defense. This is a normal reaction.

As you work with The Power Model System™ and continue to gain self awareness about your internal system, you'll learn how to exercise "impulse control." Impulse control is when you think about your response with good intention, before you actually respond, rather than responding automatically.

Story Time

When Susan came to one of my workshops, she let the group know that her sister had gone through the Power Model System™ System four months previously and that she had noticed a big change in her. Because of this, she decided to try it.

Although Susan was forty-two years old, she looked more like twenty-nine. She was friendly, talkative, and dove right into the workshop material. During the workshop she shared the following with the group:

"I had been trying and trying to further my career and could not figure out why I was not climbing the ladder in my company. Well now I know; I have been told I wear my feelings on my sleeve, but I never realized how unproductive that was in my life until now. I now realize that my reaction to stressful life situations was to emote."

Susan decided to come and see me privately for a few sessions. In our first private session, she wanted to address the issue of why she is so emotional in her personal and professional life.

"I have no control over my emotions; they take me over," Susan said.

Susan shared how she is unable to identity her feelings until they take her over in any given situation. She stated she gets worn out physically, emotionally, mentally and spiritually. She no longer felt as connected to God as she used to be. Susan and I used various activities from the Power Model System, including *impulse control* to teach her how to identify her emotions and practice the Five Steps to Centeredness.

One day Susan said, "I am now doing the Five Steps to Maturity. Wow!" She saw that she was maturing and learning not to react to situations but instead look at her choices and make her decisions with the help of her Higher Power, which she called God.

Getting Stuck in the Thinking Component

Now let's consider the "thinking" part of you. This is where your belief system resides. Have you ever tried to change what you think of yourself by writing down statements (affirmations) on pieces of paper and placing them around the house? If so, did you wonder why it didn't work as well as you hoped? When you wanted to adopt a new belief system, how long did it take to construct it, and how long did it "hold" for you? How much energy does it take to keep telling yourself the same thing over and over again? How much effort does it take to quiet your mind from the old "tapes" in your head?

Your attempts to change your thinking by re-patterning your brain can be successful, but first you have to identify your fight-or-flight behavior. Only then can you make a conscious choice and quiet the mind. But how you do this without getting exhausted and burning out is the million-dollar question!

You may be thinking, *if it's more difficult on the mind and body to stay centered than to engage in fight-or-flight responses, is it worth wasting energy trying to change?* Staying centered doesn't come naturally, so it can be exhausting. In addition, you'll need to reap rewards along the way to continue moving through the changes. (If changing is viewed as "all work and no gain," people generally aren't self-empowered enough to succeed.)

Instead of thinking how difficult changing is, why not consider what it would be like to "have it all"—to not be afraid of reverting. The Power Model System™ will show you how to "have it all." You'll know how to re-pattern your brain, change your perception of yourself and others, and maintain this success the rest of your life!

Story Time

I think and so I am!

I remember meeting Sam in a workshop. He was twenty-two years old, had lots of energy, a great smile, and did not talk much. However, Sam did let all of us know that he was a thinker; if anyone had a problem, he had the solution!

I asked Sam if he knew his IQ, and he said all he knew was that it was high. He was an engineer and loved it. He did very well financially. His problem area was relationships. As the workshop went on, he let his small group know that getting into a relationship was not a problem, but after six months, it was over. The girls were nice about it but said he just was not their type. As we went through the Feeling, Thinking, Behavior Chart, Sam yelled out, "I got it!" As we went further into our discussion, others in the workshop understood what Sam was saying. He had discovered, as he gathered The Power Model System™ information, that he put everything through a thought process. He didn't connect with his emotions or spiritual beliefs at all. What was so surprising to him was that when he was in a relationship, he solved all his partners' issues. He remembered over and over being so impatient with his partners because they did not follow his advice. After all, he had thought it all out for them. "Wow!" he said. "I wonder how they must have felt with me doing all their thinking."

Sam went on to learn a lot about himself in the next few days, but this remained his big "Wow!"

I asked him to stay in touch, which he did for about one year. In the last note I received from him, he said that he was in a relationship and that he was not going to think for both of them. He also was in the process of showing her The Power Model System™ workbook that he kept.

Getting Stuck in Your Physical Component (Behavior)

Next, consider the Behavior part of you, where physical action resides. As I mentioned before, I suspect you've tried to change your physical behavior and within forty-five to ninety days reverted to your old behavior (or you didn't integrate your new behavior within you like you wanted). For example, you promised your partner that you'd change your physical behavior. The desired change held for a while, but then you slipped back into your past behavior. Why didn't the change hold? You believed that if you kept practicing, you'd change your life, but at some point the new physical behavior faded away and you reverted back to your old reactive behavior.

In doing the Environment activity, you learned that your environment pushes the buttons of your unresolved issues and the emotions connected with them. When that happens, you feel you're at the mercy of your environment. Events trigger unresolved issues you're unaware of and you regress back to the age when a similar event happened. (This is "going on autopilot," which was discussed in Chapter 6.)

You want to be different and have tried method after method, but something is always missing. Every time you revert back to your old behavior, you're more stuck in your illusions. You find that you use more energy to stay where you are, leading to symptoms and consequences (like those listed earlier) that stress your system. The cycle continues. The four human components—emotional, mental, spiritual, and physical— become accustomed to working *against* each other. Staying in an illusive state becomes reinforced within you.

Story Time

Meet Janice, a thirty-two-year old runner who loves sports. She was having a communication problem with her thirteen-year-old daughter, so she thought she would do The Power Model System™ workshop to learn better communication skills. Janice was extremely quiet, took a lot of notes, and listened all through the first day. As Janice was leaving at the end of the first day, she walked up to me and let me know what the "big bang" for her was. She said, "I take great pride in my running ability and sports. Whenever I get upset with my daughter, I just leave and go running. I feel much better when I get back. Today, I got that nothing has been solved with me and my daughter. I just feel better after running. Now I know why the same issues keep coming up—we never solve them. I come home after running feeling relaxed and figure everything should be okay. I am going to go home tonight and let her know what I learned about myself and that in the future, I will sit down and talk out the issue with her after running." She was smiling as she walked out of the room.

The next day, Janice shared with the whole group her awareness of how she'd let her physical component carry all her stress and the results of telling her daughter. She said her daughter let her know that she herself could not figure out what was going on. All she knew was that her mother left every time they fought and came back calm and happy. They had never talked about the issue.

Janice did give me a short phone call two weeks after the workshop to let me know the new method was working. She also said she was able to talk about her emotions with her daughter and not get upset.

Janice's situation is a good example of how the physical component can dominate the other three human components.

What is the secret in creating true change in the areas of emotions, thinking, behaving, and reality itself?

Being told how I should behave, think, and feel only puts me out in the world as an actor. To be authentic, change has to come from within.

FEELING, THOUGHTS, BEHAVIOR CHART

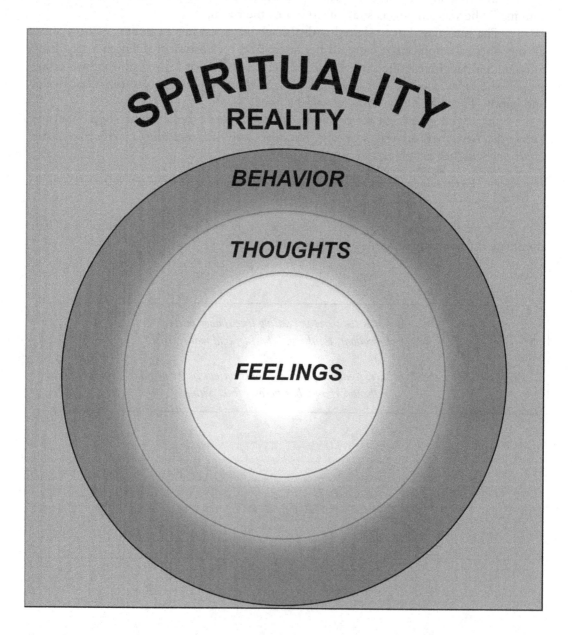

Spirituality is gained through the flexibility and harmonious interaction of your feeling, thoughts, and behavior.

Figure 9.1 ~ Feeling, Thinking, Behavior Chart   *The Power Model System™ | Copyright © 2007 – HumanWisdom LLC*

Chapter 10

THE PYRAMID OF SUCCESS

Although each of us obviously inhabits a separate physical body, the laboratory data from a hundred years of parapsychology research strongly indicates that there is no separation in consciousness.
Russell Targ

The Pyramid of Success (Figure 10.1) is an all-encompassing visual informational tool of The Power Model System™. At a glance, you can see what you may need to refer back to in The Power Model System™ or what activity you may need to repeat.

The Pyramid of Success assists you in determining where you might be in your growth process. You can use it to see where you're stuck at different times of your life and in different situations. You can also use it to see where you're growing and becoming your "authentic self." Many HumanWisdom workshop participants hang The Pyramid of Success chart in their office, bedroom, and/or study room because it helps them at a glance. If they are frustrated and are having a difficult time figuring out what level they're at or where they're stuck, they can simply review the chart.

Note how power extends from the bottom of the pyramid to the top. The question is, is your power being expended or acquired? If part of your life resides at the pyramid's bottom, then your power is being expended by resistance, resentment, and revenge. If you raise yourself up to the next level, then your power is acquired through commitment, self-empowerment, and pro-action. This leads to the next level of self-discovery through awareness, acceptance, and real action. Only after reaching the peak level can you achieve your true desired results and spiritual power.

When locating where you are on the Pyramid of Success, be easy on yourself. Traveling straight up a mountain is almost never done, even by the most rugged mountain climbers. Instead, travel up the pyramid on a winding road. For example, you may be starting at the bottom right stage of feeling vengeful. From there it is much more productive to travel left than straight up, as this path will give you an understanding of what resentments brought you to this stage. Only through this understanding of your illusionary state can you travel up to the next level and have the balance and stamina to stay there. Then you can prepare for the higher levels that will ultimately lead you to your goals.

The 3 A's

As you climb up the pyramid you will notice the decisive difference between experiencing Illusions versus Reality is whether you go through the 3 R's or the 3 A's. If you are in Reality, you have progressed from the 3 Rs to the 3 A's, *Awareness* (with Emotional Power), *Acceptance* (with Mental Power) and *Action* (with Physical Power). These are the polar opposites of the 3 Rs of Resistance, Resentment, and Revenge. The 3 Rs disempower you (dismember you from within) while the 3 A's empower you (center you from within). With the 3 A's, you respond to life using your strengths and acquired wisdom, rather than being on automatic pilot and reacting from your defense system.

Now let's take a look at the Pyramid of Success and see how your Power can be acquired in Reality or lost in Illusion through each of your human components.

Emotional Power

Private Self: This is the emotional, private part of you. Only you know how you feel emotionally. This is where your childhood issues reside. This is the first place you need to explore to find out who you really are. This is the part of you that, if not explored, can lead you into believing you have control over others and keep you in resistance of exploring your *private emotional self.*

Illusion (Level 4)

Resistance and Control: This is the beginning of the 3 Rs, resistance to change. If you stay at this level, you resist looking at yourself and how you participate in creating what's in your life. At this level, you may become sick and tired of being sick and tired of the results in your life. This is when most people start to look at themselves.

Reality (Levels 1-3)

Awareness and Commitment: Emotional awareness leads to reality. You begin handling your emotions appropriately. You become aware of how this one human component of emotions can play a role in your spiritual connection. This is where you become committed to real honesty and growth.

You begin addressing, owning, and identifying your cover-up and authentic emotions.

Mental Power

Personal Self: This is the part of you regarding your personal mental thoughts. Until you become aware of your thought processes, you'll be dependent on others to think for you. This is because you won't trust your *personal mental self.*

Illusion (Level 4)

Resentful and Dependency: Here you're dependent on others to think for you, yet you resent them for telling you how you should think. At this level, you refuse to accept the responsibility for your own *personal* thoughts and resentment.

Reality (Levels 1-3)

Acceptance and Self Empowerment: This is where you practice impulse control, identify your internal/external boundaries, and discover healthy ego strength. You also begin to identify your defense system behavior, how you justify this behavior, and then make a choice whether or not to stay on autopilot.

You now accept that it's okay to have been where you were and to be where you are in your growth process. You also start forgiving yourself for resisting learning about yourself and resenting others and yourself. You learn that there are great rewards in simply letting go. This is the wonderful place of forgiveness, forgiving you, and forgiving others.

This is the turnaround level, the level of self-empowerment. This is the place that will impress you about yourself. Your perceptions of yourself and the world will continuously improve. With this knowledge, you can change yourself. You can move forward and take action to recreate your authentic self.

Physical Power

Professional Self: This is the behavioral part of you—how you treat yourself and others; how you respond or react to events in your life. Often your behavior will be radically different at home and at work. By this I mean you may act out at home but not at work. You convince yourself that the problem is not with you but with someone at home. This deepens your illusionary state of being *professional* in the world.

Illusion (Level 4)

Revengeful and Reactive: When in a vengeful mood, you *react externally* to situations in your life instead of being proactive. You're into addictive behavior. This is how you exercise revenge on yourself for not being all you think you should be.

Reality (Levels 1-3)

Action and being Proactive: Here is where you become proactive in your life. You start reaching out to people who are supportive of the changes within you and who are changing themselves. You are able to let them assist you in a supportive manner as you move towards maturity. You physically address your addictions and learn more about their effect on you. You start taking good care of yourself physically with good food, enough sleep, and play.

Since your perceptions have already started changing due to all you have learned about yourself, you find much of your reactive behavior falling away. Your maturity begins to show itself. You become action-focused with full awareness of what you are doing and why.

Spiritual Power

Only by having the 3 A's entrenched in your daily life can you finally move into your own spiritual domain, which takes you to the highest Level. At Level 1, you approach everything in your life from a centered, spiritual perspective. Being centered, you are able to connect with your Higher Power. With this consistency in your life, you can now attract the desired results in your life.

Desired Results

As your emotional, mental, and physical power work harmoniously together, you attain true power to achieve your desired results. You move toward your desired spiritual goals and become one with them instead of fighting against them.

Now let's see how to use the Pyramid of Success through an activity.

Activity: Pyramid of Success

Monitoring Your Growth by Using the Pyramid of Success

Figures 10.1 and 10.2 relate to this activity.

1. At the top-right side of the pyramid (Level 1) in Figure 10.1, write one goal you want to reach in your life.

   See example in Figure 10.2 for reference.

   Goal Examples:

   - Finish this book;
   - Take a workshop to further your self-knowledge;
   - Check the local community college for classes available on self-improvement;
   - Make an appointment with a therapist;
   - Call a friend to discuss a problem;
   - Go to a meeting for an addiction you may have;
   - Perform a search on the internet for needed information;
   - Contact someone who will give you honest feedback;
   - Look back over some of the activities you have done, and perform them again to find out more about yourself and how much you have learned already;
   - Learn how to laugh at yourself and maintain your sense of humor;
   - Recognize what you want to change.

2. Start at the bottom of the pyramid, slowly move along (left to right) and up each level, and circle where you are now, emotionally, mentally, and physically, in relation to the goal you have identified in Step 1 of this activity.

   Example: Look at Level 4 of the pyramid and circle where you are in achieving your goal. Are you in *resistance* of trying to achieve this goal? Are you *resentful* that you need to achieve it at all? Are you acting out on yourself or others (*revengeful*)?

3. Now you know your current status. Look at what you have circled in Level 4 and go directly up to Level 3. Circle one or more items what it is going to take for you to get un-stuck.

Example: You might have circled *resistance* about having to achieve this goal. That would mean you need to *commit* to learning to identify your emotions.

4. Now go to Level 2 and see what you need to do to continue on your journey to your goal.

    Example: Now that you have become *aware* of your feelings, the next step is *acceptance*. You'll need to perform self-empowerment activities to achieve *acceptance* towards yourself and your goal.

5. Now take action on what you have circled on Level 3. Resolve to be pro-active and commit to succeed regardless of difficulties. On the right at Level 2, write down the most important action you need to take. Often, life will test you to see if you are serious. This will only strengthen you. If you choose to press on despite unexpected challenges, you will acquire wisdom.

    Example: You may take a college course.

6. Going from Level 4 to 2 will inspire you. Without action, there is no success. Fear of the unknown is normal, but don't let it stop you from taking action. Desire, commitment, and action are all necessary to remove the stumbling blocks in our lives. Remember, rewards will come only when we take *action*.

<u>Example (Figure 10.2)</u>

I will use someone named Mike for the following example:

1. Mike's desired spiritual result is to be aware of his life purpose.
2. He looks at the pyramid levels and sees that he is at Level 1 in the resentful stage. He blames his parents for his situation.
3. He looks further along the pyramid path and realizes he is dependent on his parents and resents it. He knows that he can't get in touch with his life purpose as long as he is resistant and resentful.
4. He starts exploring his emotions.
    a. Emotional:
        *   The fear of exploring the unknown and not knowing the results.
        *   Identifying feelings. Not being able to control others. Wanting to resist exploring.

    b.   Mental:
- Fear brings resentment because he never learned to take risks.
- He starts learning what is blocking him. His Defense System.

    c.   Physical:
- He reaches out to a support group that can assist him.

    d.   Spiritual:
- He connects with his Higher Power and stays on his journey of reaching his goal.

5. He has his chart. He now takes positive action.
    a.   He moves from resistance to awareness.
    b.   He studies his defense system and learns which defensive behavior is blocking him.
    c.   He finds a group of individuals who can assist him in exploring his life purpose.

This is difficult, but there is no turning back. You will succeed in finding your sense of self and purpose.

How does one achieve all this?

Challenging yourself takes courage, strength, and faith. The road to any achievement can be thwarted by your defense systems and over reactive emotions. But you don't always have the tools to get through your defenses and become aware of your true feelings and respond to them appropriately at any given moment. The rest of this book will give you those tools; and when applied will lead you towards a true sense of self. With a true sense of self, all your challenges become easier and you no longer waste energy battling yourself. You will climb up the pyramid of success faster and more easily than you thought possible.

PYRAMID OF SUCCESS

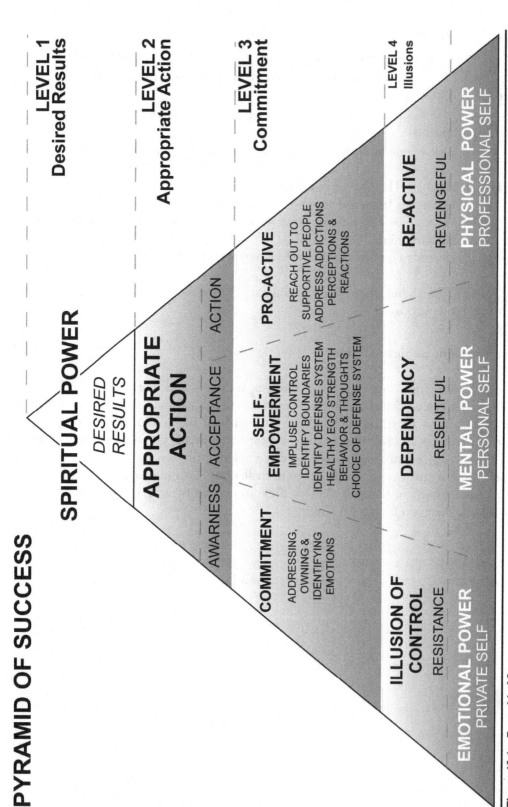

Figure 10.1 ~ Pyramid of Success

EXAMPLE
PYRAMID OF SUCCESS

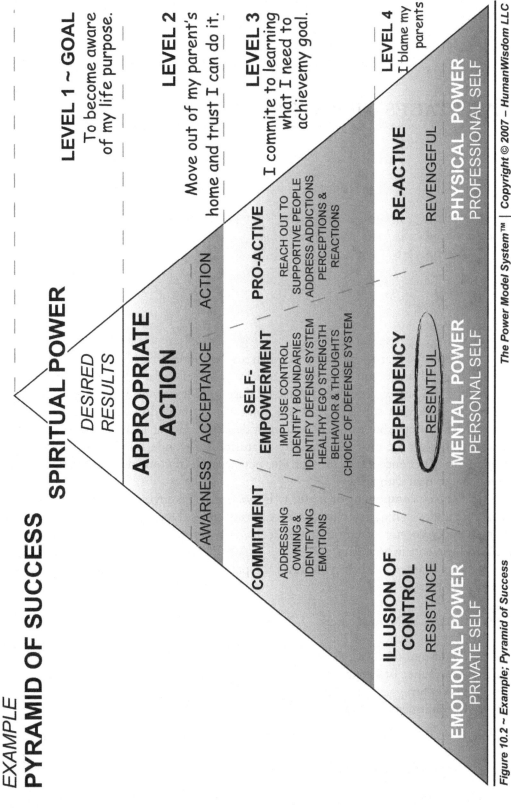

SPIRITUAL POWER

LEVEL 1 ~ GOAL
To become aware of my life purpose.

LEVEL 2
Move out of my parent's home and trust I can do it.

LEVEL 3
I commite to learning what I need to achievemy goal.

LEVEL 4
I blame my parents

DESIRED RESULTS

AWARNESS | ACCEPTANCE | ACTION

APPROPRIATE ACTION

COMMITMENT
ADDRESSING OWNING & IDENTIFYING EMCTIONS

SELF-EMPOWERMENT
IMPLUSE CONTROL
IDENTIFY BOUNDARIES
IDENTIFY DEFENSE SYSTEM
HEALTHY EGO STRENGTH
BEHAVIOR & THOUGHTS
CHOICE OF DEFENSE SYSTEM

PRO-ACTIVE
REACH OUT TO SUPPORTIVE PEOPLE
ADDRESS ADDICTIONS
PERCEPTIONS & REACTIONS

RE-ACTIVE
REVENGEFUL

PHYSICAL POWER
PROFESSIONAL SELF

DEPENDENCY
RESENTFUL

MENTAL POWER
PERSONAL SELF

ILLUSION OF CONTROL
RESISTANCE

EMOTIONAL POWER
PRIVATE SELF

Figure 10.2 ~ Example; Pyramid of Success

Chapter 11

FIVE STAGES OF MATURITY

If you understand, things are just as they are;
If you do not understand, things are just as they are.
     Zen proverb

"Reality" is far more satisfying than an "emotional high." True, an emotional high feels good while you're in it, but usually you feel awful when you come down, especially if the high was achieved while in illusion. Not only do you have a tired body but you're stuck with consequences you don't like. So how do you get out of illusion? The answer is simple but not easy: you must desire it. Having a true desire to get out of illusion will spark the onset of maturity. Maturity is a wonderful place to be. You will continue to experience stress in your life, but because of your maturity level, you'll be better able to deal with it.

The key component of maturity is *awareness*. This involves looking at life as an adventure and watching for clues to solve its mysteries. Doesn't that sound better than riding a roller coaster of emotion and feeling victimized with all the ups and downs dictated by events in your life?

This chapter will help you travel the path to maturity. Each step along the way will be your choice.

The Five Stages of Maturity are:

1. Honeymoon in Awareness
2. Acceptance of Reality
3. Power Struggle in Reality
4. Commitment to Higher Power
5. Co-Creation in Action

FIVE STAGES OF MATURITY

Honeymoon in Awareness

Acceptance of Reality

Power Struggle in Reality

Commitment to Higher Power

Co-Creation in Action

— *JOY* —

You will quickly notice that these stages are the polar opposites of the Five Stages of Illusion. In the Five stages of Maturity you learn the great importance of the 3 A's—Awareness, Acceptance, and Action.

Let's look at how we humans progress through these stages.

Stage 1: Honeymoon in Awareness

The Honeymoon Period is the early calm and harmony you experience when starting something new, for example, a relationship, job, hometown, etc. In this stage, you are learning many new things about yourself, others, or a new environment. Why are you learning? Because you choose to remain *aware* of what is going on inside you and around you. During this period, you have a tendency to act differently from who you really are. If you remain aware, you can keep this tendency in check and still be playful. You can choose to remain true to who you are and still discover joy in the new experience.

You are also aware of others. You are becoming aware of what you want in a relationship with yourself and others. You recognize this relationship for what it is. If you enjoy it, you stay on the path. If you don't enjoy it, you can choose to make changes. You are being mature by choosing to remain awake while life is happening. You don't halt your self-awareness journey just because you discover something you don't like about yourself or the experience.

Awareness Is a Choice

Without awareness (the first of the 3 A's), growth is impossible. In the Honeymoon Period, people have a tendency to sacrifice awareness for the sake of magical thinking.

In this Honeymoon, you'll recognize that there are things you don't want to look at, but you'll still do what you need to do to see them in reality. We are all human. The simple *thought* of not wanting to look at something is just a *thought*; you don't need to act it out and, thus, fall into illusion.

Awareness is a choice, which is why some people say, "I like keeping my head in the sand" or "What I don't know about myself won't hurt me." At some point in time, not knowing who you are *will* hurt you.

The Honeymoon Period is the stage where maturity comes into play. You want to be aware of your actions, your choices, and their positive or negative consequences. You're responsible for them and seek to learn as much as you can from them. You see your life full of opportunities, not problems, which is a huge perception shift from the illusion stage. You enjoy the Honeymoon periods in life for what they are, not for what you want them to be.

Story Time

I want to introduce you to Tena. She is thirty-five years old, has a great personality, and a smile that captures your heart. Tena had an anger problem and was convinced it was everyone else's fault. She did not like the results of her rages, but felt she would be okay if only others would change. When Tena became aware that her rages were affecting her second marriage, she wanted to change. She said, "This has gone on long enough." As she worked through the first stages of maturity, she became fully aware that her anger was her responsibility, not everyone else's. Her perceptions about her angry episodes changed. It became a game to see how soon she could catch herself getting angry. The more she practiced, the less reactive she became. She stated, "I love the feeling of empowerment I feel with this awareness. Now I can do something about my anger." She did do something about it, and her marriage is now doing well.

Awareness is the key towards changing. Without it, we will forever stay the same.

Stage 2: Acceptance of Reality

Acceptance of Reality is a difficult stage of maturity. This is where you're able to accept your weaknesses and turn them into strengths, look at the reality of yourself and others, and accept what you see. Only then can you start to build the essential bridge between who you thought you were and who you really are.

A bridge from awareness to acceptance is what you need to make the journey through recovery.

During this self-discovery stage, you may become overwhelmed with shame, hurt, pain, and other emotions as reality sinks in. You recognize how often you've continued to go around in circles, but because of acceptance (second of the 3 A's), you now have the strength to experience it and grow through it.

As you go through this process, remember that it's taken every second of your life and everything you've been through to get you to this point. Not one second has been wasted, no matter what you've done up to this point. You've been on your personal soul's journey, a journey of wanting to awaken. You've done it in *your own* time. Allow no one to judge you on how long it took to get you to this place, this book, and this page.

<u>Reinforcing Acceptance</u>

So how do you gain acceptance of yourself? Here are a few essentials:

1. Accept yourself with as much love as possible at this moment. When the next moment comes, repeat this step. Small, continuous waves can deepen the deepest canyon. Your love for yourself can be as deep as that canyon. All you need to do is add a few drops of love every day.
2. Know that your Higher Power loves you, and know that you can love yourself.
3. Use your sense of humor. If you don't think you have one, start practicing being funny a little every day.
4. Accept that some of the emotions you're feeling will be resolved as you go through your process of self-growth.
5. Hand your addiction, your emotional pain, and your life over to your Higher Power. Accept that you were never in control of any person, place, or thing in your entire life. Practice this a little every day. It will become easier and easier.

Story Time

We are now going to hear from two teenagers, aged sixteen and seventeen, who were in a workshop with other teenagers. Joseph and Bill were best of friends and came to the workshop with other people they knew. Participants in this workshop were thirteen to eighteen years old. It was a great group, and we all were having lots of fun when Joseph raised his hand and stood up. He got everyone's attention. Joseph then shared with the group how he was so glad he was there. He then went on to say he had an anger problem and knew it and admitted it, but had never had any real acceptance of what he could do about it. He went on to tell us how his anger was destroying the relationships that were close to him. He then had the urge to yell out, "I accept my anger problem and that I can do something about it." He then sat down, smiling. The whole group then realized how a little acceptance can change the whole situation. We all praised him for his self-discovery. I then told him to write down what he'd just accepted, and before the workshop was over he would have a working solution to his anger. By the last day, Joseph was practicing things he had learned in the workshop from day one. Even more wonderful was that his friends did the same. They felt the things they learned were magical, because as soon as they started practicing they could see the miracles in their lives and how this affected those around them.

In the acceptance process, you'll discover your inner *interdependence*, which means your emotional, mental, physical, and spiritual components will begin to connect in a balanced way. It's time to ask yourself, *Am I willing to accept my illusive state and start working towards reality?* When you answer that question with a "yes," something magical will happen. You'll be able to observe yourself and accept what you see as if watching a movie because the universe has heard your "yes," even if it's just a whisper.

> *"Alone" (al-one) equals "all one with the universe." Be still and know. You didn't create yourself alone, and you can't recreate yourself alone. So take your reality and hand it to a Higher Power.*

Stage 3: Power Struggle in Reality

Power Struggle in Reality? How can this be?

It is human nature to want life to be easy. When you are mature and start accepting things the way they are, you may begin to experience an internal struggle within yourself. This happens because you realize you may need to change or give up control due to the reality of a situation. In truth, you don't have to change or give up anything. You have a choice. Being mature, you are aware of this, but you may not like your choices or letting go. This is where the power struggle begins. This is normal for everyone.

How do you know you have a power struggle going on inside of you? A common form of internal power struggle is when your emotions and mind don't agree. This creates turmoil in your head and/or your gut.

Power Struggle with Others

Have you ever observed yourself while speaking to others? If you have an answer in your head before the other person finishes what they're saying to you, you aren't listening to them. If you're power struggling with the other person, you're not listening and just want to say what you want to say. Listening to others while they're talking to you will improve your ability to know what you are feeling and hear your own thoughts without an internal power struggle. Take it slowly. And remember, we're not perfect human beings; we're *practicing* human beings.

Getting Through Your Power Struggles

You may remember that the Power Struggle Illusion Stage was characterized by confusion and anger. This is where, in illusion, you're angry with yourself or someone else. In this stage, your emotions may be out of alignment. Later in the book, you'll perform some activities that will help you bring your emotions back into alignment by helping you understand the differences between action and reaction, and being aware of your real authentic emotions.

With this new understanding you will no longer see this reality stage as a problem. You will perceive it as an opportunity to practice alignment. What a shift in perception! You'll be well aware when you're in conflict with what you think and what you feel. You may still have a problem listening to someone or have thoughts in your head saying two different things to you. You're in a human body, and it's normal for this conflict to occur. But you'll be able to identify your emotions and express them in an appropriate way. You can put them aside and connect with your spiritual beliefs while you think clearly and enjoy being in a calm body. Tapping into your defense system becomes a choice. You *choose* the actions you want to take. You're no longer on automatic pilot.

This stage is about observing yourself when you're off balance internally, accepting that this is where you are. Power struggles will occur. See this as a chance to practice alignment. The more you practice, the faster you'll realign. After you've made the decision to move towards maturity and reality, the patterns of your brain and your body may continue to pose challenges because they've been functioning on autopilot for so long. But continue to observe and catch yourself when you go off balance. Don't shame or blame yourself or others. Accept what is. This is where you decide it all— every day and sometimes every second—until the re-patterning is ingrained in your mind, body, and spirit. This will take time, so be patient with yourself!

Each area of your life will be a challenge; don't overwhelm yourself by attempting all your changes at once. Take it slow and easy. It's better to do one change at a time and reach your goal, than to go fast and miss it.

In one lifetime, you can recreate yourself as many times as you choose. The first time takes longer, but after that, it gets easier.

Story Time

Gena, a fourteen-year-old, red haired, green-eyed, and very expressive person who talks with her hands, attended one of the teen workshops. She was aware that she yelled at her parents when she didn't get what she wanted and accepted that she wasn't getting the results she wanted from her parents, to say the least. The last day of the workshop Gena came up to me and asked if she could share her story with the class. I had told all the participants they would have the opportunity to tell their adventure story of how The Power Model System™ had improved a given situation. I say "adventure story" because we were all looking at this workshop as an adventure going on within ourselves to learn the mystery of how we work internally.

Gena began her story by describing her past behavior when her parents wouldn't give her what she wanted or let her do something she wanted to do. She said she went home and did an experiment. She asked her mother and father for something she knew she wouldn't get. Even though she was only experimenting, she could feel herself wanting to yell and get mad. She said she was able to identify her autopilot behavior. Her Power Struggle in Reality was to observe herself wanting to yell, while at the same time, knowing the yelling wouldn't work. She experienced firsthand that even though she wanted to change, it would take time. We all supported Gena in her continuing efforts to practice using impulse control. She was amazed by the experience and realized that she does have choices in her behavior. Later, she told her parents about the experiment and all three of them sat down and laughed. Her parents expressed how proud they were of her.

Stage 4: Commitment to Higher Power

In the Five Stages of Illusion, the stage of Commitment refers to being committed to your addiction. The *Commitment* stage in the Five Stages of Maturity requires you to ask yourself this question: *Am I committed to change with the assistance of my Higher Power?* (It's okay if you don't know what your definition of Higher Power is yet. You'll be creating your definition later in the process.)

When people ask me how I know there's a Higher Power, I tell them I can't ever remember not believing in one, as I know it to be. I spent a lot of my life being silent about my beliefs, but as I became more confident in myself I was able to speak out. While my concept of a Higher Power has changed over the years, I don't remember a time when I didn't believe that all people are given assistance in life from a Higher Source. Awareness of a Higher Source comes first, followed by an interdependent relationship with that Source. Then you are able to tap into all the available power in the universe. This power comes from a Higher Power belief system. This may be a religion or something that exists beyond your humanness.

Is there a Higher Power? My answer to that question is this: I know because I know because I know. I don't know how I know, but I do. You have the right to believe or not. For me, Higher Power just is. I can see the daily miracles in my life and in the lives of others. I haven't lost my awe of these daily miracles. Many times I have seen individuals without a spiritual component living in pain or numbness. When they decide what religion or spiritual belief to believe in and want to follow it, I see and experience their souls awakening. There's a radiance about them that can't be denied. I see the light turned on in their eyes. I see the glow. And I see their soul shining through their humanness.

Getting in touch with your Higher Power belief system is like everything else in life. You need tools and techniques to learn how to go within yourself. Your Higher Power is always with you, even if you don't believe it.

For now, think of a place or a scene that makes you feel peaceful inside just by being there. It might be a stream, a mountain, a tree, a sunset, or a formation of clouds you've seen from an airplane. Have this peaceful place represent your Higher Power, what you perceive as a thing of perfection on this Earth. It's a great place to start. As you continue visualizing this place and performing the Power Model System™

activities, you'll be sensing your Higher Power more and more. For now, keep it simple. When you feel stressed, visualize in your mind's eye your picture of a Higher Power. You'll find yourself relaxing as a result.

Story Time

A great, old, wise, recovering AA member told me this story one night. I will always be grateful for the lesson it teaches.

A large black dog and a little brown puppy were fighting all the time. The storyteller asked me which dog I thought would win in the long run. I said, "The black dog, of course. He's bigger, stronger, and more experienced in fighting than the puppy."

He said, "Okay, but what if you decide you want the little dog to win? Could you do anything to change the situation?"

I laughed and said, "Well, I could kill the black dog."

The old-timer said, "Wait a minute. That's not in the rules. You have to find a way the puppy can win without killing the big dog."

I thought and thought. No matter how hard I tried, I couldn't come up with a solution. "I don't know," I said finally.

He just sat there, smiling. Then he said, "The dog that wins will be the dog you feed the most."

Of course! After a while, the big dog would grow weak while the puppy would gain strength and grow up.

I said, "It would take a while."

He smiled and told me this: "The big dog is you with your *old* ways of living, and the puppy represents you learning *new* information. It will take a while for you to shift from your old habits to your new ones, and the only way you'll be successful is to starve your old habits. Every time you replace an old way of thinking with a new way of thinking, just picture that big dog going hungry and the puppy growing stronger. And remember, as the big dog is going hungry he'll be eager to trick you into feeding him, so be careful not to fall into your familiar old behavior and thinking."

Today, every time I start to create a shift for myself, I remember this story. It speaks to my heart and reminds me this is a lifetime journey. I love this story and have now given it to you. I encourage you to make it your own and pass it on.

Now that you have awareness, acceptance, and commitment in your consciousness, are you ready to be proactive in your life? If so, move on to the final stage of maturity, Co-Creation in Action.

Stage 5: Co-Creation in Action

Do you remember reading about the Co-Creation in Despair Illusion stage? You became a co-creator with your addiction of choice. This was the stage of despair and death of self.

This isn't the case when you're in reality. In the maturity stages, you and your Higher Power work together to co-create a new you. Anything is possible. You are no longer a victim in this world. You have nowhere else to travel except straight to your goals. *At this stage, you take full responsibility for your emotions, thoughts, reactions and actions, and spiritual beliefs.* You co-create with your Higher Power in the re-patterning of your brain and body. As I've said, this takes time and patience, so hang in there!

Action is the last and most important component of the 3 A's. If you're not proactive in your life, you won't achieve maturity or shift internally. When you're connected with a Higher Source, you have all the power you need internally. As you co-create your life with your Higher Power, you'll be aware of how you keep working through the stages of *awareness* and *acceptance* and how you take *action* to change yourself.

When you're aware and accept that *you are a miracle*, you will receive and accept miracles from outside yourself. What you are inside creates what you are outside. When you realize you're a miracle inside, everything else will follow.

Living a Miracle

As you and your Higher Power co-create a new you in the present, your future will naturally be affected. As your power balances within you, know that you're capable of achieving anything you want in your life. You've had this power all along but didn't have the tools to make the necessary shift that would unleash it.

In the maturity stages, you have the power to change yourself and, thus, change your life. Remember, with change come internal struggles. You've been living in illusion for so long that you will be tempted to return to the familiar (one of the stages of illusion) instead of working through the challenges of maturity. Know that this, too, is part of the process. Internal power struggles occur in all of us. The secret is to become aware of them and be able to continually refocus on balancing. This is where miracles happen. Don't give up. Life does get easier. You are the miracle!

Story Time

Larry, forty-eight years of age and successful in the investment business, has a great family and wife. Larry came to a workshop because of his spending habits. Larry's habit was to spend all the money he had. He and his wife had tried many ways to correct this problem. So here they were, both wanting to try The Power Model System™, since nothing else had worked. Larry said to the group one day, "I have never taken action on this problem. I admit I have it. I accept I have it. I struggle with it daily, and I keep praying for God to remove it, but I have not taken action." He had all our attention then. Some of the people asked him, "What do you mean, you have not taken action?" Larry then went to the front of the group. I sat on the side in a chair. I knew Larry was on a roll. He then said, "I let my wife take care of the money. I go to her if I need any, and I let her deal with our accountant, etc. I do not do any action about taking care of money." Silence was in the room. Everyone could see the awareness on Larry's face. He said he now realizes he needs to Co-Create with his Higher Power, meaning he had to do more than just pray to God. So someone asked, "What kind of action do you think you need to take?" That was the magic question and Larry was now ready with an answer. He said, "From now on, I will sit with my wife and our accountant as they do our budget. I will deposit money into savings. I will do mature actions behind this problem. It is my problem, and my wife has to do extra work due to my problem, and that does not make sense to me anymore." Larry's wife had a big smile on her face, as we all cautioned Larry to start with small steps and gradually take on bigger steps. Obviously, Larry had to really dig deep and discover his illusions and defenses in order to get to this point, and it paid off.

This is just one of the many miracles I get to watch during my workshops.

Love and Joy, Joy, Joy

As you practice the Five Stages of Maturity, you'll experience true joy. In the process, you may experience the following:

- The joy of never being alone because you're *al-one* with your Higher Power;
- The joy of being a co-creator in your life;
- The joy of knowing you're a practicing human being, rather than being perfect all the time;
- The joy of developing awareness of your internal power struggles faster;
- The joy of being aware of your own personal miracles;
- The joy of watching yourself change for the better and loving every minute of it.

Activity: Visualizing Your Power Struggle

1. Take a blank piece of paper and make two columns. Label one Illusions and one Reality.
2. Be still and ask yourself why you should continue learning about yourself through this book or any other program.
3. Listen to your thoughts.
4. Write down under Illusions all the reasons you should stop.
5. Write down under Reality all the reasons to continue.
6. Look at these two columns. You now have in front of you the struggle that goes on internally on a conscious and subconscious level. Amazing, isn't it?

Perform this activity every time you sense a power struggle within yourself. Remember, repetition is the key to change and success.

Reality isn't always an easy place to be. As you start learning about your true reality, you'll start seeing how much into the illusive stage you are (or were) in. This causes some people to stop and say, "That's enough. I'll go back to the old me. It's easier." That's right, illusions are sometimes perceived to be easier to live with than reality, but the rewards of reality and maturity are far greater.

ACTIVITY
Visualizing Your Power Struggle

Illusion	Reality

Chapter 12

BOUNDARIES

Life's a journey, not a destination.
       Amazing by Aerosmith

Boundaries: *That which indicates or fixes a limit or extent, or marks a bound, as of a territory; a bounding or separating line; a real or imaginary limit.*
                                                    Webster's Revised Unabridged Dictionary

Why are boundaries—yours and/or other people's—so important?

Let's say you were buying a piece of property. If you didn't know the boundary lines of the property, how would you know how much land you were purchasing? You wouldn't be able to tend to, pay for, or protect this piece of property without clear boundaries. The reverse is also true—you wouldn't know what part of the property was *not* your responsibility.

The same is true for *you.* You need to know your *external* and *internal* boundaries and how they affect you emotionally, mentally, spiritually, and physically. In other words, you need to take responsibility for you. Armed with this information, you'll know when someone has *crossed* your boundaries and when you have crossed someone else's. You'll have a sense of self and, thus, higher self-esteem.

With internal boundaries, you know who you are and who you are not. With external boundaries, you know where you stop and someone else starts. You know when and how to tell others what kind of behavior you will or won't accept. This allows you to meet your needs and limit your over-reactions.

Learning to set boundaries with yourself and others will ensure that you are who you are, wherever you go, whatever you do, whomever you're with.

Internal Boundaries

There are four ways to approach internal boundaries:

1. No boundaries
2. Broken boundaries
3. Walled boundaries
4. Balanced boundaries resulting in sense of self

No Boundaries

The "no boundaries" approach applies to all four components: emotional, mental, physical, and spiritual. This means anything you feel or think is expressed with no concern for yourself or the other person involved. In no-boundary relationships, abusive behavior (physical, mental, and/or emotional) becomes dominant. This violence can extend to children in the family. People who have no boundaries with the outside world have no impulse control within themselves. They put their body, mind, and spirit through abuse, alcohol, drugs, rage, endless judgments, and other addictions. Outwardly, they treat others the same way they feel inside. They feel like a victim in many situations and, thus, create victims within their lives. They take no responsibility and have no accountability for themselves or with others. The opposite are people who want to do everything for others and yet expect no respect for themselves. They're very nice and don't want to say anything to upset anyone.

People without boundaries tend to put themselves in dangerous situations (even if they see "red flags") and blame others for their problems in life.

How you respect yourself depends on your internal boundaries. How you allow others to treat you determines your external boundaries.

It's absolutely essential to have boundaries in order to develop a sense of self.

Individuals with no internal boundaries have one or more of the following characteristics:

- Feel everything
- Feel others' emotions
- Cannot contain their emotions
- Over-disclose; tell too much to others
- Depend on others for sense of self
- Get too close too fast to strangers
- Feel like victims
- Experience prolonged resentment
- Become overwhelmed and preoccupied with others
- Say yes when they want to say no
- Feel responsible for others' emotions
- Tie identity to being in an intimate relationship
- Overcompensate
- Expect others to meet their needs
- Take too much and act extremely "needy"
- Do not respect the rights of others
- Do not like being alone
- Touch others without asking
- Allow others to touch them even when it's uncomfortable or inappropriate
- Unaware of their own need for privacy
- Impose on the privacy of others
- Allow their physical space to be invaded
- Overreact to the feelings and behavior of others
- Personalize everything
- Let others influence their behavior
- Act unpredictably
- Limit bonding to others in family
- Yell and scream
- Belittle others in relationships
- Make others the object of their anger with humor
- Become addicted to drugs, alcohol, or other substances
- Become involved in physical and/or sexual abuse
- Use sexual humor

Story Time

Imagine growing up in a home where your parents and siblings could walk into your bedroom at any time without knocking. You don't like it, so you ask them to please knock. Your parents respond by saying, "If you have nothing to hide, then it shouldn't matter." Eventually you accept that you can't change the situation, so you become used to it, even though you're angry every time someone barges in. After a while, you adjust so much that you barge into your younger sibling's room. As you become older, you are drawn to individuals who don't respect your personal space. Your partners go through your wallet and you know it, get angry, and just let it go. You don't let them know you have a boundary issue about people going through your wallet. But each time this happens, your anger builds. Out of the blue, you blow up and tell them you don't like them going through your wallet. At that point, there are no boundaries on your anger. When you blow up, you abuse your nervous system and may abuse others by yelling and screaming.

If you grow up in a no-boundary environment, you're likely unaware of your personal needs. You overreact to stress and experience outbursts of rage or run away from problems. When stressed, you might not have coping skills to draw boundaries for others and yourself. You might take everything personally because you're unable to distinguish which comments are about you and which ones aren't. No-boundary people either tell everything about themselves to people they barely know or they reveal nothing about themselves, regardless how long they've known a person.

If you're in this situation, you have a need to compensate some way or another for the constant crises you lived in the past. Remember that you developed your defense system from your childhood environment. If a crisis environment is familiar to you, you'll be attracted to people who come from that type of environment. You didn't like the results when you were in that environment, and you might not like the results now, but you'll recreate this environment over and over in your life until you become aware of what you're doing and make a conscious decision to re-pattern yourself inside.

In effect, you choose the no-boundary environment in which you were raised (including any emotional, mental, spiritual and physical abuse) and recreate it inside yourself. If you've come from an abusive background, you will pass on the abuse, either internally to yourself or externally to others, because that is all you know. And until you learn something new, you will do the best you can with what you have.

What are some results of having a no-boundary childhood?

- No boundaries on your emotions. You act first and think about your actions afterward.
- You don't know how to identify your emotions, so you act them out.
- There is a good possibility that you will pile fear or anger on top of most of your other emotions.
- You don't practice impulse control because you don't have any. You go on the destructive path of being on autopilot.

Broken Boundaries

Broken: *to part or pierce the surface of. To find an opening or flaw.*
The Merriam-Webster Dictionary

Behavior with broken boundaries is similar to behavior with no boundaries except that it is unpredictable. People with broken boundaries show characteristics of fluctuating conduct—one day a certain behavior is acceptable and the next day it's not. Unpredictable behavior is difficult to adapt to, so it is particularly frustrating for spouses and children.

If children are raised in an unpredictable environment, they get confused. One day they face consequence for misbehaving, and the next day that same behavior is acceptable. They develop rigid or healthy boundaries in some circumstances and fragile boundaries in others, particularly in intimate relationships.

Story Time

My friend Jan came to me because she was stressed over her job. She said, "I love my job, I work hard, and I like who I work with except for one person—my supervisor Judy. She makes a rule one day and changes it the next. I'm going crazy with her. For instance, I'd read all the rules and regulations for our workplace and followed them to get my billing work done. I've worked here for eight years and I know I'm good at what I do, if I say so myself. Judy has been here for six months, and every month she finds something wrong with the billing form I use and makes changes. So I do it the way she instructs me for the current month, and the next month she says she doesn't want those changes. I know that in one or two weeks she'll change the rule again."

Jan and I reviewed the concept of boundaries, what they are, and how they work. Then I suggested she get any change of rules for billing in writing from Judy. Not surprisingly, Judy wasn't willing to do something as time-consuming as writing. I let Jan know that this behavior wasn't unusual. Writing is an adult action. Someone with broken boundaries doesn't function like an adult but acts according to how they feel at a particular time. Once Jan knew what was going on, understood that it was not her fault, and knew the only thing she had control over was her reaction, she learned to take it in stride.

Walled Boundaries

Walled: *a continuous structure of masonry or other material forming a rampart and built for defensive purposes.*

The Merriam-Webster Dictionary

People with walled boundaries are just that—walled up—which is part of their defense system against the world. They have been hurt and are in pain, so they build walls to handle stress. The inside of these walls is made up of hurt and pain, and the outside is comprised of aloofness and anger. These people usually avoid discussions involving their emotions.

Addiction is common in these individuals, not just with alcohol or drugs but with work, money, etc.. Work is a very common addiction because there they can talk with others. They keep conversations on a surface level. When challenged by people living with them, who complain that they are "so closed up," they reply, "I get along great with people at work. At work they think I'm funny." Individuals with walled boundaries do a lot of acting "as if." This means they act "as if" they're having a good time. They'll act "as if" you're their friend, but there is never an emotional connection because they don't know how to connect emotionally. You might think you know them well, but you don't because they keep things bottled up inside.

Balanced Boundaries (Sense of Self)

Someone with balanced boundaries is a true, self-empowered individual. This is the kind of person you strive to become—someone who is aware of, perceives, and understands his or her own identity and has boundaries in place, both internally and externally.

People with a strong sense of self have a love for self, which means they are kind, gentle, firm, and honest with themselves. They have a Higher Power connection and are comfortable with it. They don't insist that everyone have the same spiritual beliefs as they do. They accept that others are different from them, and have no need to judge them for these differences. They have inner peace, although not all the time. They know how to center themselves.

They foster "win/win" situations in their lives. They know that we are not perfect human beings but *practicing* human beings. When people have a sense of who they are, they're able to handle healthy criticism and makes changes as needed. Because they have self-esteem, they question themselves and can promptly admit if they've made a mistake. They know where they're going in life. Their life purpose is important to them, and they do what it takes to accomplish it.

What are you able to do when you have balanced boundaries?

- Make physical boundaries clear to others;
- Respect the needs and rights of others;
- Negotiate and compromise;
- Ask permission before touching others;
- Share feelings appropriately and directly;
- Be assertive;
- Exercise interdependence internally (be flexible with emotions, thoughts, spiritual beliefs, and behavior);
- Have the ability to identify choices;
- Make mistakes without damaging your self-esteem;
- Have an internal sense of personal identity;
- Comfortable with others' differences;
- Tolerate and accept differences of opinion without altering your own;
- Be sensitive to feelings of others (empathic).

See Figure 12.1 for symptoms of all four types of *internal* boundaries.

External Boundaries

External boundaries are boundaries you use to let others know about your needs. When you have external boundaries, you are able to identify your needs and express them to others. External boundaries are the mirror images of internal boundaries. Remember, what you create internally is mirrored externally. In other words, how you treat yourself internally dictates how you treat others and how you allow others to treat you. See Figure 12.2 for symptoms of the four kinds of *external* boundaries.

Activity: Setting Internal and External Boundaries

Figures 12.1 and 12.2 relate to this activity.

This activity will help you discover what boundaries you have and which ones are missing.

1. Review the Internal and External Boundaries in Figures 12.1 and 12.2.

2. Circle what applies to you under all the internal and external boundaries.

3. Pick one broken Internal Boundary and one broken External Boundary you would like to change. "Broken" here means a boundary that you did not exercise or apply.

4. Write each of those boundaries down below. We will come back to these later in the book.

Broken Internal Boundary:

_____

Broken External Boundary:

_____

INTERNAL BOUNDARIES

NONE

- Don't like being alone
- Not aware of personal needs
- Over-react to others with rage outbursts
- Let others influence my behavior
- Unpredictable behavior
- Everything that is said is taken personally
- Act out others' emotions
- Feel like a victim
- Get too close to others too fast
- Cannot contain feelings - Act them out
- Over-disclose myself

BROKEN

- Have mood swings
- Expect others to read my mind
- No tolerance for differences of opinion
- Don't know my needs
- Change my internal boundaries from day to day
- No consistency with myself
- Share addiction with other addicts

WALLED

- Seek outside gratfication
- React from defenses most of the time
- Feel pain/rage internally
- Fear changes of any kind
- Have difficulty looking internally at myself
- Act with rigidity/black and white thinking

SENSE OF SELF

- Interdependent internally with emotions, thoughts, and spirituality
- Can make mistakes without damage to my self-esteem
- Have a sense of personal identity
- Have emotional tolerance
- Sensitive to feelings of others (empathic)
- Have impulse control (internally)
- Pro-active toward internal growth and have balance in my life

Figure 12.1 ~ Internal Boundaries

EXTERNAL BOUNDARIES

NONE

- Touch others without asking
- Not aware of own need for privacy
- Do not respect others
- Depend on others to give me a sense of well-being
- Experience resentment
- Give or take too much
- Become overwhelmed/preoccupied with others
- Say yes when meaning no
- Share addictions with others
- Rage on others

BROKEN

- Make threats to others
- Assume others know my needs and won't give me what I want
- Want other people to tell me how I should feel
- Use physical intimidation
- Don't allow others to have privacy
- Change boundaries from day to day
- Inconsistent behavior with others and self
- Share addiction with other addicts

WALLED

- Aggressive
- Share addiction with other addicts
- Want others to fulfill my wants and needs
- Will not tolerate change in my environment
- Blame others for problems in my life
- Unaware of my walls and have little desire to explore
- Physically abusive towards others

SENSE OF SELF

- Share feelings appropriately and directly with others
- Assertive
- Able to identify choices
- Allow differences in others
- Tolerate/accept differences of opinion without altering my own
- Respectful and sensitive to the needs and rights of others
- Make boundaries clear to others

Setting Boundaries

Boundaries act as a guide in all your relationships. While you are in the process of changing, share honestly about the process to avoid misunderstanding and confusion with those close to you. If you've set a certain boundary that you want to keep and others want you to change, you have a decision to make. If these people still want to be in your life, they will respect your choices. If they choose to not be around you (not respect your boundaries and/or your choices), that's their decision. At first, this might feel uncomfortable, but in the long run you will have more energy and will meet others who have the same respect for boundaries as you do.

So how do you set and maintain boundaries? One of the most important skills you need to achieve permanent boundaries is *impulse control.*

Impulse Control

Impulse: *A sudden pushing or driving force. The effect of an impelling force; motion produced by a sudden or momentary force.*
Control: *Authority or ability to manage or direct.*

The Merriam-Webster Dictionary

Let's start by discussing impulse control during the "terrible twos," a developmental stage of growing up. During the terrible-twos stage you learn about impulse control, making choices, and how to express emotions appropriately. At age two, your body learns how to tolerate emotions and connect with your thoughts, even though words may be limited. You learn how to communicate and negotiate with others, letting your needs be known through facial expressions, behavior, expressions of emotion, and a limited vocabulary. Then you take what you've learned during this stage out into the world.

Because many parents haven't gotten past the terrible twos stage themselves, going through this stage with their children is difficult. It doesn't help that both parents often work outside the home, return home tired and have limited time with their children. Because of this, many aren't willing to spend the time it takes to correct their children when they misbehave—for example, holding time-outs, giving them choices, and reinforcing acceptable behavior. Parenting takes time, effort, and consistency.

As a two-year-old, you learn whatever it takes to get what you want. You learn to survive in your environment (however you perceive it to be). And you hopefully learn that there's always a consequence.

Story Time

Let's say you and your five-year-old daughter go to the grocery store seven days before her birthday and she asks for a toy. You know she wants a bike for her birthday, so you ask, "Which do you want, a bike for your birthday next week or this toy now?" She whines and says she wants both. Hopefully, you hang in there without shaming her, keeping your voice consistent, and wait until she gives you her answer.

At first she'll think her life is out of control because she's not getting what she wants. Then, when you give her a choice, she learns she's able to take control again by choosing which toy she wants and when. It's not necessary for her to *like* the choices. Rather, it's about making a decision. Hurrah! She has exercised impulse control. She gets to question and decide where her life is going—does she take the toy in front of her (instant gratification), or does she wait a week to get a bike (impulse control)?

Impulse control must be taught and practiced, if not as a child then as an adult. Without exercising impulse control, your life will spiral out of control. Many examples of no impulse control are listed in the *No Boundaries* Section of this Chapter. Setting boundaries on your emotions helps you start exercising impulse control. One thing I know for sure is this: if you don't learn to exercise impulse control, inside and outside, you will continue to have opportunities to learn this skill. Why? Because life will always challenge you! If you haven't yet learned this lesson, it's okay. You'll continue to do what you do and get what you get, until you stop looking at others and start looking inward and changing you. Situations will keep coming into your life until you are able to move past them. Because you have free will, each time you'll have the choice to either learn or blame.

> *If you want to achieve the goals you set in life, impulse control must be achieved. Without it, all is chaos, both internally and externally.*

Acknowledgements

At this point, I would like to acknowledge Pia Mellody[13, 14]. She has developed a lot of material on boundary systems and how they affect our lives. See some of her books referenced at the end of this book.

Activity: Achieving Impulse Control

Now let's perform an impulse control activity so you can focus on some events where you did not exercise impulse control.

Use Figure 12.1 to fill out the information below.

1. Write down events when you could have practiced impulse control and did not.

   Example:
   I was talking to my co-worker, who kept interrupting me to tell me something. I did not ask her what. I became overwhelmed and impatient with her. Instead of using impulse control, I got up and walked away.

2. Write down the consequences that came out of those events due to your not exercising impulse control.

   Example:
   My supervisor came up to me and said I was inappreciative with my co-worker. He told me he had sent her over to give me a message, and I walked away. He took me into his office and wrote me up for my angry actions.

3. Now write down some of the possibilities that you think you may have had if you had exercised impulse control.

   Example:
   I would have received the message from my supervisor. I would not have had a write-up, which in the long run, affects my job and future pay raises.

ACTIVITY
Achieving Impulse Control

1. Write down events when you could have practiced impulse control and did not.

_____
_____
_____
_____
_____
_____
_____

2. Write down the consequences that came out of those events due to your not exercising impulse control.

_____
_____
_____
_____
_____
_____
_____

3. Now write down some of the outcomes that could have occurred if you had exercised impulse control.

_____
_____
_____
_____
_____
_____
_____

Chapter 13

LIFE SPARK

A traveler am I and a navigator, and every day I discover a new region within my soul.
Khalil Gibran

Authentic: *1) conforming to fact and therefore worthy of belief. 2) conforming to fact and therefore worthy of trust, reliance, or belief:* an authentic account by an eyewitness. *3) Having a claimed and verifiable origin or authorship; not counterfeit.*
Emotions: *The part of the consciousness that involves feeling.*

The Merriam-Webster Dictionary

Have you ever looked into a baby's eyes and noticed how clear and shiny they are and how much they sparkle? The joy in them is clearly visible. You can clearly see the baby's "life spark." Ideally, as the child grows up, he or she is able to process life internally as it happens. If the child is loved and protected throughout childhood, this joy of discovery and life spark will remain vibrant into adulthood.

This describes the ideal life, but it's not always realistic. In reality, there are many influences in your life from birth, and not just from your family of origin. Your authenticity is influenced by life events, society, institutions, your peers, and other environmental factors. Many of these influences are often negative and thus you begin to cover up your authentic emotions, and your life spark begins to disappear. When this happens, the sparkle in your eyes begins to diminish. The suppression of this spark results in the loss of your connection with your authentic self. You can see this in pictures of yourself when you were younger. Look at your eyes. After a certain age, they may have lost their glow. Many say the eyes are the windows to our soul. I believe as we grow farther away from our soul's journey, our eyes lose their sparkle.

So, how can your authentic self, your life spark, get lost? When you were little and trying to cope with your environment, the adults in your environment gave you a sense of what emotions and behavior were acceptable. If you felt sad and sensed that tears weren't acceptable in your environment, instead of crying you likely expressed another *emotion* that was considered acceptable. So, as a child, you may have learned that sadness was not good but showing anger when something sad happened was okay. Without words, you learned that this makes you brave and, thus, you incorporated the behavior into your belief system. Yes, it happens that fast and that subtly!

As the years pass, forgetting that sadness was your authentic emotion (not anger), you continue to display anger when you're sad. Eventually, you can't identify your authentic emotion of sadness and find yourself not grieving over the loss of people, places, and things in your life—not because you aren't experiencing sadness but because you identify sadness with anger and angry behavior. When you experience a loss in your life, you get angry. When someone asks you to identify how you feel about a loss you have gone through, you say, "I'm angry." Are you really angry? If your mind tells you this, you believe you are. If the behavior that follows shows that you are, you must be. That's the dilemma. You believe you are angry, not sad.

You have placed a second emotion—anger—on top of the original *authentic* emotion. You have been doing this for so long in your life that you are on automatic pilot. Anytime something happens you don't like you revert to a secondary emotion that is more comfortable for you, thus piling layers of emotion on top of each other. No wonder you think that if you start identifying your *authentic* emotions, you won't be able to handle them!

But that's not true. The activity at the end of this chapter will give you a method of recognizing your *authentic* emotions in a short period of time.

If you do not become aware of the connection between the past and the present and have resolution, you will repeat the past in your future.

Story Time

George came to see me as a result of a court order to get help. He said he needed anger management, and with that statement, he handed me a piece of paper from his parole officer. George said, "I have been to so many counselors—four of them to be exact—all for anger management. I keep learning these new ways to behave, you know, like 'time out' and all that stuff. But before long, I always go back to busting walls, yelling, screaming, and scaring my wife until she calls the cops and they let me know I need help. So the judge sends me to another counselor, and I am given counseling on anger management." He then said, and not in an arrogant way, "I guess you and I are going to go through anger management again, huh?"

"No, George," I replied. "We're not going through anger management." I handed him a binder and said, "We are going to go through The Power Model System™."

He looked inside the binder and said, "I've never seen anything like this. Is it new?" At that time I had been using it in my private practice for ten years, but I knew it was new to him. So I said, "It's new, it's fun, and it's all about you. You're the expert."

I could immediately see George relax and smile. He then asked the million-dollar question, "Will it work? Will I stop being so angry? I'm tired of going to jail and seeing the same judge, who says the same thing to me, grow up. I don't want to leave my wife and two kids. But she told me if I did not get my temper under control, she would leave with both the kids."

I told him, "I can let you know that stopping is up to you. First, let's see if you are angry or if anger is the only emotion you know."

I could see that George didn't know what I meant. So I just said, "Let's take a look at George and see what we find."

As we progressed though The Power Model System™, George worked hard. He self-discovered that he was taught to be a "big man" all his life, including when he was young. His father raged, and his mother yelled back. As we moved along with the activities in the system, George shared that no one really talked much in his family.

The big "Wow!" came for George when we got to the life spark. He put the words "anger" and "shame" on top of all emotions. "How can that be?" George asked. "No wonder my wife is upset. I can see the fear in my kids' eyes when I start to say something to them. When I do, I feel shame and then anger. Other times, I feel anger and then shame."

After that activity, whenever I asked George how he was feeling about something, he would look at his life spark sheet. From it, he was learning to identify his authentic emotion, and it wasn't necessarily anger. As we continued to build his personal blueprint, he started experiencing more of his emotions.

I remembered the first time he cried, he told me he was afraid he wouldn't be able to stop. I assured him that he *would* be able to stop and the roof wouldn't fall on top of us, either. He kept crying, and the roof didn't fall on us. He continued to learn what his authentic emotions were and practiced feeling them instead of feeling anger or shame. As he did this process, he referred to his life spark less and less. He began experiencing a full range of emotions.

As this soul proceeded to self-discover who he really was, changes took place. He was glad he was able to identify things about himself and said, "I feel like I have control over me." I let him know that he did. And as he became more committed to his process of becoming balanced, he wanted less control over those around him. At my suggestion, George put his two children, aged eight and ten, into counseling, and he gladly went to counseling sessions with them. Soon they were able to heal some of the fear and anger that had been in their family.

After the four months of sessions in my office had ended, I saw George around town. He always waved or stopped to tell me how well he and his family were doing. He also told me that the process with me had taken more courage than anything he'd ever done in his life, but he could now experience different emotions and the anger outbursts had stopped.

The Life Spark Chart in Figure 13.1 is an effective tool in visualizing how you cover up your authentic feelings. The center of the circle is your Life Spark. It shines brightly if your authentic emotions are expressed appropriately as shown in the middle ring. The outer ring is where your cover-up feelings reside. Cover-up emotions can become more socially acceptable and form a barrier around your authentic emotions, which results in the smothering of your Life Spark. For example, you can use anger to hide how sad you really are, or tears to hide your real anger. And that is where the problem lies. Now let's discover your authentic emotions.

There are no good or bad emotions. Any emotion can be authentic or be used to cover up another.

Activity: Life Spark

Figures 13.1 and 13.2 relate to this activity.

Use the LIFE SPARK chart to identify your authentic feelings. To feel safe, you learned to mask your authentic feelings with ones that were more acceptable in your environment at that time. The middle ring in the chart represents your authentic emotions, while the outer ring represents your cover-up emotions. Review Figure 13.2 for an example.

Let's start with one of the "authentic" emotions on the LIFE SPARK chart, for example, "anger."

1. Look at the slot in the outer ring next to "anger" and think back to when you were young. Was anger acceptable in your environment?
2. If not, what feeling did you put on top of your anger?
3. Did you smile or cry?
4. What was accepted in your environment in place of anger?
5. Look around at the ten emotions listed and see which one fit for you. Perhaps you received attention if you cried, but if you expressed anger you were told that was bad. (If you select "happiness," that probably means you smiled as if everything was okay.)
6. Put "happiness" or "sadness," or whatever emotion you put on top of anger, in the empty space in the outer ring next to "anger."
7. Repeat Steps 1 through 6 for all the emotions.

Cannot Identify Your Cover-up Emotion?

You may not have cover-up feelings for all your emotions. In that case, leave the respective slot open. If you think you have a cover-up emotion but can't identify what it is, try the following exercise:

Visualize in your mind's eye a situation where you were experiencing the authentic emotion you want to know about. Now see yourself experiencing that emotion, and watch everyone in the situation with you. Just play the movie in your mind. Watch the way you are behaving. Observe your facial expressions. See if you are showing the emotion you're experiencing. If not, what are you showing? Write it down. Good work! Now go on to the next authentic emotion and complete the chart.

THE LIFE SPARK: MY AUTHENTIC FEELINGS

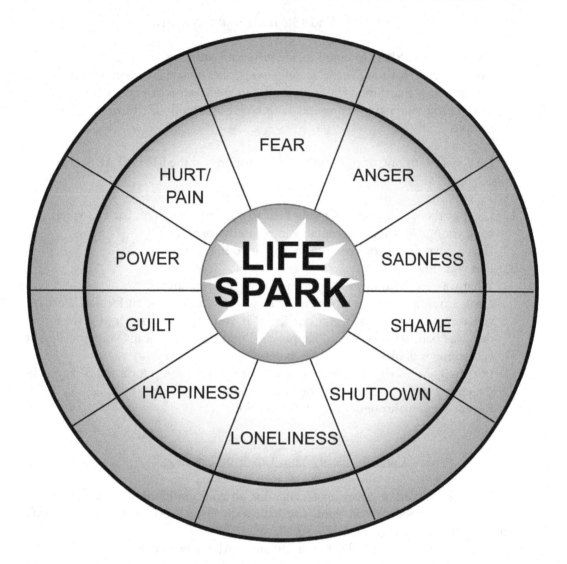

The inner circle is your Life Spark.
The middle ring represents your authentic emotions.
The outer ring is where you write down your cover-up emotions.

Use the Life Spark to identify your authentic feelings. At a young age, we all learn ways to cover up our authentic feelings as a means of self-protection. To feel safe, we learned to mask our true feelings with other feelings that were more acceptable in our environment at that time. For example, when you were a child, was showing/feeling anger acceptable in your environment? If not, you may have covered up your anger with false smiles and laughter or some other kind of artificial emotions.

EXAMPLE
THE LIFE SPARK: MY AUTHENTIC FEELINGS

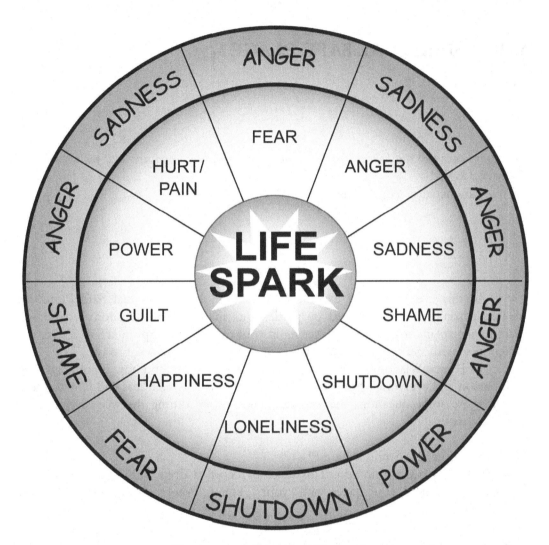

The inner circle is your Life Spark.
The middle ring represents your authentic emotions.
The outer ring is where you write your cover-up emotions.

Use the Life Spark to identify your authentic feelings. At a young age, we all learned ways to cover up our authentic feelings as a means of self-protection. To feel safe, we learned to mask our true feelings with other feelings that were more acceptable in our environment at that time. For example, when you were a child, was showing/feeling anger acceptable in your environment? If not, you may have covered up your anger with false smiles and laughter or some other kind of artificial emotions.

Chapter 14

YOUR SPIRITUAL SAFE PLACE

There is a Power that will light your way to health, happiness, peace, and success, if you will but turn toward that Light.
Paramahansa Yogananda

In this chapter, I will explain what I mean by a "Spiritual Safe Place" by answering some questions posed by participants in my HumanWisdom workshops. Also, I will explain how by visually seeing in your mind's eye a Spiritual Safe Place, you can connect with the very essence of who you are and who you want to be.

In HumanWisdom workshops, we discuss spirituality and how it connects with each person and everyone's Spiritual Safe Place. We review what it is and why we need it. Below are some questions that are frequently posed during the workshops, along with the answers:

Question: What is a Spiritual Safe Place?
Answer: It's a place within you. This place is recorded deep within your soul. It's a spiritual connection you have with your Higher Power (however you define Higher Power).

Question: Do we all have a Spiritual Safe Place?
Answer: We all have our own Spiritual Safe Place. If you're in a human body, you have one.

Question: How do I know I have one? I'm not consciously aware of mine, and I couldn't describe anything to you right now about a spiritual place.
Answer: You don't have to be consciously aware of your Spiritual Safe Place to have one. It came with you when you were born and will never leave you. It's there for you to self-discover.

Question: Why am I not aware of mine? I'm very visual. Shouldn't I be able to see or imagine what it looks like?

Answer: When you choose to go within yourself and look for it, you'll find it. It's a choice. It comes when you're ready to take a journey within yourself.

Question: Why is it called a Spiritual Safe Place?

Answer: To fully answer this question I need to make references to these four words: *prayer, meditation, centeredness, and intervention*. Let's look at some definitions for these four words along with *Spiritual, Safe and Place*. The answer lies in their meaning.

Prayer:

1. *A reverent petition made to God, a god, or another object of worship.*
2. *The act of making a reverent petition to God, a god, or another object of worship.*
3. *An act of communion with God, a god, or another object of worship, such as in devotion, confession, praise, or thanksgiving.*
4. *The slightest chance or hope.*

Meditation:

1. *The act of mediating; intervention.*

Centeredness:

1. *Self-confident, goal-oriented, and well balanced: "He's a centered guy. He's always seemed to know what he wanted, and gone after it in a concrete way."*

Intervention:

1. *Interference so as to modify a process or situation.*

Spiritual:

1. *Of, relating to, consisting of, or having the nature of spirit; not tangible or material.*
2. *Having concerned with or affecting the soul.*
3. *Of or belonging to a church or religion; sacred.*

Safe:

1. *Secure from danger, harm, or evil.*
2. *Free from danger or injury; unhurt: safe and sound.*
3. *Free from risk: a safe bet.*
4. *Affording protection: a safe place.*

Place:

1. *An area with definite or indefinite boundaries; a portion of space.*
2. *The particular portion of space occupied by or allocated to a person or thing.*
3. *A building or an area set aside for a specified purpose.*

The American Heritage® Dictionary of the English Language, Fourth Edition

When you look at the definitions of *prayer,* meditation, *centeredness, and intervention,* you see the connection between them. Usually when we go into prayer, meditation, centeredness, and intervention, we make a conscious choice to do so. We set aside time and space to participate in getting connected with our Higher Power. What if I told you that you can be connected with your Higher Power all day long with your eyes wide open while speaking to a group of people or while you're reading, as you are now. Exciting, isn't it?

In your mind's eye you can practice visualizing yourself and your Higher Power connected in a Spiritual Safe Place. This is your connection with your soul. Once you identify this place, it's yours! You'll relate to the nature of *your* spirit, not someone else's. You'll experience a sense of safety you've never known before. No harm or danger will come to you in your Spiritual Safe Place. This place is a definite space for you, with boundaries that are specifically designed for you to feel safe and remain safe. This is the place where you'll be assisted in revealing to yourself your higher purpose in life and how to achieve it.

I believe that with practice we can all walk in the world continually connected to our Higher Power. You'll notice I said, "with practice." This connection must come from within each of us. My connection may look different from your connection—that's to be expected. Your challenge is to be able to go into your own individual Spiritual Safe Place to make the connection. It's a soul connection. It's all about who you really are, not who you think you are based on your mind's limitations.

As this part of The Power Model System ™ came together for me, I realized that only when I could identify my Spiritual Safe Place could I really begin my inward journey to my spiritual self. What I thought was growth before was minor compared to the way I moved forward in my life achievements after discovering my Spiritual Safe Place. And it is gratifying to watch other people self-discover their own personal Spiritual Safe Place and the rapid self-growth that follows.

You're meant to be so much more than you think you can become. This is about peace, internal balance, success as a human being, and achieving your life's purpose. This is about benefiting from all of what your Higher Power has to offer you. This is about experiencing prayer, meditation, centeredness and intervention all throughout your day.

Your spiritual self is within you, you were born with it, and breath is the bridge of connection.

Using Your Spiritual Safe Place

Let's see how your Spiritual Safe Place benefits your emotional, mental, physical, and spiritual components through The Power Model System ™ process. This is where you can observe, without judgment, how your four human components strengthen, interact, conflict, and/or compete with each other.

Emotional Benefits: Your Spiritual Safe Place is where you place your emotions without the vulnerability of the outside world. This exercises your impulse control immediately. *The trigger for the brain to consciously shift away from reacting off your emotions is your visualization of your Spiritual Safe Place.*

Visualization is a very powerful tool. Through this practice you'll experience an emotional release. This is because even though you may not always be able to express your emotions to the outside world (as it is not always safe or necessary to do so), you will always be able to acknowledge them (rather than deny them) from within.

Once you are able to acknowledge your emotions and put yourself into your Spiritual Safe Place, you achieve the automatic connection with your Higher Power. It's this connection that shifts your emotions into neutral and then releases them or puts them on hold until you can deal with them later. With this ability to emotionally release, you'll keep your body relaxed and your mind clear, regardless of your environment. The more you exercise impulse control, the more you will be able to direct your life towards the goals and successes you desire.

Story Time

James and Judy have been married ten years. They took The Power Model System™ workshop because they wanted to learn how to resolve their communication problems. When Judy tries to communicate with Jim, he complains she talks on and on with details he doesn't need to know. He just wants the facts. Judy says, "This is the way I have communicated all my life. I do not know how to change it. I like to tell a story around my message, and James just wants the basics. We both end up getting so angry at each other that we forget what we needed to talk about and fight about how each of us communicates."

After the workshop, James communicated the following story to me, which illustrates just one of the benefits of a Spiritual Safe Place:

James and Judy have a business that is jointly owned by them and other business partners. Judy was telling James about what their business partners had to say about a new client. James kept asking Judy for just the facts, and Judy kept talking about how the partners felt about the client. James was trying to piece the story together, but he found himself getting more frustrated the longer Judy talked without revealing the facts. Judy was very expressive, which James had found cute in the beginning of the relationship, but in the end he just wanted to hear it straight. This became more of an issue as they began to work together in the business. Eventually, their lack of communication resulted in a fight between them. Of course, both thought they were right in what needed to be said.

In the workshop, James and Judy learned how to put their emotions into a Spiritual Safe Place. They came up with a key word in order to remind them to start their Five Steps to Centeredness (discussed later in this book). The word was *Safe*.

When James felt anger inside, he would say in a firm but gentle voice, *Safe*. With that word, they paused, took a deep breath, and visualized their Spiritual Safe Place. In their mind's eye, they could see themselves standing in their Spiritual Safe Place. James told me he could feel the tension leave the room while they both relaxed.

Story Intermission

Mental Benefits: Very little understanding occurs in chaos and turmoil. We all have stories we tell ourselves (the voices in our head) as I have discussed before. These stories stem from our childhood belief system. The only way that I know your brain can re-pattern itself is with the help of your Higher Power connection. This connection will assist you in creating a new positive, evolving belief system that is strong and flexible. Through this, you will realize that you were born for success—you just needed to be reminded of that fact.

In your Spiritual Safe Place, your mind will become clear and you'll experience an instant connection with your Higher Power. You'll be connected with the universal information shared between your mind and your Higher Power. You will have many more choices in your life than before. When this process occurs internally, you automatically start re-patterning both sides of your brain and changing the way you think and respond to everyday events. This is beneficial because the right brain is where you visualize things and the left brain is where your logical thinking processes occur. This balancing unites your emotional, physical, mental, and spiritual components, which results in self-empowerment. You will also be in harmony with the universe, which means you'll be connected to infinite ideas and energy.

Story Time Continued

Once James and Judy visually placed themselves in their individual Spiritual Safe Places, their bodies calmed down. With their eyes wide open, they could see the change in each other as well as feel the change internally within themselves. With their emotions out of the way and their minds calm, they were aware of the dilemma but didn't judge it. Each started to think about what to ask for or say at this time.

James realized how precious Judy was to him. He loved her and needed to let her know that. He also needed to ask her direct questions concerning the situation with the new client and partners.

Judy looked at James and thought, "What a guy. So he doesn't like stories. He prefers facts. I can choose to save the story for dinner and just give the facts now."

James expressed how thankful they both were for such a simple activity to connect them to their Higher Power. The benefits of being able to put emotions aside, clear the mind, and think were amazing to both of them.

Story Intermission

Physical Benefits: As you continue practicing visualizing your Spiritual Safe Place, your physical energy will increase. This is because most of our energy in life is expended through internal conflicts with our own emotional, mental, and spiritual selves. Most of us are simply not aware of the many internal conflicts that drain our energy. Once you're able to maintain balance and stability in your Spiritual Safe Place, this energy is conserved and, in fact, amplified. This energy then flows through the body and powers our actions and desires to change our lives.

We are made up of energy. How we use this energy is the deciding factor in achieving our goals. Without physical energy, we cannot achieve our goals. The lighter our bodies are, the higher they can fly!

Story Time Continued

Only after James and Judy came up with their solution did they realize how much energy they had expended while attempting to change each other. By the time the arguments were over they had little energy left for the rest of the day's activities. This is the miracle of letting go—you have so much more energy to change the things you can.

Story Intermission

Spiritual Benefits: Your Spiritual Safe Place is more than just a peaceful place to be. The uniqueness of this place is a part of you, a part of your soul. You discover it. You visit it. You and your Higher Power created it just for you. You cannot lend your Spiritual Safe Place to anyone. It's uniquely for you. Every section of it holds a part of you. The more you visit it, the more you become intimate with yourself and your Higher Power.

Story Time Continued

James and Judy let me know that going to their Spiritual Safe Place brought them closer to their personal Higher Power and each other. This, in turn, has brought faith into their relationships. Achievement comes from admitting they are practicing human beings. Continuing to practice moves them forward together in new directions.

Hologram: *A three-dimensional diffraction pattern of the image of an object made using holography.*
The American Heritage Stedman's Medical Dictionary.

You may want to think of your Spiritual Safe Place as a three-dimensional hologram. You'll find holograms in many museums—where a virtual image of a real object is projected into a three-dimensional space representing a little world. Your Spiritual Safe Place, however, is much more expansive, deep, and alive. So, every time you visually enter this Spiritual Safe Place, I truly believe you are entering, shifting, and changing yourself, becoming truly balanced on a cellular level. Your heart softens, your mind becomes silent, and your only desire is to connect with your Higher Power.

If I wrote for the next year, I still wouldn't be able to fully explain to you the spiritual benefits of your Spiritual Safe Place because the experience is beyond words. But I'll give it my best try.

From the moment you self-discover your own personal Spiritual Safe Place, something starts happening between you and your Higher Power (whatever you believe it to be). An energy shift occurs internally. I have seen this happen in people over the years and experienced it within myself. The more you visit your Spiritual Safe Place, the more you connect with your Higher Power and your soul. You find yourself working towards and becoming all you can become in this lifetime. You do this simply because you are inspired from within. You start truly believing you can achieve goals in your life that you believed were unachievable before. The more time you spend in your Spiritual Safe Place, the more spiritual you become.

People have made major changes in their lives with little effort. Many have stated that they didn't realize life could be so effortless. They thought perhaps they were doing something wrong, as they weren't stressing about life as much anymore!

The Practical Value of Visualization

The best way to discover your Spiritual Safe Place is through visualization. Visualization has been used for thousands of years to assist human beings to explore themselves beyond the bounds of the physical world. It also helps to reduce the stress from living in the physical world.

What causes symptoms such as headaches, trembling, night sweats, nervous tension, heartburn, heart disease, chronic infections, and respiratory problems? Contributing factors include internal and external human conflicts, working too hard, addictions, exposure to pollution (noise, smog, or chemicals), fast foods, unhealthy diets, genetics, and the list goes on. Through generations, the external environment (traffic, noise, fast-paced lifestyles, technology, work hours, etc.) has developed faster than human internal organs can adapt. (For example, your liver and spleen have to work overtime to deal with pollution, diet changes, etc.)

Anxiety is a more common problem than researchers once thought. It affects people from their teenage years through middle age and into old age. Common problems caused by anxiety include panic attacks, agoraphobia, social phobia, insomnia, preoccupation with physical illness, and obsessive-compulsive disorder. What do people do to address these problems? In America alone, people ingest *billions* of tranquilizers every year!

Visualization is a natural process that eases anxiety and relaxes the body, mind, and spirit. It's used in many cultures to teach people to relax and tap into their creativity. The process of creative visualization involves exploring, discovering, and changing your deepest most basic attitudes toward life.

Some of the things you'll experience when using visualization are:

- New perspectives
- Perception changes
- Less judging of self and others
- Increased empathy and self-acceptance
- Alertness to new options
- A sense of freedom
- Increased creativity
- Reduction in anxiety and insomnia
- Awareness of mental processes, emotional states, and sensations
- A new vocabulary for introspective conversation
- Mindfulness without hypnosis
- Changes in beliefs and attitudes that are emotionally driven

You can use visualization along with the other activities within The Power Model System™ to change your life and take you where you want to go!

Now let's see how you can visualize on your own, in your own way, and at your own pace.

The process of creative visualization involves exploring, discovering, and changing your deepest most basic attitudes toward life.

Activity: Making Your Own Relaxation Tape

You will be making your own relaxation tape that will assist you in reaching your Spiritual Safe Place. Using your own voice will initiate your connection with your internal observer. This will awaken the observer inside you and facilitate a true sense of connection and oneness with your Higher Power.

Supplies needed: Crayons, color pencils, paint, stickers, or any other art supplies you like.

Put all the art supplies beside you before getting comfortable and ready to go through this exercise. You will need a recorder to pre-record your own relaxation tape.

1. Read through the relaxation exercise below where it says *Start Recording Here.* Stop reading where it says *Stop Recording Here.* Read it through quietly to yourself at least three times (or until you feel comfortable enough to read it out loud.) After you have read the relaxation exercise to yourself, go back through it, this time reading it out loud. Do this a few times. Now you are ready to start recording your voice so you can play it back to yourself and/or your group as a relaxation tape.
2. Now turn your recorder on and read the relaxation exercise again. After recording it, play it back to see if any corrections are needed.

You have nowhere to go, nothing to do, but to be here and now.

Start Recording Here

I slowly close my eyes and know that in doing this visualization, I won't be going anywhere in my mind that I don't want to go. I'll be exploring only the places within me that I am ready to explore. I will just relax and adjust my body to a comfortable position.

I have nowhere to go, nothing to do, but to be here and now.

I continue to be aware of my breathing as I have my eyes closed and experience my body relaxing even more. I continue to *breathe in deeply through my nose and release my breath through my mouth.* When I release my breath, I will let all the air out of my lungs. I am emptying all the stale air out of my body and filling it back up with fresh oxygen. And I am sending oxygen to all parts of my body to assist in this relaxation and visualization process.

I have nowhere to go, nothing to do, but to be here and now.

1. As I continue to breathe, I go deeper and deeper into relaxation. If I need to reposition myself to feel more comfortable, I do it. I continue to go deeper and deeper into a relaxed state.
2. If thoughts come into my mind, I will let them pass through. I don't need to stop the thoughts. I will let them pass through. As I go deeper into relaxation, the thoughts will automatically quiet down. If I find myself trying to stop my thoughts, I won't judge myself. If I do, I won't judge the judger part of me. I am just continuing to focus on my breathing. If my mind strays from my breathing focus, I just gently bring it back to my breathing.
3. I breathe in through my nose and out through my mouth. I am going deeper and deeper into relaxation. Down and down I go, spiraling into relaxation. With each breath I take, I am feeling more and more relaxed.
4. I can hear outside sounds, but they don't bother me. They're slowly fading into the background until all that's left is the sound of my voice.
5. I am relaxed, warm, and the only sound I need to hear is the sound of my voice

I have nowhere to go, and nothing to do, but to be here and now.

I am now visualizing myself in my mind's eye. In front of me and at the top of my head is my favorite color. I can see in my mind's eye the color moving down through the top of my head and into my head. I am continuing to breathe in and out as I bring the color all the way down my face, forehead, eyes, ears, nose, and mouth. As the color moves down, if I see any blockages I just breathe the color through the blockages. It may take a while—the color may start coming in as a slow breeze—but I continue to visualize it coming through.

I take my time. I have nowhere to go, nothing to do, but be here and now.

I can see the color move down my neck, body, shoulders, arms, fingers, and then out of the tips of my fingers. I see the color come through the pores of my skin and around my body. In my mind's eye, I see myself continuing to breathe color through my body as it comes out the pores of my skin. I see it wrap around my whole body, and wherever I go my color comes with me.

I am now completely safe, warm, and relaxed.

I am now ready to go on my inner journey. In my mind's eye, I see myself on a beautiful tropical island. I can hear the waves on the beach in the background. As I walk on the beach, I can feel the warm sand under my toes, the sun on my skin, the light breeze in the air, and the fresh smell of salt water. I continue to walk down the beach with the sound of the waves singing in my ears. As I look ahead of me, there's a path leading off into the trees. I can still feel the warm sun on my skin and the warm sand under my toes. I am aware of my favorite color being inside of me, keeping me warm and relaxed.

As I walk down this beautiful path, I can see the lovely colorful flowers along the sides of the path. I smell the fragrance from all of the different flowers that I see blooming. As I continue to walk on this path of sand with flowers and trees, I can feel a cool breeze whispering against my body. I just walk and relax.

I have nowhere to go, nothing to do, but to be here and now.

I go deeper and deeper into relaxation. As I look around this paradise, I reach out and feel the leaves on the trees, I can smell the flowers as I pass them, I hear the birds sing, and feel the path solidly under my feet.

My body is s-o-o-o-o relaxed as I go deeper and deeper into relaxation. As I walk along, I can see the path in front of me. Not far off is a bend in the path, and as I walk along I find myself so contented. As I come to the bend in the road, I see there is a door in the middle of the path. I say to myself that I will count to five as I walk towards the door and open it on five to see what is on the other side.

ONE: I feel very safe as I go deeper and deeper into relaxation.
TWO: I continue to approach the door.
THREE: I am now facing the door, feeling wonderfully relaxed and peaceful.
FOUR: I place my hand on the doorknob.
FIVE: I open the door. On the other side is my Spiritual Safe Place.

My Spiritual Safe Place can be indoors or outdoors. It might be a place I've been to before. It could be a place I've dreamed about going to. I look around. Everything I need and want is here for me to feel safe. As I look around and walk to different parts of this place, I find myself touching, smelling, listening, and observing everything around me. This is *my* unique Spiritual Safe Place. It is not anyone else's. It is uniquely mine.

I decide to sit down and enjoy myself as I continue to experience all the colors, sights, sounds, and wonderful smells in this wonderful place. I become aware of my body and how I feel in my safe place. I start looking around to see if I can find a message or a symbol just for me. I continue to look. I will find it if it is here. I decide to stay in my Spiritual Safe Place for a while. This is who I am, relaxed and safe. This is how my body, mind, and spirit can be. I will stay here three minutes to enjoy this.

Leave Three Minutes of Quite Time on the Recorder

It's time for me to get ready to leave my Spiritual Safe Place, just for now. As I wake up, I'll be able to recall everything about this wonderful part of me. I'll also be able to return as often as I'd like. If I discovered a message left for me—whether it's a note, a color, an object, or a symbol—I'll remember what it is. I look around. This is a place that's with me wherever I go, whoever I'm with, and whatever situation I'm in. This is my Spiritual Safe Place.

I'm now going to count to five backwards. As I do, I will start to move slowly toward the door in my Spiritual Safe Place. On one, I'll open the door and walk through it, back into my paradise, walking on the path. As I return to the path, I will feel lots of energy and relaxed.

FIVE: I look around and experience how my body feels in my wonderful Spiritual Safe Place. I will remember that I can return anytime.

FOUR: I will now look at my message if it's in writing, a color, an object, or a symbol. I will remember it when I leave here.

THREE: I'm now approaching closer to the door.

TWO: I am walking to the door and placing my hand on the doorknob.

ONE: I now turn the doorknob, open the door, and walk through.

I am on a sandy path in a paradise of trees and flowers. I look around and see that my favorite color is still all around my body. The sun is shining, and I can feel it on my skin. I can feel the warm gentle sand beneath my feet. I hear the birds singing, and I smell the gentle fragrances in the air.

I continue to walk down the path. I'm so relaxed and joyful. I'm experiencing a level of joy I've never experienced before. Life is good. I continue to enjoy the sounds, sights, and fragrances in the air.

As I continue to walk down the path, I see another door in the middle of the path. This is the door leading me back into my present room. I might have some hesitation about walking up to it—I'm so relaxed and joyful; I might want to stay where I am. But it's time to go through the door. In doing so, I'll stay as relaxed as I am now and with the same level of joy I feel now.

I place my hand on the doorknob and open the door. I see myself in my mind's eye surrounded by my favorite color, feeling warm, relaxed, and joyful.

As I count to five, I slowly become aware of my surroundings.

ONE: I'm experiencing my body being relaxed and joyful.

TWO: I am coming up from the level of relaxation I've been in. My muscles feel good, and my nervous system is calm.

THREE: All my pain and discomfort is reduced or gone from my body. My mind feels clear and quiet. I am starting to become aware of my breathing patterns—in through my nose and out through my mouth.

FOUR: I can move my fingers and toes, even if I don't feel like moving them yet. I feel totally relaxed, joyful, and in the here and now.

FIVE: I slowly open my eyes. I don't move my body. I am opening my eyes and becoming aware of how my body feels. I continue to remain still for a while until I get my bearings. As I become aware, I slowly get up. If I received a message in my visualization, I write it down.

Stop Recording Here

The more you use this tape to relax and go to your Spiritual Safe Place, the more you'll be able to observe yourself throughout the day without judgment. When you're able to observe yourself and not make judgments about yourself, the changes from within will come faster and become permanent.

Now let's perform an activity for discovering your Spiritual Safe Place. This will involve drawing your Spiritual Safe Place in order to make it as real as possible to you in your everyday life.

Activity: Discovering Your Spiritual Safe Place

Figures 14.1 and 14.2 refer to this activity.

This activity can be done alone or in a group.

1. Now you can use your relaxation tape whenever you need it. This tape can be used for relaxation in the future for pain control and many other stress issues you may have. When you use it, be sure you will not be interrupted. Turn off all phones, wear comfortable clothes, and take off your shoes. Use a blanket for warmth, if needed.
2. Begin by standing and stretching your body. Lean over and touch the floor with your hands or bend as far down to the floor as you can. When you get as far down as you can reach, hold your body there and take a deep breath in through your nose and out through your mouth. When you breathe out, relax your back, legs, and arms even more, and then you'll be able to reach further down. Remain in that position for the count of ten. Gently relax your back, neck, and shoulder muscles. Good work! Do this a few times so your body is thoroughly relaxed.
3. Bring the recorder near to you, turn it on, and begin your visualization.
4. After your visualization, quietly (you and whoever else is with you) take some art supplies and start recreating what you saw in your visualization exercise on the blank sheet in this book or any paper you want to put it on. There should be no talking or communicating until everyone in the group finishes their artwork. If you are alone, do not be distracted by the phone or do anything else until you have finished your artwork. This helps to bring realism to your connection with your Higher Power.
5. If you do this exercise with a group, you may want to have a discussion on how each person experienced their inner journey and what they learned from it.

Tips about your Spiritual Safe Place:

- This is not about artistic talent. This is about soul contact. Take as long as you want and enjoy the process.
- When you're finished, hang your drawing in your house where you can look at it. This is your Spiritual Safe Place from inside you. You have this place wherever you go, whatever you do, and whoever you're with.
- Practice visualizing your Spiritual Safe Place at least twice a day or more—in the morning when you wake up and before you go to sleep.
- Be aware of what you experience in your body, mind, and spirit while you're visualizing your unique safe place.

CREATING A SPIRITUAL SAFE PLACE

EXAMPLE
CREATING A SPIRITUAL SAFE PLACE

Chapter 15

YOUR INTERNAL SYSTEM

Do not wait for a leader; do it alone, person-to-person.
Mother Teresa

What is our Internal System? The Power Model System™ defines it as "what we all need within ourselves to function and care for ourselves while living in reality."

The structure of your internal system and how it functions determines how you embrace (or reject) the world, respond to other people, experience yourself, achieve your goals in life, and experience joy through it all. This structure is composed of your *defense system, boundaries*, and your *Spiritual Safe Place* as shown in Figure 15.1.

When you exercise your boundaries (impulse control) and are aware of your defense system, you are able to put your emotions in a safe spiritual place, connect with your Higher Power, and create a calm mind where you can consider your choices in any given situation. How well you are able to do this will determine your dependence, interdependence, and/or independence in life. So the question is: are you living as a dependent, interdependent, or independent person?

This chapter will review how The Power Model System™ activities so far have assisted you in discovering these stages. The goal is to achieve interdependence within yourself so you can go out in the world as an independent person. By "interdependence" I mean that your emotional, mental, spiritual, and physical human components are interacting in harmony with your internal system. A stable, interdependent system gives you a sense of self, which leads to your goal of independence.

The Power Model Activities have guided you in the self-discovery process of the Dependent, Interdependent, and Independent Stages as follows:

Dependent

Dependent: *unable to exist, sustain oneself, or act appropriately or normally without the assistance or direction of another.*

The Merriam-Webster Dictionary

In this case the word "dependent" means that you may often rely on others to identify your emotions, do your thinking for you, and tell you how to behave and what to believe. The activities in the Dependent Stage were designed to educate you about emotions—how to identify them and how they function within you. Without awareness of your emotions, you reactive to events in your life and are unable to think your way through situations. As a result you become a "dependent" human being.

The following activities assisted you in discovering where in life you are dependent:

The Present Self: Chapter 3 (Figures 3.1 and 3.3)

You identified how you are (emotionally, mentally, spiritually, and physically) in the present, how you respond to life events, how you respond to stress, and how staying dependent on old coping skills is causing consequences in your life that are no longer acceptable to you.

Environment Activity: Chapter 4 (Figure 4.1)

This activity showed how you're dependent on your emotions and react off them. You learned how your environment can cause you to regress and be reactive off your past. You self-discovered how a present day event can trigger the reaction to a past event in your life.

Three Faces of Illusion: Chapter 5 (Figures 5.1A and 5.1B)

You went on to learn about how being in illusion emotionally, mentally, spiritually, and physically affects your life. You learned how staying in illusions leads to the 3 Rs, Resistance, Resentment, and Revenge.

Automatic Pilot/Autopilot: Chapter 6 (Figure 6.1)

You looked at how autopilot (automatic reaction) works unconsciously. You learned that you established emotional, mental, spiritual, and physical reactions to life's situations in your youth and that you're still reacting off these established patterns in your adult life.

The Five Stages of Illusion: Chapter 7 (Figure 7.1)

You covered the Five Stages of Illusions and learned that you can choose to stay in illusion for a lifetime or move forward. You discovered how in illusion it's possible to sink deeper and deeper until your very life is threatened. You faced the undeniable fact that your life is all about choices that only you can make.

Defense System: Chapter 8 (Figure 8.1 and 8.3)

This exercise gave you your "top ten" defenses, which are part of the invisible force that has stopped you from achieving your goals in life. You learned that your defenses are always based on fight or flight, and you discovered what the consequences of these defenses have been in your life.

Feeling-Thinking-Behavior Chart: Chapter 9 (Figure 9.1)

When looking at the Feeling, Thinking, Behavior chart, you learned how flexible you need to be with these components if you want to live as a balanced human being and make a connection with your Spiritual component. You learned that you will not be whole or complete unless all these human components are in balance.

Pyramid of Success: Chapter 10 (Figure 10.1)

The Pyramid of Success shows you what growth level you're on in any given situation and what your next step is so you can achieve the goal you set. In this activity, you determined what you needed to do to get through each level to reach your desired spiritual results.

Interdependent

Interdependent: *having a reciprocal relation between interdependent entities (objects or individuals or groups) [syn, interdependency]*

The Merriam-Webster Dictionary

In the Interdependent Stage activities, you learned that interdependence exists between your four human components, your defense system (your system of fight-or-flight) and your Spiritual Safe Place (your connection to your Higher Power). You learned that without boundaries and impulse control, your defense system can prevent you from connecting to your Higher Power. When you are interdependent, your emotional, mental, physical, and spiritual powers work together, empowering you to freely respond to virtually any event in your life.

The following activities assisted you in achieving interdependence:

The Five Stages of Maturity: Chapter 11 (Figure 11.1)

You learned to recognize the important growth stages of maturity. You also learned the difference between being in illusion and being in reality.

Discovering Internal Boundaries: Chapter 12 (Figure 12.1)

You learned what you need to change internally in order to care for yourself physically, emotionally, mentally, and spiritually. Your internal boundaries provide you with discipline and guide you in treating yourself and others with tolerance, compassion, and love.

Discovering External Boundaries: Chapter 12 (Figure 12.2)

You learned how to develop and communicate your external boundaries to others in order to keep you safe in this world. With some people, you need to make your physical, emotional, mental, and spiritual boundaries very clear.

Life Spark: Chapter 13 (Figure 13.1)

You now know you were born with a Life Spark that only you can uncover. By becoming aware of your cover-up emotions, you start to identify and experience your authentic emotions. In this chapter, you were able to create a map relating each of your authentic emotions to your cover-up emotions.

Creating a Safe Spiritual Place: Chapter 14 (Figure 14.1)

You must be silent to hear the gentle voice of spirit. To do this, you created a relaxation tape for yourself. From this silence, you are now able to go to a place deep inside you that has always been there waiting to be rediscovered by you. From this place you can hear messages and receive insight relating to your life. To make this place real, you drew and colored this beautiful Spiritual Safe Place. This is where your soul is awakened.

My Internal System: Chapter 15 (Figure 15.1)

The review of the Power Model System™ so far shows you how your internal system works and why it is so important. Without recognizing its existence you simply cannot function in life for very long successfully. Without managing it, you cannot cross over from illusions to reality, much less recognize what's real and what's not.

Understanding and managing *Your Internal System* allows you to achieve the following:

- Your emotions can be placed in your mind's eye in your visual Spiritual Safe Place;
- You know your defense system, thus you are aware of your choices;
- You put internal boundaries on your emotions when you place them into your Spiritual Safe Place;
- You exercise and communicate your external boundaries to others;
- You can see how your defense system, Spiritual Safe Place, and boundaries work together inside of you, allowing you to practice full impulse control in any given situation.

Your Internal System is extremely important, so let's look at it again.

In the chart in Figure 15.1, you see *impulse control* is right next to boundaries. This shows that you have taken a very important step. When you refrain from acting off your emotions and have boundaries on your emotions, you automatically have impulse control. This in turn gives you a clear mind in which to think through situations instead of reacting to them. Being aware of your defense system empowers you to exercise the mental choice of acting from your defense system or looking at new choices available to you. Instead of just reacting from your emotions, you are able to exercise impulse control and make decisions using your mental abilities, with the help of your Higher Power connection in your Spiritual Safe Place. You have progressed from being *dependent* to *interdependent* and are well on the way to becoming an *independent* human being.

As you can see, you are gathering information on self-discovering "you." Later on, you will put all this information together for the final stage of achieving *Independence*.

YOUR INTERNAL SYSTEM — INTER-DEPENDENT

1. Your defense system is in place.

2. In your Spiritual Safe Place, you connect with your Higher-Power and place boundaries on your emotions. Your defense system becomes a conscious choice.

3. Every time your emotions and defense system connect with your Higher Power, you strengthen your impulse control.

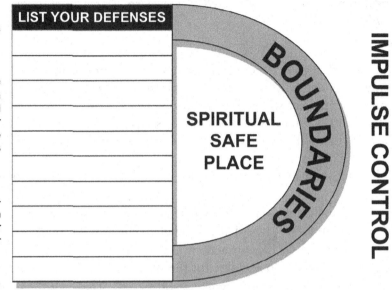

LIST YOUR DEFENSES

SPIRITUAL SAFE PLACE

BOUNDARIES

IMPULSE CONTROL

Figure 15.1 ~ My Internal System - Inter-dependent

Independent

Independent: *free from the influence, guidance, or control of another or others; self-reliant: an independent mind.*

The Merriam-Webster Dictionary

With your three human components (emotional, mental, and spiritual) working interdependently, you'll come up with the right action to take (exercising your physical component) that will give you independence. This balanced internal system gives you the ability to make independent decisions and take actions that are best for you—actions that reflect your values and morals and aren't influenced by your peers.

Here are some major characteristics you will exhibit as an Independent Person:

- You are able to physically take action on your decisions, knowing this is the right action for you and that your Higher Power is with you.
- If the results of your actions aren't what you expected, you won't feel victimized; you'll take responsibility for the situation and make changes.
- You will grow and evolve stronger and wiser with everything that happens in your life, because you treat all situations as a learning experience.

In Chapter 18, on a single chart, you will compare your *Internal System* with how you respond and exist in the real world, which I call your *Personal Blueprint*. This will allow you to track in real time how your Internal System is actually performing in the real world.

Remember, without your internal system in place, it's impossible to distinguish between illusion and reality.

So now that your internal system is in place, let's look at *Reality*.

Chapter 16

REALITY

The only thing harder than forgiveness is the alternative.
            Philip Yancey

Have you ever wondered what it would be like to be completely authentic? To be all you were meant to be? To be fully open to what life offers every day? To be comfortable in any given situation you find yourself in and not react to past events in present situations? Have you wondered what it would feel like to be comfortable and accept your present condition, whatever that might be?

Am I asking too much? I don't think so. This is what reality has to offer. Being yourself—being real—is one of the most important and rewarding things you will ever achieve in your lifetime.

So what does reality (being authentic) really mean?

Being authentic does <u>not</u> mean:

- Saying whatever comes to mind about anyone and/or anything and acting out on any and every emotion you experience;
- Being justified in abusing or hurting anyone else verbally or otherwise, or doing something despite the consequences;
- Refusing to accept responsibility for your actions;
- Making up your own rules of living and expecting everyone else to follow them.

Being authentic means:

- Being able to genuinely live in the reality of your own life;
- Acknowledging your four human components, taking responsibility for them, personally identifying with them, and maintaining harmony and balance between them while living in the present;
- Being aware that you're always learning, forever journeying through the events and opportunities that go along with being alive;
- Perceiving all events, joyful or painful, as opportunities for growth;
- Understanding that you can stay *in* a problem forever if you choose to;
- Knowing that the longer you stay in a problem, the further you get from solving the problem.

---

*If you stay in the problem and dwell on your emotions,
you start building a case for how you've been victimized.*

We are the Obstacles to Experiencing Reality

If you wonder why you're failing in your relationships within your marriage, family, workplace, community, or career, remember this: *you can't control anyone, or any place, or most situations.*

Even though you may want to be in control of everyone, everything, and every place, the truth is that *control is an illusion.* So if you can't control others, what's left? You! When you change yourself, it's amazing how effortlessly you can journey through reality. If you develop a close, loving relationship with yourself, everything else will follow.

I'm reminded of the book *Don't Sweat the Small Stuff* by Richard Carlson, who contends that, "everything is small stuff." A person's perception makes things bigger or smaller than they are. It may be easy to say to yourself, "Don't sweat it." But perceiving day-to-day events as "small stuff" is nearly impossible if you're not balanced internally.

The *real you* has already been established within and is just waiting to be self-discovered and expressed outwardly. I'm amazed by how many people have said to me over the years, "This is the way I am," or "I can't change, no matter how hard I try," or "This is who I am; this is the real me. Take it or leave it." Take a minute and repeat these statements. Do you see how limiting this attitude of refusing to change can be? By adopting this perception of yourself, you're declaring that *how you are inside* at the age of twenty will be exactly the same at age thirty, forty, fifty, sixty, and so on.

Having this false perception causes you to:

- Limit your choices and opportunities;
- Confine yourself to stagnation for the rest of your life;
- Build the walls of your own prison in your mind and take those prison bars out into your life.

Why do people living in illusion do this? *Because they believe that being right is more important than being happy.*

When you're in illusion, being right is preferable to being balanced, so you struggle with yourself to prove that you're right. In Richard Bach's *Illusions*, he made this idea clear by saying, "Fight for your limitations and they are yours." Also, you stick with what you know rather than continuing to learn, observe, and grow. If you keep basing your reality on experiences you had when you were young, daily living can seem overwhelming. In fact, that's how The Power Model System™ defines "illusion." Rather than perceiving life from a mature, balanced adult's perspective, you perceive it from a child's perspective.

The good news is that you've chosen to read this book, which suggests that you are no longer satisfied with that limiting belief system. By reading this book, you're taking action to change.

> *Don't allow old belief systems to interrupt the reality of a new situation.*

The Path to Your Soul is Through Reality

Think of your emotions and thoughts as being opportunities to exercise boundaries and impulse control so the *real* you can come out. Remember, you are *not* your emotions, your thoughts, your actions, or your spiritual beliefs (although you're responsible for all these). You are your *soul*. The other stuff in your life simply assists you in reconnecting with who you really are, your soul.

Where does your soul reside? Is your higher purpose contained within you? *Where is the real you?* Many of us simply aren't in touch with our soul, but that doesn't mean it doesn't exist. It just means we aren't aware of it. Only through real experiences in the present can you discover your true self, your soul.

> *In today's society, we* don't learn *that taking time to learn balance within oneself can be more important than earning a college degree.*

The Power Model System™ based on Your Present Experiences

The kind of reality that The Power Model System™ addresses is based on having an awareness of your Internal System and becoming balanced internally. This allows you to learn from your past experiences and move quickly into the present. It's about developing present spiritual beliefs and present authentic emotional systems with balanced internal and external boundaries. It's also about achieving impulse control and, thus, maintaining the connection with your Higher Power. Only then will you listen to what your physical, emotional, mental and spiritual components are saying to you *in the present* and make appropriate decisions—and thus achieve true internal interdependence. When you have developed an interdependent relationship with your four components *internally*, you'll learn how to have interdependent relationships with other human beings *externally* with minimal conflicts.

When you live in the present, you:

- Spiritually and mentally acknowledge that a Higher Power exists;
- Recognize that the world doesn't need to revolve around you;
- Are able to identify your emotions and stresses instead of hiding them;
- Consciously choose your fight-or-flight defense system instead of reacting automatically (autopilot);
- Learn how your body works; you know what you need to do to take care of yourself, and you do it;
- Have a spiritual agreement with yourself to be kind, firm, loving, gentle, and intensely honest with yourself;
- Are supportive to yourself in your mind;
- Are accepting of *you*;
- Are on a journey of connecting with your soul.

With these elements of reality in place, you:

- Look for solutions to problems;
- Self-discover how you can make changes with accountability;
- Take full responsibility for your life, with your Higher Power at your side;
- Live in the present reality and accept the hardships and the miracles in life;
- Have a sense of internal stability and calmness, even if the world around you is chaotic.

- Use your spiritual power beliefs to assist you through all events in your life rather than to separate yourself from others;
- Enjoy having interdependent relationships in the present with others;

Life is a process. There are no mistakes, only lessons to be learned. As a mature human being, you fully understand the words of W. Mitchell: "It isn't what happens to you, it's what you do with it."

Now let's see how your four human components keep you in reality. With this awareness, you will discover why it's nearly impossible to stay in reality when one of your physical, emotional, mental, or spiritual components is either missing or out of balance.

Emotional Power in Reality

When you're in your Emotional Power, you're able to:

- Identify your emotions;
- Confirm for yourself that you are experiencing authentic emotions, rather than cover-up emotions.

You are able to do this because you used the Life Spark Chart found in Chapter Thirteen to visually confirm your authentic feelings. Over time, you will intuitively know at any time if you're using a cover-up emotion. This is truly empowering because you are able to remain firm about who you are in virtually any situation. Being firm about your emotional identity allows you to respond decisively, yet compassionately, to real events in your life. You stay in reality only if you stay empowered.

If your authentic emotions become overwhelming in certain situations, you can always retreat to your Spiritual Safe Place, where you can visualize the stress leaving your body and mind. Remember, emotional power comes from being *real*. Being real means acknowledging that reality will occasionally surprise you with unexpected events. You must prepare yourself for life's surprises, even the painful ones. A good time to practice going to your Spiritual Safe Place in your mind's eye is when you're not under stress. Even though you aren't under stress, you'll find that your body will go into deeper relaxation. Eventually you'll be able to do this automatically, even in stressful and unexpected situations.

Mental Power in Reality

With your emotions in your Spiritual Safe Place and your spiritual power aligned with your mental abilities, your choices become unlimited. You become aware that anything is possible. You'll want to do your decision-making from this place of reality, where your intuitive abilities tune into the "music of the universe."

This is how you establish "healthy ego strength." Ego comes from the mind. When your mind is healthy and balanced, your ego is healthy and balanced. When your ego is balanced, it has no need to dominate anyone else or any situation. When you are at peace with yourself, you are at peace with those around you.

Healthy ego strength is your bridge between *conscious awareness* that you're in control of your thoughts and behavior and *understanding* how this will affect your external reality. A healthy way to strengthen your ego is by staying connected with your Higher Power.

Healthy ego strength will develop faster if you're able to be *firm, loving, kind, honest, and gentle* with yourself and others. Your Higher Power will speak to you in this way, and you'll want to treat yourself and others with the same respect.

Let's look at these five words in depth.

> **Firm:** *Constant; steadfast.*
> **Loving:** *A deep, tender, ineffable feeling of affection and solicitude toward a person, such as that arising from kinship, recognition of attractive qualities, or a sense of underlying oneness.*
>
> The Merriam-Webster Dicticcfonary

Before we can truly show love toward others, we need to learn how to love ourselves. Go to the mirror, look at the face in the mirror, and then say, "I love you." How do you feel about loving that person in the mirror? If at first it feels fake or false, keep practicing until it feels authentic.

> **Kind:** *Having feelings befitting our common nature; congenial; sympathetic; as, a kind man; a kind heart.*
>
> The Merriam-Webster Dictionary

Kindness will develop when you remind yourself that you are a "practicing" human being and that perfection is an illusion. Are you sympathetic and kind with yourself? If not, you need to start practicing self-compassion in any situation where you constantly criticize yourself. This can be difficult and take time, so be patient with this for as long as it takes.

Honest: *Characterized by integrity or fairness and straight- forwardness in conduct, thought, speech, etc.; upright; just; equitable; trustworthy; truthful; sincere; free from fraud, guile, or duplicity; not false.*

The Merriam-Webster Dictionary

Courage is all about being able to take an honest look at yourself, seeing the truth about who you think you are and what you need to do, and then rearranging yourself internally to become who you really are.

Gentle: *Not harsh or severe; mild and soft: a gentle scolding; a gentle tapping at* the *window.*

The Merriam-Webster Dictionary

When you discover a weakness in yourself, how do you talk to yourself about it? What do you say when you try to reach a goal and don't make it the first, second, or third time? Do you speak gently and support yourself in going for a fourth attempt? Accepting that you make mistakes and learn from them will lead you to being open to new ways of improving yourself.

Using Both Sides of Your Brain to Stay in Reality

The left side of your brain is where you do your *linear thinking.* It's where your organization, mathematic, scientific, and verbal skills reside. This part of your brain goes through The Power Model System™ step by step. The left brain seeks the logic of the Power Model System™ and wants to make sense of things on an intellectual level.

The right side of your brain is the side that's spontaneous and visual; it sees in pictures. This is the creative, artistic, and musical side that integrates ideas and situations. When you're dancing, singing, and laughing, you're using this side of your brain. It's also responsible for your intuitive processes of feeling, thinking, problem-solving, and decision-making. The right brain is where you learn the Power Model System™ through visuals, activities, self-discovery, and drawings.

As you learn how to place your emotions in your Spiritual Safe Place and align with your Higher Power, you'll be able to return to your Mental Power in Reality and have the use of both parts of your brain. With left brain and right brain working in harmony, you'll be in harmony with the universe, therefore connected to infinite information and energy.

> *To achieve your goals, you must transcend your beliefs about the way you think things are accomplished in life and see how reality actually works.*

This means that in all your activities you're able to list the facts of a situation as well as combine your feelings, thoughts, and spiritual knowledge to develop your intuitiveness and come up with many new possibilities in your life. You're functioning at an extremely high level and are able to take physical action if and when the reality of the situation requires it.

Spiritual Power in Reality

Spiritual Power in Reality will give you awareness on a soul level. Only then will you be able to accomplish great things against great odds.

It is difficult to explain to people without eyesight the beauty of the stars and sky. Explaining the move from Spiritual Power in *illusion* to Spiritual Power in *reality* is equally difficult, as no words can adequately describe it. Suffice it to say that as you continue to apply The Power Model System™ and move from illusion to reality, you'll feel like you've woken up from a dream. This is what the word "power" in the model stands for. The more you walk in balance with your four human components, the more you'll awaken from your dream world and enjoy a sweet life. Yes, even with the hardships, the challenges, the pain, and the reality, life is sweet when you know who you really are and where you're going!

So how does spiritual power empower you to stay authentic and real?

As you may recall, the Five Stages of Maturity from Chapter 11 are:

1. Honeymoon
2. Reality
3. Power Struggle
4. Commitment
5. Co-creator

Let's look at these Five Stages of Maturity within the context of growing into your Spiritual Power in Reality.

Spiritual Honeymoon

In this experience of Spiritual Awakening, you make a connection with your religious or spiritual beliefs and see the world and yourself differently. You no longer feel alone. At last, you feel connected to everything around you, including the universe itself. Your body feels lighter, and you have hope for yourself and the entire world. You may feel like you're walking on a cloud! Life is a joy.

Spiritual Reality

As time goes by, the Honeymoon seems to fade away. As the reality of life starts sinking in, you realize that your spiritual awakening is just that—an awakening—and now it's time to apply your spiritual beliefs to life and its challenges. In this stage, you learn to let go and allow your Higher Power to assist you in all situations in your life. You realize that you must create/adopt/modify your own belief system and not simply rely on what you've been told. In other words, life teaches you, and you're flexible and willing to change and grow through the process.

Spiritual Power Struggle

This is where your past meets your present. This stage will come and go throughout your life. Doubts from your old thought patterns will resurface. Then you'll rebound and say to yourself, "I want to keep believing there is hope and I can change." It's normal to have this power struggle going on in your mind. When you begin making changes in your life, you struggle with your old self. It's no different with your spiritual component.

Sometimes difficult events occur and you'll be challenged to keep believing there's a Higher Power. Know that this, too, will pass and that you'll progress to the next stage of commitment. Remember, we all go in and out of these stages. This struggle is a test of faith, so don't give up!

Your Higher Power doesn't give you what you want, but what you need.

Spiritual Commitment

Once you've chosen a path of spiritual belief, you commit to it. You realize that other people don't need to have the same spiritual belief system or definition of a Higher Power as you do. Your path might involve an organized religion or other belief system, perhaps even the same religion your parents followed. You've come full circle: you belong; you believe; you feel a close connection to your soul. Being in this stage doesn't require that you subscribe to the same belief system for the rest of your life. You just know that a Higher Power exists and can now start maturing spiritually.

You become aware of your past behavior, your addictions, and what you need to make amends for. Sometimes we hide this truth from ourselves, but with the help of all four of your human components and your Higher Power, you can come to a resolution within yourself about yourself and how you have affected others. When this is done, you'll experience peace, faith, and joy. The new joyful feelings will take the place of all your hidden emotions, thoughts, and old reactive behavior. With each resolution, you will remember that your Higher Power gives you free will and that no matter what events happen in your life, it will always help you grow if you look at it a certain way.

I continue to marvel at the spiritual capacity of human beings to get through the most horrendous events in their lives. Once we become aware of our human spirit (soul), we can overcome great odds, while remaining kind, gentle, firm, honest, and loving to ourselves and others. This maturity and knowledge gives us the ability to go on to the fifth stage, which is spiritual co-creation.

Spiritual Co-creation

In this stage, you become aware that your relationship with a Higher Power is a partnership. By being in partnership with your Higher Power, you connect with your own soul. You're aware that human balance and soul growth are the keys to having a peaceful existence. Like any other relationship, you have to spend time on your relationship with yourself and your Higher Power. But unlike your human relationships, this one has to come first, before anyone or anything else. If it doesn't come first, you will have no other relationships. (If you think you do, you're in illusion.)

In this close relationship, you and your Higher Power are co-creators in your life. You and your Higher Power can re-create you as many times as you choose. You no longer believe that if you don't get what you want in life, this higher source doesn't exist. As you reflect on events and opportunities in your life, you acknowledge what you've learned from each event and how each one has strengthened you. Remember, painful situations can provide insight into the lessons of the past.

It might take time to shift your perception, but in time you'll start looking at life differently. When that happens, you'll develop a knowingness that you and your Higher Power are co-creators—and that you have to hold up your end of the relationship.

Defining your Spiritual Safe Place and working The Power Model System™ will help you recognize and realize your spiritual stages. You'll pass through the Honeymoon period, through the Reality stage, through the Power Struggle stage, and onto the Commitment stage of choosing your spiritual belief system. At that point, you'll be able to take full responsibility and accountability for your life. With this knowledge and awareness, you're well on your way to obtaining wisdom.

Physical Power in Reality

The reality of physical power takes effect only when your emotional, mental, and spiritual components are in alignment. You're able to make the right decisions and take the right action *for you*. You focus on solutions, not problems. You not only take responsibility for your life but accept accountability for it. You know what you want to accomplish. You write out the steps you'll need to take to achieve your goals and then take the right action to achieve them.

Let's look at what "right action" means. When you're balanced—your emotions are in a Spiritual Safe Place, your right and left brain are connected and working together, your intuition is at its peak, and your connection with your Higher Power is at its fullest—you will know the right action to take when making daily decisions. Your maturity will shine through your actions.

I would be misleading you if I said we are all either in illusion or reality. You'll need to look at each area of your life. You may be in reality in some situations and in illusion in other situations.

Now let's determine what areas of your life are in illusion, and then cross over to reality.

Activity: Crossing from Illusion to Reality

Figures 16.1A, 16.1B, 16.2A and 16.2B refer to this activity.

This is where you discover you have the ability to cross back and forth between illusion and reality. Hopefully, as time goes by, you will choose to stay in reality more and more. The more you develop discipline and flexibility, the faster you will transfer from an illusion state to a reality state and remain there for longer periods of time.

Now let's piece together all four of your human components in reality.

Read through the activity, look at the example, and then begin the activity.

1. In Figure 16.1A, under each of the Illusion Sections (emotional, mental, physical, and/or spiritual power) write two of the illusions you discovered from Chapter Five (Figures 5.1A & 5.1B).
2. Now circle in the Reality columns what you could do to move out of the illusion and into reality. What would it take for you to be able to cope with the reality of the illusion? Add any unique reality items to the list that you believe you need to do or fully understand.
3. Perform Steps 1 and 2 above for all your emotional, mental, physical and spiritual illusions.
4. After you finished, ponder over what you have discovered here. Why can't you do this every day? Choose reality over illusion any day?

Good work!

<u>Example</u>

Let's look at Sue who was in the example (Chapter Five). Let's take her circled illusions in Chapter Five and move them into reality. (See figures 5.2A and 5.2B.)

Example: Emotional Power

Illusion: *I have been victimized*
Sue states she has felt like a victim all her life. She has ended up in abusive relationships and has a hard time getting out of them. At her workplace, she seems to be the one people yell at if they find an error.

Reality: *I am not a Victim*
Sue in reality is able to identify her emotions. She realized that underneath her victim role she felt anger, hurt, and shame, so she checked these emotions in the Reality Authentic Column.

Example Mental Power:

Illusion: *I can't hear my choices due to defenses*
Sue found that one of her defenses was to be constantly mentally abusive (talking to herself) whenever she is stressed. She believes she can't quiet her mind enough to hear herself think. This internal behavior invites others to treat her the same way.

Reality: *My defense system is a choice (I can observe my own behavior)*
When Sue goes to her Spiritual Safe Place, she realizes her defense system is a choice. In her Mental Power in Reality, she can now quiet her mind, which allows her to observe her authentic emotions along with her strength and weaknesses. She thinks the situation through and, thus, realizes her choices. With this, she puts her life in her own hands rather than relying on magical thinking.

Example Spiritual Power:

Illusion: *My Higher Power punishes me when bad things happen in my life.*
Sue stated that she learned at a very young age that if she was good, all good things would come to her. So when something goes wrong, she automatically believes she is being punished.

Reality: *My Higher Power is present at all times to assist me in learning and becoming stronger from my experiences.*
With a new belief system in place, Sue has learned that her Higher Power gives her free will, and it is always there to help her through any events in her life. This connects her with her Higher Power and keeps her in reality mentally, emotionally, and physically. This allows her to remain firm, kind, and honest in difficult situations.

Example Physical Power:

Illusion: *I act based on how I feel*
Sue realized it was hard for her to leave abusive relationships because she was basing all her actions on the emotion of love. So she stayed and took the abuse because she loved them.

Reality: *I can act in such a way that keeps me safe while still caring for others.*
With Sue's emotions identified, her mind calm, and her connection to her Higher Power established, she is able to set boundaries for herself and others. This allows her to act with true power instead of blindly reacting. She takes care of herself by removing herself from abusive situations.

REALITY

SPIRITUAL POWER

Kind - Loving - Gentle   CENTERED   Firm - Honest

Spiritual Illusion (not connected)

Spiritual Reality (connected)
- My Higher Power is at my side in difficult times
- I can connect with my Higher Power
- I can create/choose my own belief system
- I am comfortable with other's having a different belief system

EMOTIONAL POWER		MENTAL POWER		PHYSICAL POWER	
Illusion	Reality Authentic	Illusion	Reality	Illusion	Reality
What are my emotions?		*What am I telling myself?*	*What are my choices?*	*What is my reactive behavior?*	*What do I choose to do?*

EMOTIONAL POWER — Reality (Authentic)

- ☐ Anger
- ☐ Hurt/Pain
- ☐ Shame
- ☐ Guilt
- ☐ Shutdown
- ☐ Saddess
- ☐ Fear
- ☐ Power
- ☐ Loneliness
- ☐ Happiness

MENTAL POWER — Reality (What are my choices?)

- I have healthy ego strength
- I can identify my emotions
- I have tolerance for my feelings
- I have tolerance for human characteristics
- I have sympathy for others
- I calm down and investigate my choices
- I know my internal/external boundaries
- I am a friend to myself
- I have a sense of self
- I know my strengths/weaknesses
- I can observe my own behavior
- I self-discover what I need
- My childhood reactions are not needed as an adult
- I cannot control people, places, and things
- My life is in my hands
- My Spiritual Safe Place helps me focus

LIST OF DEFENSES

PHYSICAL POWER — Reality (What do I choose to do?)

- I exercise impulse control
- I am aware of what affects my body
- I rely on my Higher Power
- I exercise by internal/external boundaries
- I have predictable behavior
- I can take action to change my perception
- I pay attention and confirm if I am understood
- I am responsible for my actions
- I take care of myself
- I am dependable
- I practice playing

AWARENESS
Dependent

ACCEPTANCE
Interdependent

IMPULSE CONTROL

ACTION
Independent

Figure 16.1A ~ Reality   The Power Model System™ | Copyright © 2007 – HumanWisdom LLC

REALITY cont...

SPIRITUAL POWER

Kind - Loving - Gentle | CENTERED | Firm - Honest

Spiritual Illusion (not connected)	Spiritual Reality (connected)
My Higher Power is at my side in difficult times I can connect with my Higher Power	I can create/choose my own belief system I am comfortable with other's having a different belief system

EMOTIONAL POWER

Illusion	Reality Authentic
What are my emotions?	

☐ Anger
☐ Hurt/Pain
☐ Shame
☐ Guilt
☐ Shutdown
☐ Sadness
☐ Fear
☐ Power
☐ Loneliness
☐ Happiness

AWARENESS
Dependent

MENTAL POWER

Illusion	Reality
What am I telling myself?	*What are my choices?*

- I am a practicing human being
- I focus and get what I need today
- I offer/receive constructive criticism
- I see problems as opportunies
- I know change is normal
- I gain strength in solving problems
- I trust those who respect my boundaries
- I ask what others are thinking
- I let others know my needs
- I am responsible for my problems
- I know I'm not the "all" in the world
- My defense system is a choice
- I practice being in the present
- I explore new possibilities
- I continue self-growth
- I am aware change starts with me
- I am creative at home and in the workplace

LIST OF DEFENSES

ACCEPTANCE
Interdependent

IMPULSE CONTROL

PHYSICAL POWER

Illusion	Reality
What is my reactive behavior?	*What do I choose to do?*

- I am proactive in life
- I go to my calming Spiritual Safe Place
- I ask for feedback
- I take action on lifestyle changes
- I have a balanced lifestyle
- I am a team player
- I study successful people's habits
- I consider others before I speak
- My playtime is golden
- I take a walk when I'm angry
- I take responsibly for my anger

ACTION
Independent

Figure 16.1B ~ Reality Cont...

The Power Model System™ | Copyright © 2007 – HumanWisdom LLC

EXAMPLE
REALITY

SPIRITUAL POWER

Kind - Loving - Gentle   CENTERED   Firm - Honest

Spiritual Illusion (not connected)
I believe my Higher Power punishes me when bad things happen in my life

Spiritual Reality (connected)
My Higher Power is at my side in difficult times
I can connect with my Higher Power

- I can create/choose my own belief system
- I am comfortable with other's having a different belief system

---

EMOTIONAL POWER

Illusion	Reality Authentic
What are my emotions?	
I have been victimized	[X] Anger
	[X] Hurt/Pain
	[X] Shame
	[ ] Guilt
	[ ] Shutdown
	[ ] Sadness
	[ ] Fear
	[ ] Power
	[ ] Loneliness
	[ ] Happiness

AWARENESS
Dependent

MENTAL POWER

Illusion	Reality
What am I telling myself?	What are my choices?
I can't hear my choices due to defenses	I have healthy ego strength
	I can identify my emotions
I have magical thinking	I have tolerance for my feelings
	I have tolerance for human characteristics
	I have sympathy for others
	I calm down and investigate my choices
	I know my internal/external boundaries
	I am a friend to myself
	I have a sense of self
	I know my strengths/weaknesses
	I can observe my own behavior
	I self-discover what I need
	My childhood reactions are not needed as an adult
	I cannot control people, places, and things
	My life is in my hands
	My Spiritual Safe Place helps me focus

LIST OF DEFENSES

IMPULSE CONTROL

ACCEPTANCE
Interdependent

PHYSICAL POWER

Illusion	Reality
What is my reactive behavior?	What do I choose to do?
I decide/act based on how I feel	I exercise impulse control
	I am aware of what affects my body
I have no boundaries	I rely on my Higher Power
	I exercise by internal/external boundaries
	I have predictable behavior
	I can take action to change my perception
	I pay attention and confirm if I am understood
	I am responsible for my actions
	I take care of myself
	I am dependable
	I practice playing

ACTION
Independent

Figure 16.2A ~ Example: Reality

The Power Model System™ | Copyright © 2007 – HumanWisdom LLC

EXAMPLE
REALITY cont...

SPIRITUAL POWER

Kind - Loving - Gentle   CENTERED   Firm - Honest

Spiritual Illusion (not connected)   Spiritual Reality (connected)

PHYSICAL POWER

Illusion	Reality
What is my reactive behavior?	What do I choose to do?
	• I am proactive in life
	• I go to my calming Spiritual Safe Place
	• I ask for feedback
	• I take action on lifestyle changes
	• I have a balanced lifestyle
	• I am a team player
	• I study successful people's habits
	• I consider others before I speak
	• My playtime is golden
	• I take a walk when I'm angry
	• I take responsibly for my anger

ACTION
Independent

IMPULSE CONTROL

MENTAL POWER

Illusion	Reality
What am I telling myself?	What are my choices?
	• I am a practicing human being
	• I focus and get what I need today
	• I offer/receive constructive criticism
	• I see problems as opportunies
	• I know change is normal
	• I gain strength in solving problems
	• I trust those who respect my boundaries
	• I ask what others are thinking
	• I let others know my needs
	• I am responsible for my problems
	• I know I'm not the "all" in the world
	• My defense system is a choice
	• I practice being in the present
	• I explore new possibilities
	• I continue self-growth
	• I am aware change starts with me
	• I am creative at home and in the workplace

LIST OF DEFENSES

ACCEPTANCE
Interdependent

EMOTIONAL POWER

Illusion	Reality Authentic
What are my emotions?	
	☐ Anger
	☐ Hurt/Pain
	☐ Shame
	☐ Guilt
	☐ Shutdown
	☐ Sadness
	☐ Fear
	☐ Power
	☐ Loneliness
	☐ Happiness

AWARENESS
Dependent

The Power Model System™ | Copyright © 2007 – HumanWisdom LLC

Figure 16.2B ~ Example; Reality Cont...

Chapter 17

GIFTS OF EMOTIONS

Grace is not fair.
    Philip Yancy

When you performed the Life Spark exercise in Chapter Thirteen, you uncovered your cover-up emotions. In doing so, you self-discovered your authentic emotions and set up a circle of strength and balance. As you continue to reveal your Life Spark by expressing authentic emotions, you'll strengthen each of your four human components.

The goal in this chapter is to bring you closer to knowing how to use what you've learned to gain greater wisdom. Wisdom is far more than knowledge itself. *Wisdom is having a respect for knowledge, knowing when to apply that knowledge, and understanding how knowledge affects your life.*

Let's examine this further through the concept of gifts.

> *Energy is neutral. You can use it for you or against you. You yourself are the creator. Energy is just energy. Don't make it more than it is. You are the creator of how this energy is used.*

How Authentic Feelings Bear Gifts

Once you've experienced your authentic emotions, you'll want to keep bringing them into your Spiritual Safe Place. This will allow you to wisely and consciously (rather than randomly) express these feelings at any given moment in an appropriate manner. This energy will transform these emotions into many gifts that circle around and come back to you, further strengthening your four human components.

<u>Emotional Gifts</u>

Hurt/pain: As you deal with the authentic feelings of hurt and pain sparked by a past or present event, and you stay connected with your Higher Power, you'll experience an increased amount of *knowledge* about what you need to do to take care of yourself and others. Once you understand why you feel hurt or pain and how to avoid it wisely, you'll strengthen your *Mental Power in Reality.*

Fear: It's okay to experience fear when attempting to reach new goals or when looking at past and present events in your life. *It's what you do with the fear that determines your end results.*

Fear becomes a gift when you treat it with respect and compassion. You do this by bringing your fears to your Spiritual Safe Place where you can look at them objectively without judgment. Sitting with your fear quietly without judgment is like sitting in the dark for a period of time. Eventually, your eyes can see through the darkness. When this happens, you begin to put your fears into perspective and not overreact to them.

Embracing your fears neutralizes them and transfers the energy into wisdom. Remember, knowledge is Mental Power in Reality, while wisdom is Spiritual Power in Reality. By seeing through your fears, you will gain a higher level of *Spiritual Power in Reality.*

Anger: Anger gives you energy and strength. You can use this energy to rage on yourself and others, or you can put the energy into action, which turns it into Physical Power in Reality. You do this by placing the emotion into your Spiritual Safe Place.

Putting anger in your Spiritual Safe Place is like stopping time; everything is at a standstill. At first, many of us feel justified in our anger. We want to react, usually destructively, to a given situation. With everything at a standstill in your Spiritual Safe Place, you can look through the rage and see the situation objectively. You can then say, "Okay, I don't like what has happened. Now, what can I do to make it better rather than worse?" This clears your mind, connects you with your Spiritual Power in Reality, and allows you to think about your choices for taking action in any situation. This in return will strengthen your *Physical Power in Reality.*

Sadness: When you express your authentic sadness, you're able to grieve. If you grieve your losses in life (past or present), you can *let go* and let your Higher Power take over. Letting go is one of the hardest things for humans to do because of our control issues. Even if you're completely exhausted from trying to control a situation in your life, letting go is still difficult. But the sooner you let go, the sooner you'll experience peace of mind. By grieving and then letting go, you strengthen your *Mental Power in Reality.*

Shame: Shame refers to *"who I am"* (as opposed to guilt, which relates to *"what I do"*). Shame reminds us of our humanity, which is nothing to be ashamed of. (Yes, it's okay to not be perfect!) Shame also provides us with *humility* to help us recognize a Higher Power in our life. When you possess humility, you suffer less humiliation. You give up the job of being perfect and know you're a "practicing" human being. Shame strengthens your *Spiritual Power in Reality*.

Shutdown: Shutdown occurs when you close down the emotional energy in your body. This keeps the physical body safe, for example, after a car crash or if you're experiencing something traumatic and you don't have the coping skills to handle the situation. Here's an everyday workplace example: While sitting in a business meeting, your boss tells you something that angers you. You go into shutdown mode, deciding you will deal with your anger later. In this situation, shutdown has helped keep you safe.

If someone intends to harm you physically, emotional shutdown is a good way to keep you safe. When you emotionally shut down in a dangerous situation, you're able to think more clearly and look at all your options. You can deal with your emotions once you're out of the situation, but not *during* the event. In order for it to be a healthy action, shutdown must be a conscious choice. A safe action such as this strengthens your *Physical Power in Reality*.

Loneliness: When you experience loneliness, you instinctively want to reach out to supportive people, revealing your need to have others in your life. In the movie *Oh, God!* starring George Burns as God, He said, "All of you humans want a miracle. The miracle I gave you was each other." So when you reach out, reach out to supportive people who love you and care about your welfare. By taking the action to reach out to others, you fulfill this need, which feeds your *Physical Power in Reality*.

Happiness: Happiness results when you truly appreciate what you have. When you thank your Higher Power for all the people, things, and events that come into your life, you gain more appreciation for your Higher Power. That means being thankful for *all* events, not just the ones you perceive as "good." The book *When Bad Things Happen to Good People* by Harold S. Kushner reminds us that what we *do* with those bad things is what really counts. Thank your Higher Power for *all* events because with them come the gifts of awareness and a deep appreciation for your *Spiritual Power in Reality*.

If you apply this same appreciation to every feeling you have, you'll be amazed at the results you'll experience. Remember, emotions are neither negative nor positive; *they just are*. With this awareness, you experience authentic happiness, which strengthens your *Spiritual Power in Reality*.

Guilt: Look at your life and see if there's anything you feel guilty about. If so, you might need to make amends. This means that if in the past or present you have done something inappropriate to someone, you go back and make up for what you did. This is the most effective means of ensuring you'll choose a different behavior if you encounter a similar situation again.

Making amends as soon as you realize your conduct has been inappropriate is the only way to go. Hanging on to guilt is harmful to your mind, body, and spirit. Feeling guilty tells you that you have a sense of what's right and gives you the opportunity to promptly make amends. This is a physical action you need to take. It strengthens your *Physical Power in Reality*.

Power: From the moment we're born, we constantly seek a sense of power. Power and control go hand-in-hand. Why do I consider power an emotion?

Power has been defined as "the ability or official capacity to exercise control or authority." It's the ability or capacity to perform or act effectively.

The definition of the word power says it all. We get confused between our own power and abilities and our Higher Power and its abilities. We think identity comes from how much power (money, career, possessions, etc.) we have in our lives. *If you're going down this road, you need to wake up!* None of these things will bring us happiness, peace, or balance because they are in illusion. This is where we get confused about an experience of human power and control versus an experience of Higher Power. There's really no comparison—one is limiting and the other is unlimited spiritual expansion.

When you start to become balanced internally, the first thing you let go of is your desire for power or control over people, places, and things. It's a wonderful, freeing feeling! You become more aware of the *power within you* and feel less need to control others. You become one with your Higher Power and experience free will for yourself and others. This strengthens your *Spiritual Power in Reality*.

Story Time

One rainy afternoon, I met Jack, who truly believed he had all the power, money, and material things he needed in his life. He came to me saying, "I have no idea why my wife isn't happy with me. I run an eight-lawyer legal firm that started with just me. My wife and I have all the money and status anyone could have. I give her anything she wants. We have a big house, cars, vacation cabin in the north, a retirement fund, and a financial portfolio that anyone would envy.

"Our children are grown and happy. I help out financially whenever she tells me to and when the kids need anything extra. We've been married thirty-five years, and I keep hearing the same thing over and over. She claims I don't share with her, that she can't talk with me. I've never hit her or the children. I don't drink too much, do drugs, gamble, or chase women. What am I missing here? I think I'm a good guy."

I listened as Jack spoke and knew that his wife's unhappiness with him through the years sincerely bewildered him. After about forty-five minutes, he stood up and said, "My wife is out in the waiting room. I want you to talk with her. You're a woman, and you can let her know I'm okay." I smiled, shook his hand, and went out to the reception room to meet Emma.

As we approached each other, she put out her hand to shake mine and said, "I was looking forward to meeting you." We then walked back to my office in silence. As soon as the door closed, Emma sat down and started to talk, crying as she spoke.

"I love Jack, don't get me wrong. I just want more. I know he works hard and has always provided for the family, more than enough materially. I want to feel close to him, and I never have. I just keep telling him what I want from him, and I know I'm not clear because I can't put it into words myself. When I tell him I want to feel close, he says, 'We *are* close; I love you.' That's it in a nutshell."

Emma stopped crying and sat looking at me. I asked her, "Do you have any idea what the problem really is?"

"No. It's just a feeling."

I asked her to repeat her last four words, and she said, "It's just a feeling." She looked at me blankly and said again, "It's just a feeling."

"That's it; you just said it—feelings, emotions. Do you feel emotionally connected to Jack?"

She jumped off the chair and yelled, "That's it! We don't share *any* kind of emotional connection." As she sat down, I suggested I bring Jack in, and she agreed. I asked them if they'd be willing to attend together a three-day workshop for couples the following month.

I laughed at this point, because instead of answering the question about the workshop, Jack said, "Don't you want to see us again?" He was expecting a certain form of help, and I wondered whether he'd be unhappy if there were no further meetings in my office.

"No," I said. "We've identified the problem: you two aren't emotionally or spiritually connected."

"I don't like her church," Jack said.

"This isn't about church. When you come to the workshop, you'll both be working through a system. Once you each go through your own individual work, you'll understand each other better. Are you willing to give it a try?"

I went on to explain a little about The Power Model System™, that it's a logical, orderly system presented in a step-by-step process of self-discovery activities. "In this workshop, no one tells anyone how to behave or what religion to believe in or how to think," I said.

Jack said, "Okay, I'll come. But it sounds like it's more education than therapy."

"Yes, and you'll come out of it with information about *you*," I said.

Jack said, "I'm sure glad it's none of that touchy-feely stuff."

Looking over at Emma, I could see she was very happy he was agreeing to come to the workshop.

They joined eight other couples at the workshop. As Emma and Jack worked beside the other couples, they started relaxing and having fun. We all did!

When Emma and Jack were working on their Life Spark exercise, they shared a lot of insights with their group members. But the big eye-opener came when the couples were sharing their new Spiritual Safe Place with their group. Jack said, "We discovered that we both have a Spiritual Safe Place. It's just that we each have different definitions of what it is and how it looks."

At the close of the workshop, Jack told the group, "You know, I came here thinking I had it all and there was nothing else to discover in life. What I called 'having it all' was power, money, and success. I thought that was all I needed. I'm leaving here with a very different meaning of 'having it all.'" And he was able to laugh at himself.

Emma said, "I thought Jack had to go to my church because he needed God in his life. In this workshop, I found out that he's always had God in his life; he just defined it differently."

Jack said, "While doing the Life Spark, I learned that I cover up most of my emotions with shutdown. No wonder Emma feels like she can't connect with me—I can't connect with *anyone* emotionally." He went on to say he was going to continue to practice identifying his emotions. He also stated he now could keep using this system on his own and get better at this. I thought that was great.

I haven't seen Jack and Emma since the workshop, but I enjoyed getting a Christmas card last year that ended with "We truly have it all!"

I've put individuals, couples, and families through The Power Model System™ for years, yet I never grow tired of seeing people connect with the four components and watching the lights go on in their eyes as they express their authentic emotions. I love hearing how their lives have changed for the better. It is a manifestation of true power—the connection between our internal power and our Higher Power.

Activity: Gifts of Emotion

Figures 17.1, 17.2, and 17.3 refer to this activity.

This activity will help you put your entire Life Spark system together. This includes your *cover-up emotions, authentic emotions,* and the *gifts* you receive for acknowledging your authentic emotions.

The following activity sheet will serve as one of the components for your personal blueprint—information at a glance that you can reference anytime. You'll identify your cover-up emotions, look at the Life Spark Chart, and then move from your cover-up emotions to your authentic emotions. Once you acknowledge and experience your authentic emotions, you can then process and resolve the issue at hand. You can look again at the Life Spark Chart and see the gift you've gained (outer ring in Figure 17.1) by being able to process an authentic emotion instead of being stuck in the cover-up one. With this process, you start uncovering the Life Spark you were born with. It's exciting to see how all the pieces come together!

Read over the instructions before starting this activity.

1. Go back to Chapter Thirteen (Figure 13.1) where you wrote your cover-up emotions on top of your authentic emotions.
2. Copy them onto Life Spark Chart in Figure 17.1 so you have everything in one chart.
3. Reflect on the gifts (as shown on the chart) that you're going to receive from working with your authentic emotions.
4. Now that you have this information on your Life Spark in one place, make copies for yourself. Carry one copy with you in your purse or wallet, hang one on a wall in your house, and leave one in a drawer at your workplace.

You and your Higher Power created a Life Spark system when you were very young. You and your Higher Power can also be partners in recreating (co-creating) an authentic Life Spark system now.

See Figure 17.2 for an example.

See Figure 17.3 to see how the gifts of emotion transfer to your mental, physical, and spiritual power.

Story Time (Example)

You're at work at the end of the day. Your supervisor has just said to you, "You left out a step in the project. Let me show you." As he begins to show you, you become very angry and let him know it. You say you need to go get a drink of water and you'll be right back. You were sure you thought of everything—now look what's happened. The date for delivery of this important project will now have to be delayed, and you feel it's entirely your fault. You're telling yourself all this on the way to the water cooler.

You stop. You remember the Life Spark chart and pull it out of your wallet or purse. You look at "anger" and see what authentic emotion you cover up with anger. Wow! Shame and guilt have anger on top of them. That's what you're really experiencing right now. You feel shame for not doing the project the right way and feel guilt for forgetting one of the requirements.

This is great. You now realize you aren't really angry. Instead you feel guilt and shame. You then look at the gift of these authentic emotions. Amends and Higher Power connect. You now realize you are not your Higher Power and you can make mistakes. It's okay. You can now simply make amends for getting angry, express regret for missing one of the requirements, and correct the mistake.

You now simply drink your water, walk back into the conference room with your supervisor, and say, "Sorry I missed this step. Let's go over it again so I can write it down. I'll start on it right away."

That's it. You made great use of the lessons learned about cover-up and authentic emotions. You were able to visually see the emotions you covered up with anger. You can now correct the situation without yelling, exploding, or employing other inappropriate behavior. By quickly identifying and processing your authentic emotions instead of channeling your energy into anger and rage, you retain more of your personal Life Spark energy.

GIFTS OF EMOTIONS - PART 1

The gifts of identifying and working with my authentic feelings.

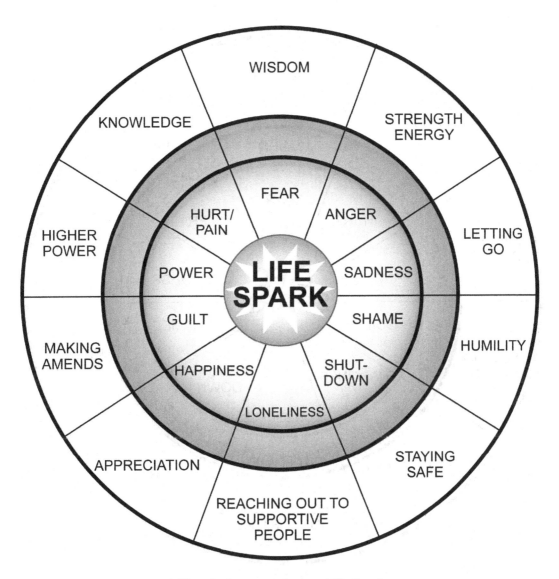

The circle center is your Life Spark.
The inner ring represents your authentic emotions.
The middle ring is where you write your cover-up emotions.
The outer ring represents the gifts you receive from your authentic emotions.

EXAMPLE
GIFTS OF EMOTIONS - PART 1

The gifts of identifying and working with my authentic feelings

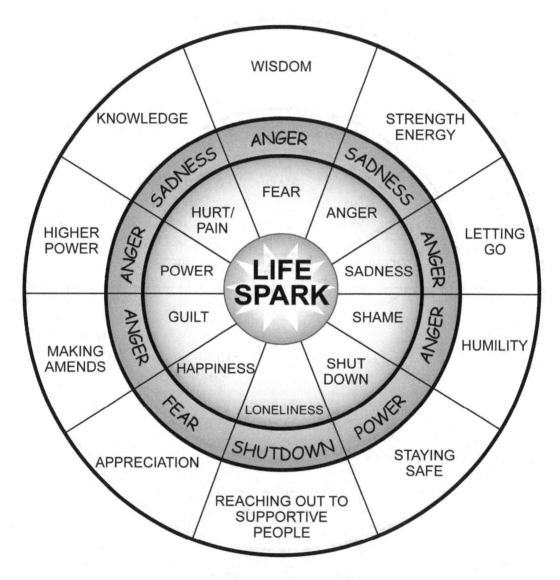

The circle center is your Life Spark..
The inner ring represents your authentic emotions.
The middle ring is where you write your cover-up emotions.
The outer ring represents the gifts you receive from your authentic emotions.

GIFTS OF EMOTIONS
PART 2

SPIRITUAL POWER

SPIRITUAL GIFTS

Shame ➤➤ Humility   Happy ➤➤ Appreciation   Power ➤➤ Spiritual Beliefs   Fear ➤➤ Wisdom

EMOTIONAL POWER		MENTAL POWER		PHYSICAL POWER	
		Illusion	Reality	Illusion	Reality
What are my emotions?		What am I telling myself?	What are my choices?	What is my reactive behavior?	What do I choose to do?
			MENTAL GIFTS		PHYSICAL GIFTS
			Sadness ➤➤ Letting go		Anger ➤➤ Energy/Strength
			Hurt/Pain ➤➤ Knowledge		Shutdown ➤➤ Action
					Lonely ➤➤ Reach out
					Guilt ➤➤ Amends
Dependent		Inter-dependent		In-dependent	

Figure 17.3 ~ Gifts of Emotions - Part 2

217

Chapter 18

YOUR PERSONAL BLUEPRINT

For your rebirth, no death is needed - rather, a transcendence.
For this transcendence, use yourself.
> Osho, Author and Mystic

If you have performed all the activities so far, you now have all the pieces of a puzzle that will make up your Personal Blueprint. This blueprint maps the way your four human components (physical, emotional, mental, and spiritual) interact with each other and affect your everyday life. It is a guide to your internal and external reactions or responses to everything you experience on a day-to-day basis.

Activity: Putting Your Personal Blueprint Together

Figures 18.1 – 18.3 relate to this activity.

This activity will help you develop your Personal Blueprint.

Part 1 of the activity will generate your Personal Blueprint on a single page.
Part 2 shows you how your blueprint can guide you in any situation in your life.

Before actually performing this activity, read through the directions twice or until you fully understand them. Follow the instructions with awareness, honesty, love, and compassion towards yourself.

Part 1: Putting Your Blueprint Together

1. Make ten copies of the My Personal Blueprint chart (Figure 18.1).
2. Now its time to fill in one of the copies with your information from the activities you have done throughout the book.
3. Write your cover-up emotions from your Life Spark chart (Chapter 13, Figure 13.1) in the Emotional Power Illusion column in Figure 18.1.
4. Go to Chapter 8, Figure 8.1 and get your list of defenses. Copy them in the Mental Power Illusion column (Figure 18.1).
5. In Chapter 14, Figure 14.1, you have a piece of artwork representing your connection with your Higher Power. Make a copy this Spiritual Safe Place.
6. In Chapter 17, Figure 17.1, you have your Gifts of Emotions. Make a copy of this Life Spark Chart.
7. Now make at least ten copies of items 4, 5, and 6 (Blueprint Chart, Spiritual Safe Place, and Life Spark Chart). You may want to use a single page, where the Blueprint Chart is on the front, and your Spiritual Safe Place and Life Spark Chart are on the back. You'll be using these for resolving your issues in the future. Retain extra copies of these charts so you can make more copies later.

Using the original ten blank charts you made in Step 1, you can make up new profiles as your cover-up emotions, defenses, and/or boundary issues evolve by repeating Steps 2-7.

Your Personal Blueprint Collection should now have three parts:

1. Your Personal Blueprint Chart (Figure 18.1)
2. Your Gifts of Emotions/Authentic Emotions/Cover-up Emotions (Figure 17.1)
3. Your Spiritual Safe Place (Figure 14.1)

Part 2: Applying Your Blueprint to any Given Situation

In Part 1, you put together the Personal Blueprint that you developed during childhood and has been active ever since. It will take practice to make changes to your belief system, cover-up emotions, defenses, and boundaries. What I can tell you is that change will come, and it will come from within you. When you re-pattern your brain, you change your perception of life. This, in return, will effect great changes in your life.

Part 2 of this activity shows you how to apply your Personal Blueprint to any given situation. In any given situation, past or present, you will combine your emotional, mental, physical, and spiritual illusions onto a single page. With this awareness, you will be able to make changes in your life. You will be able to choose what realities you could have applied or can apply to any given situation. Included in this process is your acknowledgment of what boundaries you broke or applied.

Now that you have the three parts of your blueprint, let's see how you can use it in a typical everyday event.

Part 2A: Discovering Your Illusions in a Situation

Here you will write down any illusions and boundary issues you had during an event. Use Tables 18.1 through 18.5 to assist you in realizing what illusions you may have had or what boundaries may have been broken.

1. Take one of your completed Personal Blueprint profile charts (Figure 18.1).
2. At the top of the page, write down a recent stressful situation you've experienced. Choose one in which you didn't like the outcome because of your reactive behavior.
3. Picture the situation in your mind's eye. Feel the emotions and hear the story you were telling yourself in your mind.
4. As you experience the emotions, circle them in the Emotion Illusion column. If the emotion isn't listed, write it down and circle it.
5. As you hear the stories in your mind, write them down in the Mental Illusion column.
6. Check to see if you relaxed or broke any of your internal and/or external boundaries. If yes, check the box in the Mental Illusion and/or Physical Illusion columns, and write down the boundary in question.
7. Now think for a moment. Were you connected to your Higher Power? If not, under Spiritual Illusion write what your thoughts were, if any, about not being connected.
8. Circle the defenses you used in this situation (from your defense list).
9. Did you go to your Spiritual Safe Place? The odds are if you used reactive behavior, you did not. That's okay. Just be aware.
10. Go to the Physical Power Illusion column, and write down your behavior.

Take a few deep breaths.

Part 2B: Learn, Make Choices, and Take Action

Write down what you could have done in response to the event in Part 2A in a more empowering way. Use Tables 18.1 through 18.5 to assist you in realizing what realities you could have applied.

1. Take this time to visualize in your mind's eye the same situation. Hold up your Spiritual Safe Place artwork in front of your eyes and see yourself there.
2. Now that you are in your Spiritual Safe Place, look at the emotions you circled in the Illusion column, see what authentic emotions were under them, and check those authentic emotions in the authentic column. That is all. Just be aware.
3. Stay in your Spiritual Safe Place in your mind's eye, and see if you would choose to use any of your defenses now. If you would not, use one or more of them now and put an X over the circled defenses you used at the time. Do you now feel a connection with your Higher Power?
4. If you do and are receiving messages, write them down under Spiritual Reality. Messages can come in many different forms: intuition, a thought, a feeling of strength or calmness from within, or a message from another human being.
5. As your body calms down, think about what other options (choices) you may have had in this situation and write them down in the Mental Power Reality column.
6. Now look at your options you have written down in the Mental Power Reality column. Choose one of them, then go to the Physical Power Reality column and write down which one would be appropriate to act upon and what action you would take.

See Figure 18.2 for an example of a Personal Blueprint completely filled out. If you need more room to write all your illusions/realities, use more than one chart.

I encourage you to repeat the above activity for at least three situations initially. Work with someone who is also performing this exercise. Then repeat the activity as many times as you need in your daily life until the process becomes automatic. *This is no longer about just completing an activity. It's about changing your life!* Practice, practice, rest, and then practice some more.

There may be times when you'll want to go back to the other activities in the book to gather more information. Do so. It is important. You may also come up with some issues that require professional assistance such as a councilor or therapist.

An Even Faster Way

Congratulations! You now have a complete blueprint of how you can process life's events internally and externally. Reality, experienced by you and your Higher Power, is the birthplace of Wisdom. With Wisdom, you will be able to progress through The Power Model System™ faster and faster. And that leads us to the next chapter, "The Five Steps to Centeredness," which will allow you to journey through life more quickly and easily then you thought possible.

MY PERSONAL BLUEPRINT

Situation _____

SPIRITUAL POWER

Kind - Loving - Gentle   CENTERED   Firm - Honest

Spiritual Illusion (not connected)   Spiritual Reality (connected)

EMOTIONAL POWER	MENTAL POWER		PHYSICAL POWER	
What are my emotions?	*What am I telling myself?*	*What are my choices?*	*What is my reactive behavior?*	*What do I choose to do?*
Reality	Illusion	Reality	Illusion	Reality
Authentic	☐ Broken Boundary	☐ Applied Boundary	☐ Broken Boundary	☐ Applied Boundary

Illusion

Cover-up

Authentic
- ☐ Anger
- ☐ Hurt/Pain
- ☐ Shame
- ☐ Guilt
- ☐ Shutdown
- ☐ Saddness
- ☐ Fear
- ☐ Power
- ☐ Loneliness
- ☐ Happiness

DEFENSE SYSTEM

IMPULSE CONTROL

LIST OF DEFENSES

BOUNDARIES

SPIRITUAL SAFE PLACE

| Awareness Dependent | Acceptance Interdependent | Action Independent |

Figure 18.1 ~ My Personal Blueprint

The Power Model System™ | Copyright © 2007 – HumanWisdom LLC

MY PERSONAL BLUEPRINT

Example

1) Attach your Spiritual Safe Place
2) Attach your Gifts of Emotions

Situation: I was asked to do more work, more than I could finish.

SPIRITUAL POWER

Kind - Loving - Gentle   **CENTERED**   Firm - Honest

Spiritual Illusion (not connected) | Spiritual Reality (connected)

I forgot to center myself by going to my Spiritual Safe Place | I can become centered at any time, any place by going to my Spiritual Safe Place

---

EMOTIONAL POWER

What are my emotions?

Illusion	Authentic
	☐ Anger — Hurt/Pain
	☐ Hurt/Pain — Anger
	☒ Shame — Anger
	☒ Guilt — Fear
	☐ Shutdown — Sadness
	☐ Sadness — Anger
	☐ Fear — Shame
	☐ Power — Anger
	☐ Loneliness — Fear
	☐ Happiness — Fear

· Unable to identify emotions
· In fight-or-flight
· Edgy

Awareness — Dependent

MENTAL POWER

What am I telling myself?

Illusion	Reality
☒ Broken Boundary — Blamed others too quickly.	☒ Applied Boundary — Tolerate differences of opinion without altering mine.
· Overwhelmed	
· Concentration Problems	Ask for help to finish.
· Reactive to changes	Ask for a schedule extension.
· Resistant towards looking inward.	

Acceptance — Interdependent

LIST OF DEFENSES
- Anger
- Judge
- Projection
- Rationalization
- Sarcasm
- Can't remember
- Laugh
- Pain
- Victim
- Silence

BOUNDARIES

SPIRITUAL SAFE PLACE

IMPULSE CONTROL

DEFENSE SYSTEM

PHYSICAL POWER

What is my reactive behavior?

Illusion	Reality
☒ Broken Boundary — I let others influence my behavior.	☒ Applied Boundary — I am assertive with my needs.
· Nervous system is stressed	
· High blood pressure	Go to my Boss and explain the problem, and offer real solutions that will get the job done in a more efficient manner.
· Tight muscles	
· Low pain tolerance	

What do I choose to do?

Action — Independent

Figure 18.2~ Example: My Personal Blueprint   The Power Model System™ | Copyright © 2007 – HumanWisdom LLC

EXAMPLE
Spiritual Safe Place and Gifts of Emotions
Attach These to Your Blueprint Chart
You may copy them to the back of the Blueprint chart.

GIFTS OF EMOTIONS

The gifts of identifying and working with my authentic feelings.

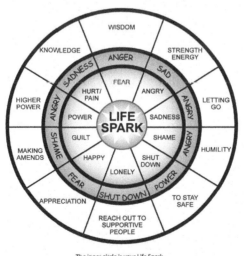

The inner circle is your Life Spark..
The next ring represents your authentic emotions.
The next to outer ring is where you write your cover-up emotions.
The outer most ring represents the gifts you receive from your authentic emotions.

Figure 18.3 ~ Spiritual Safe Place and Gifts of Emotions   Power Model System™ | Copyright © 2007 – HumanWisdom LLC

Table 18.1: HumanWisdom Emotional Illusion/Reality	
Emotional Illusion	**Emotional Reality**
Am a victim	Identify my emotions and process them
Am helpless	Connect with my higher power
Want instant gratification	Get centered and have patience
Have no emotional boundaries	Practice the Five Steps to Centeredness
Want what I want, and I want it now!	Have interdependence within myself
I am stuck in the past	I am in the present
Fight / Flight – I am on survival mode	I am able to stay present
Don't know what/how to feel	Identify my thoughts and feelings
Fear anger in others; feel others' emotions	I do not own someone else's emotions
Feel responsible for others' emotions	I go to my Spiritual Safe Place
Feel emotional about everything	I relax more
Feel nothing	Shutdown only when it's a choice
Get too close too fast with others	Take my time bonding to others
Laugh when want to cry	Identify authentic emotions (Life Spark)
Put anger on top of hurt	Appropriately let others know of my feelings
Am unable to say No	No is a complete answer
Say No all the time	Have learned to say yes when necessary
Experience prolonged resentment	I understand and process resentments
Experience prolonged resistance	I can let go
Change is a punishment to me	Changing helps me grow stronger
Rage a lot	Own my anger and express appropriately
Feel guilty when setting boundaries	I know setting boundaries is healthy
Rage when others don't know what I want	Express my needs to others
Feel safest when I am angry	Safety is connecting to my Higher Power
Am not aware of my emotional reactions	Have an observer within me
Anxiety comes from nowhere	Identify my stress as it comes
Am easily startled	I go to my Spiritual Safe Place

Table 18.2: HumanWisdom Mental Illusion/Reality	
Mental Illusion	**Mental Reality**
Have false ego strength	Have healthy ego strength
Cannot identify my emotions	Can identify my emotions
Have no tolerance for my emotions	Have tolerance for my feelings
Have no tolerance for human characteristics	Have tolerance for human characteristics
Am critical with others	Have sympathy for others
Can't hear my choices due to defenses	Calm down and investigate my choices
Have no boundaries	Know my internal/external boundaries
Have self-hatred	I am a friend to myself
Don't know who I am	Have a sense of self
Have a distorted perception of myself	Know my strengths/weaknesses
Am overwhelmed	Can observe my own behavior
Don't know my own needs	Self-discover what I need
Over-react to changes	Childhood reactions are not needed as an adult
Worry a lot	Know I cannot control people, places, and things
Have illusions/magical thinking	My life decisions are in my hands
Have concentration problems	My Spiritual Safe Place helps me focus
Judge myself harshly	I am a practicing human being
Believe in scarcity	Focus and get what I need today
Take constructive criticism personally	Offer/receive constructive criticism
Am problem-oriented	See problems as opportunity
For me, change equals problems	Know change is normal
Think problems will disappear	Gain strength in solving problems
Don't know who to trust	Trust those who respect my boundaries
Assume what others think	Ask what others are thinking
Others should know my needs	Let others know my needs
Give me solutions to my personal problems	I am responsible for my problems
Am responsible for everything	Know I'm not the "all" in the world
Make excuses about my behavior	My defense system is a choice
Daydream too much	Practice being in the present
Lie to myself about what I want in life	Get educated on new possibilities
Get bored or tired and give up	Continue self-growth
Procrastinate	I am aware change starts with me
Don't have anything to offer	I am creative at home and in the workplace
Am depressed most of the time	Look for someone to talk about my depression
Do not know what I need	Can identify my needs
Reactive to changes	Proactive in life
Sleep problems	Use relaxation techniques to go to sleep
Unable to keep my mind quiet	Use visual techniques to quiet my mind
Compromise=win/lose=resentment	Compromise is win/win
Sabotage thinking	I can identify my thought pattern
Obsessive-compulsive thought patterns (OCD)	Use the Five Steps to Centeredness to break OCD
Memory problems	Use the tools I need to remember
Resistant towards looking inward	Resolve my past, stay in the present, hope in future
Difficulty in decision-making	The wrong decision is not a mistake, only a lesson
Distorted perceptions of others and self	I am able to take my own inventory

| Table 18.3: HumanWisdom Physical Illusion/Reality ||
Physical Illusion	Physical Reality
Decide/act based on how I feel	Exercise impulse control
Have physical body reactions	Am aware of what affects my body
Have addictive behaviors	Rely on my Higher Power
Have no boundaries	Exercise by internal/external boundaries
Have inconsistent behavior	Have predictable behavior
Get headaches and fatigue	Can take action to change my perception
Have poor communication	Pay attention and confirm if I understood
Don't look at the consequences	Am responsible in my actions
Overextend physically	Take care of myself
Frequently take off work	I am dependable
Have difficulty having fun	Practice playing
Get stuck and do nothing	Am proactive in life
Get anxious and tense	Go to my calming Spiritual Safe Place
Freak out after a presentation	Ask for feedback
Have tension in my body	Take action on lifestyle changes
Am inflexible	Have a balanced life-style
Isolate myself	Am a team player
Unable to reach personal/career goals	Study successful people's habits
Talk too much and gossip	Consider others before I speak
Keep busy all the time	My playtime is golden
Become physically abusive when angry	Take a walk when I'm angry
Yell when I am angry	Take responsibility for my anger
Heart palpitations	Take deep breaths when I am tense
Become tense	Visualize a relaxing place when tense
Have panic attacks (fight-or-flight)	Aware of my breathing and slow it down.
Difficulty having fun	Plan my playtime
Nervous system stressed	Exercise
Reactive towards others	Do the Five Steps to Centeredness
High blood pressure	Relax and do Five Steps to Centeredness
Hold my breath when stressed	Do the Five Steps to Centeredness
Tight muscles when stressed	Do the Five Steps to Centeredness
Tight jaw; grind teeth	Do the Five Steps to Centeredness
Talk constantly to feel comfortable	Use impulse control
Gossip about others	Speak for myself and no one else
Autoimmune problems	Take good physical care of myself
Muscle spasms	Take care of myself
Do not care for physical needs, medical	Make all yearly doctor appointments
Low pain tolerance	Use my relaxation techniques
Unable to move forward towards goals	Use The Power Model System™ to find out why
Difficulty setting/keeping boundaries	Practice boundary setting/keeping

| Table 18.4: HumanWisdom Spiritual Illusion/Reality ||
Spiritual Illusion	Spiritual Reality
Do not know my spiritual beliefs	Create/discover my own spiritual beliefs
Know my beliefs, yet do not apply them	Practice my spiritual beliefs
Not enough quiet time	Take time to hear myself and my Higher Power
Unable to meet life on life's terms	Accept life and learn from it
My Higher Power is responsible for my life	Am responsible; my Higher Power guides me
Do not allow time to grow spiritually	Spiritual growth is very important
Try to control others' belief system	I am okay with and respect others' belief systems
Do not know the right action for myself	Trust my intuition; I research my choices
Believe I know the right action for others	Trust what others choose for themselves
When bad things occur, my Higher Power punishes me	My Higher Power is with me at all times in my life

Table 18.5: HumanWisdom Boundaries	
Without Boundaries	**With Boundaries**
Internal	Internal
Cannot contain my emotions	Apply impulse control/balance
Over-disclose, tell too much to others	Take emotions to my Spiritual Safe Place
Act like a victim	Share appropriately/directly with others
Show my resentments	Am responsible for my life
Say yes when I want to say no	Take care of myself; then help others when I can
Feel responsible for others' emotions	Communicate what I need
Not aware of my personal needs	Allow others to process their emotions
Overcompensate	Learn what I need and work towards it
Unaware of my need for privacy	Take timeout for myself
Overreact to the feelings and behavior of others	Am sensitive to feelings of others
Personalize everything	Do not take things personally
Blame others for influencing my behavior	My behavior is my choice
Act unpredictably	Am a predictable person
Change internal boundaries from day to day	Keep my boundaries constant
Addicted to drugs, alcohol, or other substances	Am in Recovery
Use sexual humor	Do not use sex as humor focus
Have mood swings	Identify my mood swings; see a counselor
No consistency with myself	Am consistent yet flexible
External	External
Allow others to touch me inappropriately	Place external boundaries
Allow my physical space to be invaded	Have a sense of self
Get overwhelmed and preoccupied with others	Accept what is; change what I can; move on
Feel or act out others' emotions.	Aware of others' feelings while being aware of mine
Depend on others for sense of self	Have sense of personal identity
Get too close too fast to strangers	Get close only to those who respect my boundaries
Tie identity to being in an intimate relationship	Have sense of personal identity
Expect others to meet my needs	Care for myself, and ask for help when needed
Expect others to read my mind	Respectfully let others know what is on my mind
Take too much and act extremely needy	Share with others
Do not respect the rights of others	Respect the rights of others
No tolerance for differences of opinion	Allow "differences" in others
Limit bonding to others in family	Have good friends outside my family
Touch others without asking	Respect others' space
Impose on the privacy of others	Respect others' privacy
Belittle others in relationships	My partner is my equal
Make others the object of my anger with humor	Respectful/sensitive to the rights/needs of others
Share addiction with other addicts	Am in Recovery
Involved in physical and/or sexual abuse	Maintain my physical and sexual boundaries
Blame self for everyone's problems	Respect others, letting them care for their problems
Put up with abuse	Remove myself from situations when necessary

Chapter 19

FIVE STEPS TO CENTEREDNESS

The mystery of life is not a problem to be solved but a reality to be experienced.
Aart Van Der Leeuw

The Five Steps to Centeredness is a step-by-step process you'll be able to use anywhere and with anyone so you can respond in an empowering way to any situation in your life. In this process, you bring together your Emotional Power, Mental Power, Spiritual Power, and Physical Power in Reality to respond to everyday events quickly and appropriately. The power and effectiveness of these five steps stem from all that you have self discovered about yourself through the previous activities. More specifically, your *Personal Blueprint* (Chapter 18) empowers you to process through *The Five Steps to Centeredness* with ease and at speeds that would not have been possible before. In addition to enabling you to respond to events quickly and appropriately, these five steps will significantly reduce stress and anxiety in your everyday life.

The Five Steps to Centeredness are:

1. Reflect on Emotions in Your Spiritual Safe Place
2. Connect with Your Higher Power
3. Make Defense System a Choice
4. Consider Your Options
5. Make Decisions and Take Action

Before we go through these steps in detail, let's look at what has been discovered in some cutting-edge research about stress in the body. The word "meditation" in The Power Model System ™ simply means "to relax, be silent, and allow yourself to become aware of your thoughts, authentic feelings, and spiritual belief system." Most of us stay so busy that much of our authentic selves stay hidden from ourselves and others. You can't give your children true attention or understanding unless you are silent, focused, and truly listening to what they are saying or watching what they are doing. The same is true for your inner spirit. Without being silent within yourself, and having the patience of a loving parent, you will have limited success in knowing yourself.

Research on Meditation and Stress

To emphasize the importance of meditation and stress management, I would like to share some important research on the subject.

Buddhist Meditation May Produce Lasting Changes in the Brain
By Jennifer Warner[6]

Nov. 10, 2004 -- Meditation may not only produce a calming effect, but new research suggests that the practice of Buddhist meditation may produce lasting changes in the brain. Researchers found that monks who spent many years in Buddhist meditation training show significantly greater brain activity in areas associated with learning and happiness than those who've never practiced meditation. The results suggest that long-term mental training, such as meditation, may prompt both short- and long-term changes in brain activity and function.

In the study, which appears in an online edition of the *Proceedings of the National Academy of Science*, researchers compared the brain activity of 8 long-time Buddhist monks and ten healthy students. The average age of the monks was 49, and each had undergone mental training in meditation for 10,000 to 50,000 hours over the course of 15 to 40 years. The students' average age was 21. They had no prior experience in meditation and received one week of meditative training before the start of the study. Both groups were asked to practice compassionate meditation, which does not require concentration on specific things. Instead, the participants were instructed to generate a feeling of love and compassion without focusing their attention on a particular object.

Researchers measured brain activity before, during, and after meditation, using electroencephalograms. They found striking differences between the two groups in a type of brain activity called gamma wave activity, which is involved in mental processes including attention, working memory, learning, and conscious perception.

The Buddhist monks had a higher level of this sort of gamma wave activity before they began meditation, and this difference increased dramatically during meditation. In fact, researchers say the extremely high levels of gamma wave activity were the highest ever reported. The monks also had more brain activity in areas associated with positive emotions, such as happiness. Researchers say the fact that the monks had higher levels of this type of brain activity before meditation began suggests that long-term practice of Buddhist or other forms of meditation may alter the brain.

Although age differences may account for some of the results that showed up in this study, researchers say that the hours of meditation practice, rather than age, significantly predicted gamma wave activity. Researchers stated more studies are needed to look at whether differences in brain activity are caused by long-term meditation training or by individual differences before training. *End: Warner*

Razor-edge research is being conducted about the power of connection with a Higher Power and the changes it can make in our entire human system, body, emotions, mind, and spirit.

We can begin to see how it's almost impossible to cultivate positive attitudes and beliefs when we're stuck in survival mode, when our heart is not open, or our rational mind is disengaged. Our consciousness is focused on fear and anger, not love. When we're overwhelmed with excessive stress, our life becomes a series of short-term emergencies. We lose the ability to relax and enjoy the moment. We live from crisis to crisis with no relief in sight. Burnout is inevitable. This burnout is what usually provides the motivation to change our lives for the better. We're propelled to step back and look at the big picture of our lives, forced to examine our beliefs, our values, and our goals.

This is what Harvard cardiologist Herbert Benson[7], M.D says about the importance of relaxation:

> The relaxation response represents a hard-wired antidote to the fight-or-flight response. The relaxation response corresponds to a physical portion of the brain (located in the hypothalamus) which, when triggered, sends out neurochemicals that almost precisely counteract the hyper vigilant reaction of the fight-or-flight response.
>
> When we follow the simple steps necessary to elicit the relaxation response, we can predictably measure its benefits on the body. These include the following: a decrease in blood pressure, diminished respiratory rate, lower pulse rate, diminished oxygen consumption, increase in alpha brain waves (associated with relaxation), and in many cases, a sense of mental and spiritual well-being.
>
> Because the relaxation response is hard-wired, we don't need to believe it will work. The relaxation response is a physiologic response, and as such, there are many ways to elicit it, just as there are many ways to increase our pulse rate (another physiologic response).

Calmness development can positively affect the anterior cingulated gyrus area of your brain. This area controls concentration and is directly related to the hippocampus area, which governs learning. As the message moves through the brain, a chemical reaction is set off to neutralize the norepinephrine reaction that makes you feel edgy and tired. It's a fact, then, that lack of calmness can cause mood swings and restlessness.

At the University of Wisconsin Madison[9], a research study on relaxation revealed that:

During an alpha relaxation session the brain actively switches from the right side of the prefrontal cortex to the left side of the brain. This cortex is directly related to anxiety-producing reactions and to the right side of the brain. This research also reported that positive emotions are a direct result of left-brain activation. In other words, left-dominant people are happier than right-dominant people, who tend to be more anxious.

Calmness development is a powerful trigger to the brain's energy center. Anxiety robs people of this energy, whereas calmness can help them triumph over situations that can cause exhaustion. This same calmness can alter pain thresholds by 50% according to Kabat-Zim[10] of the University Of Maryland School Of Medicine.

With all the proof of the positive side of calmness development, more emphasis should be placed on helping clients become more knowledgeable about their own abilities to lessen anxiety and produce more positive energy through activating states of mind.

In a landmark 1990 study, Stanford University psychiatrist David Spiegel[8] researched the effectiveness of relaxation on cancer patients.

A group of 86 women with metastatic breast cancer, all of whom received the same medical treatment, but only half of whom participated in group therapy. Spiegel's treatment, called "Supportive/Expressive Therapy," encouraged patients to do the following:

- Relax and tune in to their bodies and mind through self-hypnosis;
- Become aware of their needs and feelings, and then share them with the group;
- Procure social support from group members and loved ones outside the group;
- Become more expressive and assertive with doctors and family members.

Each of these features touched upon the development of attention, connection, and expression. The group participants, who increased these abilities over time, lived twice as long as the breast cancer patients who did not participate. David Spiegel's astonishing discovery suggests that people who cultivate attention, connection, and expression can improve their odds against cancer.

At Ohio State University, psychologist Janice Kiecolt-Glazer[11] performed research on how relaxation affects the body:

"Progressive muscle relaxation" was taught to a group of geriatric patients. During the exercise, the person mentally travels through the body, attending and relaxing each part. *Blood tests revealed a marked increase in the vitality of natural killer cells among patients who practiced this form of body-mind attention.* Natural killer cells are vital to our defense against infections and cancer.

As can be seen, there is overwhelming evidence for the importance of being centered in your environment and not allowing stress to consistently build up in your life. This is why the Five Steps to Centeredness is so important. By following this simple process, you'll remain centered in virtually any situation.

Five Steps to Centeredness

Step 1: Reflect on Emotions in Your Spiritual Safe Place

Upon realizing that you're in a stressful situation or before you go into a stressful situation, your emotions will need to be in your Spiritual Safe Place. This will calm you down, prevent you from over-reacting and/or freezing up, and allow you to respond appropriately to the situation.

To do this, close your eyes (or keep them open, if the situation dictates). When you feel the stress beginning to affect you (e.g., you feel like you're going to "blow up" or run), visualize your Spiritual Safe Place in your mind's eye. See yourself sitting in your Spiritual Safe Place. At first, you may need to look at your artwork drawing, but in time you'll see this place immediately in your mind's eye.

As you see yourself in your Spiritual Safe Place, experience your body and mind calming down. Leave all your emotions and stress in your Spiritual Safe Place. When you do this (Step 1), your emotional energy transcends into calm energy and your mind slows down and becomes peaceful. You gain energy while reserving your emotional and mental energy (the emotional can drain the mental). You experience *serenity* so that you can step into the reality of the situation that's before you. You don't want or need to revert to your illusive emotions, thoughts, behavior, or to be on automatic pilot.

You have calmed your body, mind, and spirit. You have done this by yourself. No one else from the outside has assisted you. You drew from one of your four human components—Emotional Power. You didn't act off your emotions, yet you were acutely aware of them. You have begun to exercise your internal *Impulse Control* (knowing how you feel but not acting off those feelings). Because you chose to visually enter your Spiritual Safe Place, you prevented yourself from adopting a defensive posture.

The chart in Figure 19.1 shows that by going to your Spiritual Safe Place (Arrow 1), you immediately avoid being in *illusion* to being in the *reality* of the present situation. In the process, you become clearer and clearer in your mind and body. As a result, you'll be in the reality of life more often.

Step 2: Connect with Your Higher Power

Once your emotions are calm and your mind is clear, you can connect your inner self to your Higher Power. This connection immediately opens up many possibilities that were previously unavailable to you. You now have access to the knowledge of yourself and the wisdom of your Higher Power. You've significantly enhanced your ability to exercise impulse control.

By connecting with your Higher Power, you are now able to respond to the situation with kindness and gentleness while being firm and honest with yourself and others. Because you're relaxed, people around you will notice something different about you, even though they may not be able to identify exactly what it is. Your eyes are wide open; you're aware of yourself and your environment. You are *present in reality*. You now have energy from your Emotional and Spiritual Power to look at the situation in a different light and see your choices. Figure 19.1 (Arrow 2) shows that when you enter your Spiritual Safe Place, you develop an immediate connection with your Higher Power.

By practicing these two Steps continuously, you will be able to maintain a quiet body and mind allowing you to hear any inner messages. "Hearing the voice" can come in many different forms: intuition, a thought, a feeling of strength or calmness from within, or a message from another human being.

When we are able to be silent, only then are we able to hear from our Higher Power.

Step 3: Make Defense System a Choice

Now that you are calm, connected to your Higher Power, you're ready for Step 3, where you'll need to consciously choose whether or not to use one of your defensive behaviors (impulse control). As you review your defense behaviors, be aware of their consequences.

If you're willing to be responsible and accountable for your choice of behavior from your defense system, then do it. If not, review your choices involving three of your human components Emotional Power, Spiritual Power, and Mental Power. Making a decision with these three human components interacting harmoniously will result in a great deal of positive energy, enabling you to make a balanced decision. I cannot emphasize enough what a gift it is to be in this position of power with your Higher Power at your side!

At this point as shown in Figure 19.1 (Arrow 3), you are truly ready to take action with the best possible outcome. You'll take action on your present life rather than reacting from your past. You won't do the same thing you always did and expect different results. You'll perform a different action and have different results.

Step 4: Consider Your Options

Now that you are connected to your Higher Power and you've chosen not to become reactive through your defense system, you are ready for Step 4, where you objectively consider your options for a given situation. What is the information you need to know? What are your options as to what you can say or do in this particular situation?

Because you have gone through Steps 1 and 2, you aren't suffering emotional turmoil inside and no old tapes are playing in your mind. Even if some of this is going on (we are all practicing here!), you don't react to it (Step 3), which is a triumph in and of itself. This gives you the foundation to ask yourself, "What are some of the ways I can handle this situation?"

To make your options immediately real, you may want to write down your available choices. If you don't know what they are, do research to gather more information. If the situation is not urgent, you can always postpone your response until you are ready. If the situation is urgent, you may have to jump to Step 5 and take action (life isn't always fair!)

If you have your Personal Blueprint sheet in front of you in a given situation, write down all your options in the Mental Power Reality column. If you don't have the sheet in front of you, take a piece of scrap paper and write down some available choices and then think through each option clearly. Remaining silent is good in certain situations, as this gives you clarity to think things through.

The simple act of considering your options will result in immediate *self-empowerment*. Instead of feeling stuck, you'll realize you have the power of choice. You can consider your options carefully and pick one you'd like to act on. Choosing not to immediately select from your options is still a reasonable choice, provided you don't feel victimized by the situation.

Many of us feel overwhelmed when we have to make a decision simply because we haven't fully explored our options. The feeling of being overwhelmed is actually a good sign; this tells you that you've skipped a crucial step in the process of becoming centered. Figure 19.1 (Arrow 4) indicates that once you are calm and connected to your Higher Power, you are ready to consider your options.

Step 5: Make Decisions and Take Action

Only by following the previous four steps will you understand what I mean by "taking real action in your life." Completing these four steps centers your energy with your emotional, spiritual, and mental components so you can move forward with your physical action.

Now it's time for the final step, without which there is no true maturity.

Having made the choices in Steps 3 and 4, you are now ready to take responsible physical action, as shown in Figure 19.1 (Arrow 5). The moment you take physical action, you'll feel a sense of completion. You'll be living in the reality of life with all four of your human components working at the same time and gathering energy.

When possible you can go through the Five Steps of Centeredness prior to a given situation, write down your choices and the action you've decided to take. This way, when you're in the situation, you'll already know your choices, decision, and action.

This is *real power* over yourself and your life. All other power is illusion. Once you experience true power in your life, you'll never be content with illusion again. But remember, you are a "practicing" human being. You will fall in and out of illusion over the course of your life. But reality behavior and the empowering experiences that follow will occur more and more often. Staying committed to this path is true maturity, and true maturity brings true happiness.

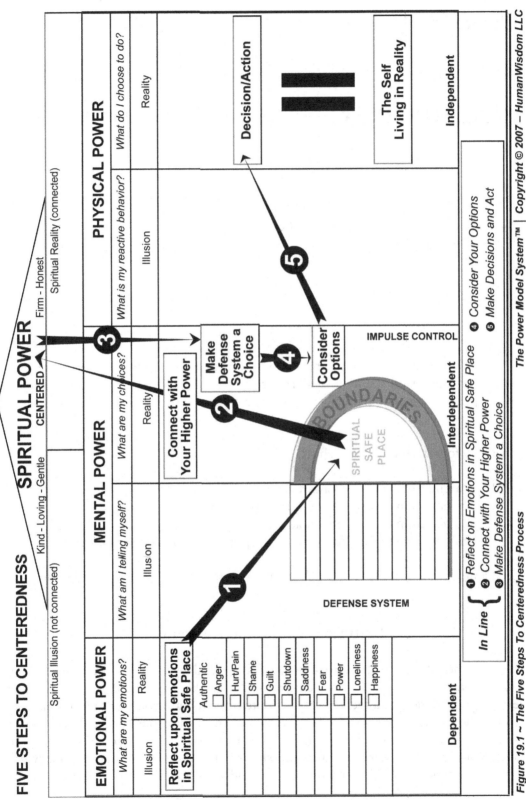

FIVE STEPS TO CENTEREDNESS

Figure 19.1 ~ The Five Steps To Centeredness Process

Chapter 20

INTERNAL SHIFT

Not only was I ignorant-I was ignorant that I was ignorant.
    Book of Illusions

What is an *internal shift,* and can you experience it within and be aware of it while it's taking place? An internal shift occurs when you have developed new patterns of living. It is where you naturally and without much effort, respond in healthy ways to everyday events.

There are four types of internal shifts

1. Shifting from control to awareness
2. Shifting from dependency to self-empowerment
3. Shifting from reactive to pro-active
4. Shifting from feeling lost to having a spiritual connection and power

See Figure 20.1 to visually see how these shifts occur and where they will take you.

Shift from Control to Awareness

When shifting from control to awareness, you'll notice more and more that you don't spend as much time in your emotions. You're able to exercise your internal and external boundaries. You feel less stressed internally because you don't feel the need to control how others think, feel, or behave. You connect with your Higher Power sooner and feel a sense of control over your own life. Your body is healthier and you're not in a fight-or-flight mode as often. Emotions stop running your life—you don't overly rely on your emotions to tell you who you are and how you should think and react to situations in life. With these internal changes, you'll find yourself being drawn to healthier lifestyles.

Shifting from Dependency to Self-Empowerment

As you shift from dependency to self-empowerment, you start to discard old mental tapes of the past and revert to new, improved mental tapes. With this shift comes self-empowerment. How wonderful it is when you start noticing how differently you feel about yourself, when encouraging thoughts from within are nurturing and developing a better you! You're able to be your own self-observer and hear yourself think and talk. You now have the ability to take your own inventory and continue to correct your character defects and reinforce your character strengths. This, in return, gives you healthy ego strength. You'll exercise impulse control. You're able to think a situation through with the help of your Higher Power. As these changes occur, you'll find yourself becoming more creative and intuitive in all areas of your life.

Shifting from Reactive to Pro-Active

You'll likely notice this internal change after the fact. In the past, if a stressful situation came up, you would have reacted first and thought about it later and not liked the consequences. But now you find yourself going through the Five Steps to Centeredness and feeling calm inside. You find yourself telling other people that you'll think about the situation and get back to them instead of thinking you must respond instantly. Later, after you have reached a solution and taken true action, you'll realize that you were able to put internal boundaries on your reactive behavior and that you were proactive. These changes may come slowly or quickly, but in every case, when you look back after the fact, you'll be able to see and feel the change.

Shifting from Feeling Lost to Having a Spiritual Connection

This shift will change how you perceive yourself, the world, and the people in it. This change is deeply personal. You'll find yourself following a spiritual path of your own beliefs. The deep loneliness will start to disappear because you're learning that you are never alone in the world. You can be by yourself and be in good company. With a Higher Power belief, you have common ground with every human being on the planet. Unlike in the past, there's hope inside you—hope for yourself and others. But if you happen to fall down (from an addiction or other past behavior), you'll be able to get back up and practice centeredness again.

Make copies of the Five Steps to Centeredness (Figure. 19.1). Make sure you keep one at work, at home, in your car, and in your wallet or purse. Repetition breeds true knowledge and lasting results. Regularly practicing the steps will help you integrate and re-pattern your brain so it will automatically respond in a centered manner to any stressful situation.

I make this promise to you: If you regularly practice the Five Steps to Centeredness whether you have stress or not, your four human components will learn to align quickly and become centered, calm, and balanced in almost any situation. (I know CEOs who've done the Five Steps to Centeredness exercise in their minds in the middle of a difficult board meeting!) Another ideal time to practice is just before you talk to an employee or to your employer.

Continue to make copies of your Personal Blueprint. That way you can fill one out before you go into a stressful situation. You'll find that you can change the results of almost any situation so they are in your favor. You'll also find that stress will leave your body.

Each time you go through the Five Steps to Centeredness, review the Gifts of Emotions, Chapter Seventeen (Figure. 17.1) to remind yourself about the rewards you're receiving and how you've strengthened your four components.

In the following activity you will be able to gage how much you've grown since you started The Power Model System™.

You can be by yourself and be in good company.

Activity: The Present Self Living in Reality

Figures 20.2 and 20.3 relate to this activity.

This activity requires four (4) colored pencils: Orange, Blue, Red and Black.

In this activity you'll be able to see "where you are now" and "what you consciously know" about your growth since you filled out the Present Self in Illusion chart in Figure 3.1.

You are the person in the middle of the chart in figure 20.2. Notice all four human components represented around the body. Each component is broken down into a set of human aspects including behaviors, reactions, physical symptoms, and beliefs. This time all the human aspects are based in Reality.

When drawing, use the color relating to the associated human component.

Human Component	Pencil Color
Emotional	Red
Mental	Orange
Spiritual	Blue
Physical	Black

1. Go down the lists of all four human components in Figure 20.2 and circle (using the colors above) any item that relates to you.
2. Take the *orange* pencil and color in the part of the body that any of the *mental* aspects (the circled items in the mental box) affects.
   a. For example: I get overwhelmed at times, but I am aware of my defense system and I have a choice how and when to respond. I circled item 11.
3. To remind yourself which item in the *mental* list you want the orange color to apply to, draw a line from each circled item to the corresponding location in the body. For example, draw a line from item 11 to the head.
4. Repeat Steps 2 and 3 above for the emotional with a red pencil.
5. Repeat Steps 2 and 3 above for the physical with a black pencil.
6. Repeat Steps 2 and 3 above for the spiritual with a blue pencil.
7. Now take time to reflect on the changes in yourself.

If you want to use more then one color for the same part of the body, divide the body section up so you can use multiple colors. If a part of the body has already been colored in, simply draw a line to the body part using the correct color. See the example in Figure 20.3.

INTERNAL SHIFT

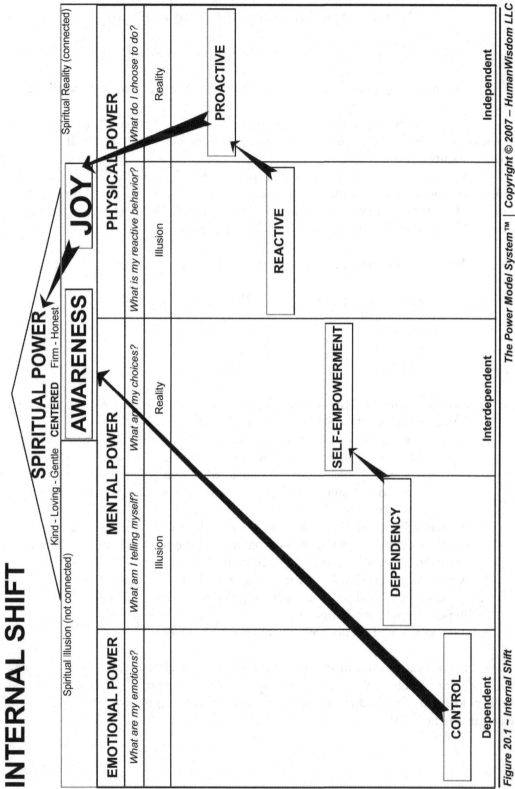

Figure 20.1 ~ Internal Shift

ACTIVITY
SELF LIVING
IN REALITY

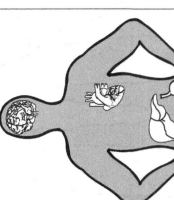

Emotional Reality (red pencil)

1. Able to identify authentic emotions
2. Able to exercise impulse control internally
3. Able to work on resolving my past issues
4. Emotional stability
5. Sense of happiness from within
6. Ability to have fun and play
7. Able to sense an emotional connection with others
8. Know when I need to reach out for support, emotionally
9. Able to keep myself emotionally safe
10. I have a sense of accountability and control over my life

Mental Reality (orange pencil)

11. Knowledge of my defense system
12. Make defense system a choice
13. Knowledge of my thought patterns
14. Process of re-patterning brain
15. Appreciation of personal growth
16. Take full responsibility for my own life
17. Able to quiet my mind
18. Continue to practice impulse control
19. Life compromise = win/win
20. Awareness that I am a practicing human being
21. Know my boundaries and can state them to others
22. Self-respect
23. Healthy ego strength; able to take and give constructive criticism
24. Honest when taking my own inventory
25. Aware of interdependent process (5 steps)
26. I meet life on life's terms
27. Know my needs
28. Able to connect with my Higher Power and become aware of my personal mission

Spiritual Reality (blue pencil)

29. Know my own Higher Power belief system
30. Have a spiritual connection with my Higher Power
31. Able to center myself in any given situation
32. Continue to practice the 5-step process with my Higher Power to re-pattern my brain
33. I believe in miracles
34. Able to forgive others and myself for past behaviors
35. Self-love
36. I continue to gather knowledge on how to connect with my higher self
37. Am aware and accept that I am the writer, producer, director, performer, and audience for my own life
38. Ability to be firm, kind, loving, gentle, and honest with others and myself
39. Ability to listen to the universe on my behalf
40. Able to establish a connection with my soul and my purpose in life and have the desire to apply it
41. Able to meet life on life's terms and know my Higher Power is here to assist me through
42. I attract spiritual, positive individuals in my life
43. I embrace life

Physical Reality (black pencil)

44. Know my goals and am taking steps to achieve them
45. Predictable behavior; I am proactive in my life
46. Able to keep myself safe, emotionally, mentally, spiritually, and physically
47. I make amends promptly to others
48. Reach out to supportive individuals who are on my path
49. Know that I have the physical energy to carry out my mission in life
50. Team player in relationships with others
51. Am aware of positive action for me, and I take it
52. Know my physical needs and take action on them
53. If I have an illness, I know that I am not my illness, and I am responsible to take care of it

EXAMPLE
SELF LIVING IN REALITY

Spiritual Reality (blue pencil)

29. Know my own Higher Power belief system
30. Have a spiritual connection with my Higher Power
31. Able to center myself in any given situation
32. Continue to practice the 5-step process with my Higher Power to re-pattern my brain
33. I believe in miracles
34. Able to forgive others and myself for past behaviors
35. Self-love
36. I continue to gather knowledge on how to connect with my higher self
37. Am aware and accept that I am the writer, producer, director, performer, and audience for my own life
38. Ability to be firm, kind, loving, gentle, and honest with others and myself
39. Ability to listen to the universe on my behalf
40. Able to establish a connection with my soul and my purpose in life and have the desire to apply it
41. Able to meet life on life's terms and know my Higher Power is here to assist me through
42. I attract spiritual, positive individuals in my life
43. I embrace life

Physical Reality (black pencil)

44. Know my goals and am taking steps to achieve them
45. Predictable behavior; I am proactive in my life
46. Able to keep myself safe, emotionally, mentally, spiritually, and physically
47. I make amends promptly to others
48. Reach out to supportive individuals who are on my path
49. Know that I have the physical energy to carry out my mission in life
50. Team player in relationships with others
51. Am aware of positive action for me and I take it
52. Know my physical needs and take action on them
53. If I have an illness, I know that I am not my illness, and I am responsible to take care of it

Emotional Reality (red pencil)

1. Able to identify authentic emotions
2. Able to exercise impulse control internally
3. Able to work on resolving my past issues
4. Emotional stability
5. Sense of happiness from within
6. Ability to have fun and play
7. Able to sense an emotional connection with others
8. Know when I need to reach out for support, emotionally
9. Able to keep myself emotionally safe
10. I have a sense of accountability and control over my life

Mental Reality (orange pencil)

11. Knowledge of my defense system
12. Make defense system a choice
13. Knowledge of my thought patterns
14. Process of re-patterning brain
15. Appreciation of personal growth
16. Take full responsibility for my own life
17. Able to quiet my mind
18. Continue to practice impulse control
19. Life compromise = win/win
20. Awareness that I am a practicing human being
21. Know my boundaries and can state them to others
22. Self-respect
23. Healthy ego strength; able to take and give constructive criticism
24. Honest when taking my own inventory
25. Aware of interdependent process (5 steps)
26. I meet life on life's terms
27. Know my needs
28. Able to connect with my Higher Hower and become aware of my personal mission

SPIRITUAL
PHYSICAL
STOMACH
MENTAL
STOMACH

The Power Model System™ | Copyright © 2007 – HumanWisdom LLC

Figure 20.3 ~ Example: Self Living in Reality

Chapter 21

REVIEW

One moment of patience, may ward off great disaster,
One moment of impatience may ruin a whole life.
Chinese wisdom

The chart in Figure 21.1 shows The Power Model System™ in its entirety. Let's review all the activities and what you achieved by performing them.

The Present Self: Chapter 3

You identified how you perceive yourself (emotionally, mentally, spiritually, and physically) in your illusions by the way you respond to life events and stress, and how you were stuck on old coping skills to get you through life.

Environment Exercise: Chapter 4

You identified that you're dependent on your emotions and how your physical behavior is determined by the emotions you feel. You experienced how the environment can trigger you to regress (into a past event). You self-discovered how a present-day event can cause you to react the same way you responded to a past event in your life. You became aware of how your past continues to affect your present and how not identifying past issues can cause emotional regression in your present-day life, which then affects your future.

Three Faces of Illusion: Chapter 5

You went on to learn how you are asleep when you are in illusion and how your emotional, mental, spiritual and physical components can work against each other. You learned about operating from a young person's belief system, which is also connected with past events in your life. You self-discovered some of your emotional, mental, spiritual, and physical illusions based on recent events in your life. You learned that the 3 Rs (Resistance, Resentment, and ultimately Revenge) can be directed toward yourself or others.

Automatic Pilot/Autopilot: Chapter 6

You learned what being on autopilot means and how and why autopilot doesn't work. You learned that you've been acting on automatic pilot most of your life because that's what you knew.

Five Stages of Illusion: Chapter 7

With courage, you uncovered the Five Stages of Illusion. You saw how you could either stay in illusion with addictions for a lifetime or move forward. You learned the enviable truth that your life is all about choices that only you can make. (In illusion you're making choices that negatively impact your life, so why not move forward into Reality, which leads to happiness?) You also discovered that staying on automatic pilot results in the Five Stages of Illusion, which can cause a downward spiral towards death of self.

Defense System: Chapter 8

This exercise gave you your "top ten" defenses, which are part of an invisible force that stops you from achieving your goals in life. You learned what your defense system is, how it works, when you developed it, and how to know when you're using it in your everyday life. This valuable information enabled you to *make permanent changes from within.*

Feeling-Thinking-Behavior Chart: Chapter 9

When looking at the Feeling-Thinking-Behavior chart, you recognized that flexibility is needed in your emotional, mental, physical, and spiritual components so you can live as a balanced human being and connect with your spiritual self.

The chart illustrated the importance of working with all four human components all at once to achieve success.

Pyramid of Success: Chapter 10

The Pyramid of Success provides a quick method for you to find out where you are in any given situation. You're able to see what you need to do to get through each growth level to achieve your desired results.

Five Stages of Maturity: Chapter 11

You are now able to recognize Stages of Maturity and compare them with the Stages of Illusion. You learned that illusion results in despair and death of self, while maturity results in joy. You know that you'll be able to recognize your growth and reward yourself.

Discovering Internal Boundaries: Chapter 12

You self-discovered what you need to do to take care of yourself and what you need from others. You discovered your internal boundary strengths and weaknesses and what you need to practice exercising your boundaries. (With practice, you'll become a more authentic you and move towards your full potential.)

Discovering External Boundaries: Chapter 12

You self-discovered what you need to change externally by letting others know your external boundaries, i.e., what behavior (towards you) you will and won't accept from others. You found out what you need to do to achieve your sense of self and maintain it while interacting with others.

Life Spark: Chapter 13

Through the Life Spark, you rediscovered your cover-up emotions. By becoming aware of them, you started to identify and experience your authentic emotions. You realized you were born with a Life Spark, a connection with your Higher Power. As you continue to work with your authentic emotions, you'll uncover more of your Life Spark and allow your love to shine through.

Creating a Spiritual Safe Place: Chapter 14

You made a relaxation tape for yourself and rediscovered a place within you that is your spiritual connection. You awoke your soul and now have a Spiritual Safe Place to continue to visit throughout your life.

My Internal System: Chapter 15

You learned that miracles begin to occur once your defense system, Spiritual Safe Place, and boundaries are understood and integrated into your life. This allowed you to exercise true impulse control. You have now begun to be proactive in your life and in the present, which is the birthplace of your future.

Reality: Chapter 16

You discovered reality is the place of internal growth and acceptance of life— where you thrive, not just survive. You found out that being in reality offers you new challenges in your life and great rewards. You learned that staying in reality allows you the comfort of not having everyday life build up inside you. You realized you are able to resolve your past and be present in your life. You learned that most of us live in the past (in illusion) our whole lives, never knowing the inner beauty of living in reality. You resolved not to be one of those people.

Gifts of Emotions: Chapter 17

Here you experienced authentic emotions resulting in spiritual gifts that strengthen each of the four human components. You learned that this reflects the perfection of the universe and that the universe takes the authentic emotional energy and transfers it back into your very being. You realized that this enables you to repeat this process over and over throughout your life (the amazing circle of life).

Your Personal Blueprint Profile: Chapter 18

This is where all your efforts came together, as I promised at the beginning of this book. You took all the information you'd gathered through The Power Model System™ and put it into three consolidated charts so you could quickly go through The Power Model System™ and practice it daily. Now you can truly be in *reality* with joy!

Five Steps to Centeredness: Chapter 19

Finally, you discovered that being *centered* is your *awakened* meditative state of being. You learned that with your eyes wide open you can go through all five steps in a matter of seconds, any place, with anyone, or in any given situation. You found out that these steps reduce stress on your body, prevent emotions from ruling your life, connect your internal power with your Higher Power, and harmonize the use of both sides of your brain, which calms and clears your mind and stimulates your intuitive abilities. You realized that the Five Steps to Centeredness gives you choices you never knew were possible and guides you to the right actions in your life. (You have the universe at your feet!)

Internal Shift: Chapter 20

In this chapter you discovered how you can internally shift from the negative to the positive in many aspects of your life. You learned how these internal shifts can dramatically affect your life.

Figure 21.1 is an overview of The Power Model System™. Use it as another guide to remind yourself of all the components of the Power Model System™ and where you can go back and continuously practice to be a growing, loving, and wise human being.

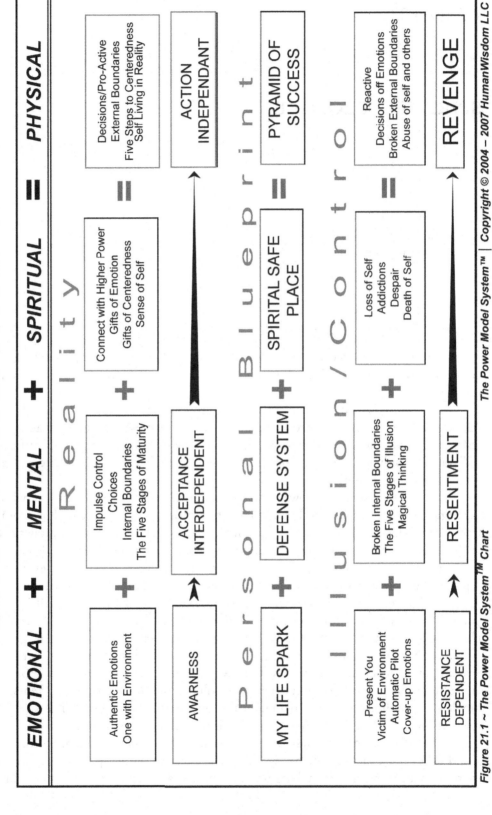

THE POWER MODEL SYSTEM CHART ™

EMOTIONAL + MENTAL + SPIRITUAL = PHYSICAL

Reality

| Authentic Emotions
One with Environment | Impulse Control
Choices
Internal Boundaries
The Five Stages of Maturity | Connect with Higher Power
Gifts of Emotion
Gifts of Centeredness
Sense of Self | Decisions/Pro-Active
External Boundaries
Five Steps to Centeredness
Self Living in Reality |

AWARENESS + ACCEPTANCE INTERDEPENDENT + = ACTION INDEPENDANT

Personal Blueprint

MY LIFE SPARK + DEFENSE SYSTEM + SPIRITAL SAFE PLACE = PYRAMID OF SUCCESS

Illusion/Control

| Present You
Victim of Environment
Automatic Pilot
Cover-up Emotions | Broken Internal Boundaries
The Five Stages of Illusion
Magical Thinking | Loss of Self
Addictions
Despair
Death of Self | Reactive
Decisions off Emotions
Broken External Boundaries
Abuse of self and others |

RESISTANCE DEPENDENT + RESENTMENT + = REVENGE

The Power Model System™ | Copyright © 2004 – 2007 HumanWisdom LLC

Figure 21.1 ~ The Power Model System™ Chart

Chapter 22

SPIRITUAL CLOSURE

Do you need proof of God?
Does one light a torch to see the Sun?
          Oriental wisdom

In this chapter we will discuss what all your changes mean spiritually. Let's put your newfound knowledge, Higher Power freedom, and ultimate happiness into perspective.

We human beings focus on internal growth, not because we are told to, but because we are usually motivated by pain or desire for pleasure and we realize our old ways aren't working. The timing or catalyst of this readiness for growth differs from individual to individual, depending on one's own characteristics, life experiences, and family and cultural upbringing.

When this urge for growth and the betterment of ourselves rises up within us, we begin to seek the means to break out of the prison we feel we are in. Some of us use traditional religions and teachings, while others seek wisdom in faraway lands. Regardless of where we get our answers, they inevitably lead us back to the understanding of ourselves. That's why so many teachings in virtually every culture repeat old universal laws and ancient knowledge about the spirit hidden within us.

However, societies around the world are now experiencing the common cultural shock of the technology, information, and communication age. Everything is changing so fast it is hard for individuals, families, and entire nations not to get lost in the chaos of it all. In this day and age, we need self-growth methodologies in our lives that are fast, direct, and self-empowering. We're in need of systems that can be used in all cultures and all levels of society, including troubled teenagers, parents, entire families, community groups, mental health and addiction fields, prisons, employee relations, with CEOs, and with government leaders around the world.

Modern self-growth systems must be flexible enough to adapt to the modern world. They must incorporate the world's belief systems, be simple, and achieve faster, more permanent results. How long will the human race continue to react off emotions triggered by our differences (thoughts, feelings, race, religion, etc.)? How long will we fail to see that what isn't resolved within each and every human being affects our world? How long will we continue to believe war is the answer to world conflicts?

> *Only through you and your Higher Power traveling together through life can you reach internal balance.*

Internal anger and fear are the ultimate causes of war. I know that puts it rather simply, but truth is truth. If each of us came to terms with our own fear and anger, our world would be safer and better for all future generations. All the wars that occur outwardly, whether in our homes or overseas, start within one person taking his/her fear and anger and reacting with others who have the same emotional makeup. To put it another way, it starts with people who are at war with themselves. If our first response to any internal conflict was to develop peace from within, there would peace throughout the world. We are in need of a fast and simple method to achieve this internal peace. The Power Model System™ is that method.

By using The Power Model System™, anyone can be at peace and become self-empowered and balanced internally. By being internally balanced, you'll be able to spiritually connect to your Higher Power, rather than just hope that this connection happens by chance some day. This system will also give you the ability to spiritually connect with others, regardless of their spiritual beliefs, age, sex, or culture.

You showed a desire for self-growth and took action in your life by buying this book. By now, you have probably realized "The Power Model System™ The Natural Path to Human Wisdom" is no ordinary book. It takes ordinary human beings through the journey of practicing a living system. It allows you to experience firsthand that *you are the expert on you* and that you have been all along. With this expertise, you have all the abilities to accumulate knowledge. With humility, you learn that all the knowledge in the world doesn't mean much if you lack a connection with yourself and your Higher Power—a connection that gives you the wisdom you need to apply your knowledge.

Wisdom: *1) the ability to discern or judge what is true, right, or lasting. 2) the trait of utilizing knowledge and experience with common sense and insight; ability to apply knowledge or experience or understanding or common sense and insight.*
Knowledge: *acquaintance with facts, truths, or principles.*

The Merriam Webster Dictionary

Eighteenth-century poet William Cowper[12] describes the relationship between knowledge and wisdom as follows:

> *Knowledge dwells in heads, replete with thoughts of other men.*
>
> *Wisdom, in minds attentive to their own. Knowledge, a rude, unprofitable mass, the mere materials with which wisdom builds.*
>
> *Till smooth and squared and fitted to its place, does but encumber who it seems to enrich.*
>
> *Knowledge is proud that he has learned so much.*
>
> *Wisdom is humble that he knows no more.*

How do humans acquire wisdom?

Our wisdom is obtained from the miracles and experiences that life brings. Wisdom isn't something you can give to or get from someone. You can go to wise teachers and learn many things. You can take exams on what you've learned, but even if you ace the test, it doesn't mean you've acquired wisdom.

As you continue to practice The Power Model System™, you'll continue to learn many lessons, all of it in the realm of knowledge. You may rest assured that with practice, experiencing *reality*, and openness to your Higher Power, this *knowledge* will be transformed into divine wisdom. *Your Higher Power is the expert on what wisdom is for you.*

I guarantee that if you continue to use The Power Model System™ and practice the Five Steps to Centeredness, you'll find yourself feeling, thinking, and behaving differently. Your impulse control will be strengthened in ways you never thought possible. You'll feel younger, more abilities will be at your disposal, and your walk with your Higher Power will be more harmonious than it has ever been. I don't need to convince you of this. You will discover it on your own as you develop your relationship with your Higher Power.

I encourage you to follow the Natural Path to Human Wisdom the rest of your life. If you do, you will achieve true enlightenment.

Here's my sincere wish for you and your future:

To assist you through your journey of life, may the Sun give you energy, the Moon light your path in the darkness, the Stars remind you there is always a dream to reach for, the Rain refresh you as it does the plants, and the Wind whisper wisdom in your ear.

Kay Bennett

References

1. Jaak Panksepp Ph.D, "Affective Neuroscience " (Oxford University Press, 1998), pp. 117-119.
2. Ricky Alan Mayotte, "The Complete Jesus: All the Sayings of Jesus Gathered in a Single Volume for the First Time" (SkyLight Path Publishing, 2006).
3. Dr. Gary Phillips (National School Improvement Project).
4. Steven K Baum PhD, "Growing Up At Any Age: How to Know when Adulthood Arrives" (HCI, 1994).
5. Ellissa S. Epel, (Proceedings of the National Academics of Sciences, Dec 1, 2004).
6. Jennifer Warner, "Buddhist Meditation May Produce Lasting Changes in the Brain" (Proceedings of the National Academy of Science on line Early Edition, Nov 10, 2004). Reviewed by Brunilda Nazarid, M.D.
7. Herbert Benson and Miriam Z. Klipper, "Relaxation Response" (Harper Collins Publishers, 2000) pp 73, 115.
8. David Spiegel MD, "Supportive-expressive group therapy and life extension of breast cancer patients." (Adv Mind Body Med, 2001 Winter; 17(1)" pp 38-41.
9. University of Wisconsin Madison, website: http://www.rsp.wiscedu/aboutrsp.html.
10. Kabat-Zim, "Research on Calmness", website: http://medschool.umaryland.edu/psychiatry/.
11. Janice Kiecolt-Glazer, "Progressive Muscle Relaxation" (News-Sentinel, Chicago Tribune, Oct. 23, 2006).
12. William Cowper, "The Task".
13. Pia Mellody, "Facing Codependence: What It Is, Where It Comes From, How It Sabotages Our Lives" (HarperCollins Publishers, 1989).
14. Pia Mellody, "Facing Love Addiction: Giving Yourself the Power to Change the Way You Love - The Love Connection to Codependence" (HarperCollins Publishers, 1992).

Appendix 1: Products and Services

HumanWisdom LLC offers speaking engagements for organizations, teams, counselors, and individuals.

Licensing of the Power Model System™ is available for commercial training courses.

To learn more about HumanWisdom products and services, please visit our website.

www.human-wisdom.com